THE BEST BUDDHIST WRITING 2007

THE BEST
BUDDHIST
WRITING
2·0·0·7

Edited by Melvin McLeod

and the Editors of the *Shambhala Sun*

SHAMBHALA

Boston & London · 2007

Shambhala Publications, Inc.
Horticultural Hall
300 Massachusetts Avenue
Boston, Massachusetts 02115
www.shambhala.com

9 8 7 6 5 4 3 2 1

First Edition
Printed in the United States of America

⊛ This edition is printed on acid-free paper that meets the
American National Standards Institute z39.48 Standard.
Distributed in the United States by Random House, Inc.,
and in Canada by Random House of Canada Ltd

ISBN 978-1-59030-497-6
ISSN 1932-393X
2006213739

Contents

INTRODUCTION *ix*

WHAT MAKES YOU NOT A BUDDHIST 1
Dzongsar Khyentse

LETTING GO 21
Judith Lief

WRITERS AND THE WAR AGAINST NATURE 26
Gary Snyder

CREATING A CULTURE OF LOVE 40
bell hooks

HE HAD ME AT HELLO 50
Perry Garfinkel

HOW TO SEE YOURSELF AS YOU REALLY ARE 61
His Holiness the Dalai Lama

LOVE WITHOUT LIMIT: AN INTERVIEW WITH
THICH NHAT HANH 67
Thich Nhat Hanh

OUR TRUE HOME 82
Thich Nhat Hanh

THERE'S NO "I" IN HAPPY 89
Matthieu Ricard

On the Shores of Lake Biwa   103
Natalie Goldberg

Wanting Enlightenment Is a Big Mistake   114
Seung Sahn

Discovering the True Nature of Mind   124
Thrangu Rinpoche

Momma Zen   137
Karen Miller

Reflections on My Mother's Love   141
Ajahn Amaro

Hardwired for Altruism   148
Daniel Goleman

Impermanence Rocks!   164
Daniel Dancer

Beautiful Snowflakes   168
Norman Fischer

Eight Flashing Lances   176
Khenpo Tsultrim Gyamtso

Reentry   192
Jennifer Lauck

Birthing   195
Nancy Bardacke

Through the Lens of Attention   200
Michael Krasner

Five Reasons to Get Cancer   208
John Tarrant

Married to the Guru   216
Diana Mukpo and Carolyn Rose Gimian

My Life in Robes 239
Poems by Leonard Cohen

Suffering Too Insignificant
for the Majority to See 243
Alice Walker

Turning Your Whole Way of Thinking
Upside Down 259
Pema Chödrön

Pitbull 265
Jarvis Jay Masters

Are You Joining a Cult? 275
Donna Lovong

What's Crazy, Really? 281
Layla Mason

The Dharma of Social Transformation 287
Charles Johnson

Healing the Earth 295
Stephanie Kaza

Mindful Marriage 307
Christopher Germer

Nirvana 312
*Gil Fronsdal, Anam Thubten Rinpoche,
and Roko Sherry Chayat*

Contributors 321

Credits 331

Introduction

If there's such a thing as Buddhist writing, and I think there is, then it's something rich, subtle, and almost confusingly diverse. In this collection you'll find memoirs and personal reflections of all kinds—on birth, death, love, motherhood, and even jail. There are think pieces on nature, the arts, medical diagnoses, racism, and the place of love in society. There are spiritual teachings on classical Buddhist themes such as emptiness, enlightenment, the causes of suffering, and the true nature of the mind, and helpful advice on working with marriage, illness, difficult parents, and on what you can do to help the environment. There are famous names from Buddhism and literature—the Dalai Lama, Thich Nhat Hanh, bell hooks, Gary Snyder, Alice Walker, Leonard Cohen—and less well-known writers whose honesty will move you and whose insight will startle you.

What joins together all these different types of writing and these very different people? What is the *Buddhist* part of "Best Buddhist Writing"? In some cases it's obvious—it's clear the writing is about or informed by a formal religion known as Buddhism—but in other cases it's not so explicit. It may be only a broad theme or even just the writer's attitude that makes it Buddhist.

To help tie it all together, let's look at some of Buddhism's underlying principles and how they're reflected in this collection of the year's best Buddhist writing. The themes I'd like to touch on, among the many I could choose, are nontheism, non-ego, suffering, meditation, wisdom, compassion, skillful means, and the teacher. Sometimes explicitly, sometimes implicitly, these ideas run throughout the book.

It's fair to say that Buddhism is not well understood in the West. Buddhist terms are bandied about in the popular culture with little concern for their actual meaning (look no further than the word *Zen*—Buddhism's most rigorous and regimented tradition—used to mean "laid-back" or "relaxed"). Without clear definition, "Buddhism" becomes something vague on which people can project their own spiritual yearnings or left-over concepts from the theistic religions they were brought up in. In fact, as Dzongsar Khyentse Rinpoche explains in the outstanding essay that opens this book, Buddhism is based on firm and specific principles. It's just that many of these principles are very different from those of other religions, and that's one reason Buddhism is so often misunderstood.

Above all, Buddhism is the great nontheistic religion, the religion without God. Nowhere in this book will you find any reference, prayer, or supplication to a higher power or external savior. In Buddhism, what you see is what you get. So the bad news is, you'll have to deal with it alone. The good news is, you can do it. You have the inherent strength, wisdom, and basic goodness to live your life, with all its challenges, in an enlightened way. What you'll find throughout this book is people looking at life without denial or escape, confident that as human beings they have all the resources they need.

Along with no God, Buddhism has no idea of a soul, no belief that we have a permanent essence or identity. This is the renowned doctrine of non-ego, described so poetically by Norman Fischer in his essay "Beautiful Snowflakes." Buddhism sees all phenomena, both beings and things, as always changing—impermanent—and without any solid core—empty. From our current point of view, that may seem pretty depressing but accepting this truth is the very answer to our suffering. Daniel Dancer's story " Impermanance Rocks!" shows how even children can receive this message joyfully, when normally we try so hard to shield them from it.

The basic problem Buddhism addresses is suffering, unlike religions that strive for salvation or transcendence. Buddhism analyzes why we suffer and offers us a path out of suffering. As Matthieu Ricard argues so cogently in "There's No 'I' in Happy," we suffer precisely because of our belief in a permanent, ongoing self, which Buddhism calls *ego*. We suffer because the struggle against change and death is futile; we attain liberation from this struggle when we are freed from the delusion of ego.

This diagnosis of the human dilemma is another unique characteristic of Buddhism. According to Buddhism, our fundamental problem is not sin or some moral failing. We suffer because of our ignorance; because we do not understand the actual nature of reality. The Dalai Lama's teaching on "How to See Yourself as You Really Are" is a step-by-step exercise in recognizing our mistaken views of ourselves and the world around us.

The medicine that heals this illness of ignorance is insight or wisdom, which we can develop through the practice of meditation. Meditation means working with our mind, the source of all we experience and do. Through the practice of meditation we become familiar with all that goes on in our mind, both its confusion and inherent wakefulness. We tame the upheavals, conflicting emotions, and mistaken views that cause so much suffering for ourselves and others, and come to know the mind's true nature, which is enlightenment. While many religions practice some form of meditation or contemplation, what's unique about Buddhist meditation is that it doesn't involve doing, changing, or creating anything. It's about stopping and resting—about relaxing at least for a moment our endless struggles and cogitations. The basic Buddhist view is that we are fine— perfect even—just the way we really are. As Judy Lief explains in "Letting Go," the practice is simply that: letting go—of all the ways we feel we have to improve or solidify ourselves. It's so simple, yet so profound and so difficult.

Buddhism is said to be like a bird, which needs two wings to fly. Wisdom is one of these wings, and the other is compassion. Wisdom heals our suffering; compassion heals the suffering of others. It is these two principles that inform all the selections in this book. Some emphasize the wisdom aspect; some the compassionate side. But at heart these two are indivisible.

Wisdom is the true nature of the mind; compassion is the true nature of the heart. This volume offers teachings by great Buddhist masters on both subjects. Some of the wisdom teachings, such as those by the Dalai Lama, Matthieu Ricard, and Norman Fischer, emphasize the emptiness aspect of the mind—they allow us to relax into great spaciousness and openness beyond the fixed concepts we normally try to impose on reality. Teachings by Thrangu Rinpoche and Khenpo Tsultrim Gyamtso take us further, pointing out that this vast openness is joined with the clarity and wakefulness called *buddha nature*, the infinite store of positive qualities that shine like the sun when we cease to cover them over with the clouds of ignorance and self-absorption.

Compassion is wisdom in action, the heart's natural desire to ease the suffering of beings and help them find happiness. Compassion suffuses this book, from the great teachings of Thich Nhat Hanh, to the heartfelt responses to the world's sufferings by writers such as Alice Walker and bell hooks, to the experiences of ordinary people facing the challenges of daily life with love and courage. I am sure you will be moved and inspired by the stories of John Tarrant, Karen Miller, Jarvis Jay Masters, Ajahn Amaro, and Layla Mason, which show us how rich is the opportunity of human life, difficult as it may be, if we approach it as a spiritual path.

From the union of wisdom and compassion flows the final component that allows us to benefit ourselves and others: skillful means. Motivated by love, not blinded by projections, fixed ideas, and selfish concerns, we are capable of working in the world with great skill. Western Buddhists are making valuable contributions in applying Buddhist principles and practices to modern life, and many of the selections in this book are about how we can act skillfully to address the challenges of our own lives and the problems of society. These range from Christopher Germer's helpful advice on mindful marriage, to the work of seminal thinkers such as Stephanie Kaza and the MacArthur Award–winner Charles Johnson on how Buddhism can help us address global issues of environmental destruction and social change.

Finally, all these ideas come down to human relationships, and no relationship is more important in Buddhism than the relationship between the teacher and the student. Because the truth is beyond concepts, words and writing are at best signposts that help us along the way. The true transmission has taken place since the time of the Buddha in an unbroken lineage of relationships between teachers and students. And thus it continues to this day, marked by the great Asian teachers such as those represented in this book and their Western students, many of whom are now excellent teachers in their own right. It is the success of this transmission—the emergence of Western teachers passing on to new generations the great gifts they have received—that gives us hope for the future of Buddhism in the West and the positive impact it can have on our lives and on our society.

It is appropriate, then, to begin my acknowledgements with heartfelt thanks to my own teachers, Khenpo Tsultrim Gyamtso Rinpoche and the late Chögyam Trungpa Rinpoche. I have had the good fortune in my life to meet many great Buddhist teachers, but to these two I have given my heart.

As editor-in-chief of the *Shambhala Sun* and of *Buddhadharma: The Practitioner's Quarterly*, I am privileged to combine my work with my study of Buddhism. Our days here at the *Sun* are frequently devoted to consideration of Buddhism's meaning and its progress in the West. I would like to thank all my colleagues, who are partners in this ongoing, fruitful conversation, particularly publisher Jim Gimian, my longtime friend and colleague Molly De Shong, and the members of the *Sun* and *Buddhadharma* editorial and art departments: Liza Matthews, Barry Boyce, Andrea McQuillin, Tynette Deveaux, Seth Levinson, Jessica von Handorf, Andrea Miller, and Scott Armstrong.

I would like to thank my good friend Peter Turner, president of Shambhala Publications, for the honor of editing this series, and Beth Frankl for editing this year's edition. Above all, I thank, and give thanks for, my wife Pam and daughter Pearl, who are my inspiration and my teachers too.

Melvin McLeod
Editor-in-chief
The Shambhala Sun
Buddhadharma: The Practitioner's Quarterly

THE BEST BUDDHIST WRITING 2007

What Makes You Not a Buddhist

Dzongsar Khyentse

This is a book of "best Buddhist writing." We're all pretty clear about what writing is, but many people are uncertain about what is really "Buddhist" and what is not. There's a misconception that Buddhism is something vague and open-ended into which we can each plug our own ideas about peace, love, and spirituality. It is true that many of the trappings and rituals we associate with Buddhism are culturally determined, even optional. But as the Tibetan teacher Dzongsar Khyentse informs us in this hard-hitting essay, there are certain core beliefs in Buddhism that are nonnegotiable. If these describe your experience of life, you are a Buddhist. If not, you're something else.

Once, I was seated on a plane in the middle seat of the middle row on a transatlantic flight, and the sympathetic man sitting next to me made an attempt to be friendly. Seeing my shaved head and maroon skirt, he gathered that I was a Buddhist. When the meal was served, the man considerately offered to order a vegetarian meal for me. Having correctly assumed that I was a Buddhist, he also assumed that I don't eat meat. That was the beginning of our chat. The flight was long, so to kill our boredom, we discussed Buddhism.

Over time I have come to realize that people often associate Buddhism and Buddhists with peace, meditation, and nonviolence. In fact many seem to think that saffron or maroon robes and a peaceful smile are all it takes to be a Buddhist. As a fanatical Buddhist myself, I must take pride in this reputation, particularly the nonviolent aspect of it, which is so rare in this age of war and violence, and especially religious violence. Throughout the history of humankind, religion seems to beget brutality. Even today religious-extremist violence dominates the news. Yet I think I can say with confidence that so far we Buddhists have not disgraced ourselves. Violence has never played a part in propagating Buddhism. However, as a trained Buddhist, I also feel a little discontented when Buddhism is associated with nothing beyond vegetarianism, nonviolence, peace, and meditation. Prince Siddhartha, who sacrificed all the comforts and luxuries of palace life, must have been searching for more than passivity and shrubbery when he set out to discover enlightenment.

Although essentially very simple, Buddhism cannot be easily explained. It is almost inconceivably complex, vast, and deep. Although it is nonreligious and nontheistic, it's difficult to present Buddhism without sounding theoretical and religious. As Buddhism traveled to different parts of the world, the cultural characteristics it accumulated have made it even more complicated to decipher. Theistic trappings such as incense, bells, and multicolored hats can attract people's attention, but at the same time, they can be obstacles. People end up thinking that is all there is to Buddhism and are diverted from its essence.

Sometimes out of frustration that Siddhartha's teachings have not caught on enough for my liking, and sometimes out of my own ambition, I entertain ideas of reforming Buddhism, making it easier—more straightforward and puritanical. It is devious and misguided to imagine (as I sometimes do) simplifying Buddhism into defined, calculated practices like meditating three times a day, adhering to certain dress codes, and holding certain ideological beliefs, such as that the whole world must be converted to Buddhism. If we could promise that such practices would provide immediate, tangible results, I think there would be more Buddhists in the world. But when I recover from these fantasies (which I rarely do), my sober mind warns me that a world of people calling themselves Buddhists would not necessarily be a better world.

Many people mistakenly think that Buddha is the "God" of Buddhism; even some people in commonly recognized Buddhist countries such as Korea, Japan, and Bhutan have this theistic approach to the Buddha and Buddhism. This is why I use the name Siddhartha and Buddha interchangeably, to remind people that Buddha was just a man and that this man became Buddha.

It is understandable that some people might think that Buddhists are followers of this external man named Buddha. However, Buddha himself pointed out that we should not venerate a person but rather the wisdom that person teaches. Similarly, it is taken for granted that reincarnation and karma are the most essential beliefs of Buddhism. There are numerous other gross misconceptions. For example, Tibetan Buddhism is sometimes referred to as "lamaism," and Zen is not even considered Buddhism in some cases. Those people who are slightly more informed, yet still misguided, may use words such as *emptiness* and *nirvana* without understanding their meaning.

When a conversation arises like the one with my seatmate on the plane, a non-Buddhist may casually ask, "What makes someone a Buddhist?" That is the hardest question to answer. If the person has a genuine interest, the complete answer does not make for light dinner conversation, and generalizations can lead to misunderstanding. Suppose that you give them the true answer, the answer that points to the very foundation of this 2,500-year-old tradition.

One is a Buddhist if he or she accepts the following four truths:

All compounded things are impermanent.
All emotions are pain.
All things have no inherent existence.
Nirvana is beyond concepts.

These four statements, spoken by the Buddha himself, are known as "the four seals." Traditionally, *seal* means something like a hallmark that confirms authenticity. For the sake of simplicity and flow, we will refer to these statements herein as both seals and "truths," not to be confused with Buddhism's four noble truths, which pertain solely to aspects of suffering. Even though the four seals are believed to encompass all of Buddhism, people don't seem to want to hear about them. Without further explanation they serve only to dampen spirits and fail to inspire further interest in many cases. The topic of conversation changes and that's the end of it.

The message of the four seals is meant to be understood literally, not metaphorically or mystically—and meant to be taken seriously. But the seals are not edicts or commandments. With a little contemplation, one sees that there is nothing moralistic or ritualistic about them. There is no mention of good or bad behavior. They are secular truths based on wisdom, and wisdom is the primary concern of a Buddhist. Morals and ethics are secondary. A few puffs of a cigarette and a little fooling around don't prevent someone from becoming a Buddhist. That is not to say that we have license to be wicked or immoral.

Broadly speaking, wisdom comes from a mind that has what the Buddhists call "right view." But one doesn't even have to consider oneself a Buddhist to have right view. Ultimately it is this view that determines our motivation and action. It is the view that guides us on the path of Buddhism. If we can adopt wholesome behaviors in addition to the four seals, it makes us even better Buddhists. But what makes you not a Buddhist?

> If you cannot accept that all compounded or fabricated things are impermanent, if you believe that there is some essential substance or concept that is permanent, then you are not a Buddhist.

> If you cannot accept that all emotions are pain, if you believe that actually some emotions are purely pleasurable, then you are not a Buddhist.

If you cannot accept that all phenomena are illusory and empty, if you believe that certain things do exist inherently, then you are not a Buddhist.

And if you think that enlightenment exists within the spheres of time, space, and power, then you are not a Buddhist.

So, what makes you a Buddhist? You may not have been born in a Buddhist country or to a Buddhist family, you may not wear robes or shave your head, you may eat meat and idolize Eminem and Paris Hilton. That doesn't mean you cannot be a Buddhist. In order to be a Buddhist, you must accept that all compounded phenomena are impermanent, all emotions are pain, all things have no inherent existence, and enlightenment is beyond concepts.

It's not necessary to be constantly and endlessly mindful of these four truths. But they must reside in your mind. You don't walk around persistently remembering your own name, but when someone asks your name, you remember it instantly. There is no doubt. Anyone who accepts these four seals, even independently of Buddha's teachings, even never having heard the name Shakyamuni Buddha, can be considered to be on the same path as he.

When I tried to explain all of this to the man next to me on the plane, I began to hear a soft snoring sound and realized that he was sound asleep. Apparently our conversation did not kill his boredom.

THE VIEW IS THE FINAL REFERENCE POINT

The *view* is the core of any religion. At an interfaith conference, we may have no choice but to be diplomatic and agree that all religions are basically the same. But in fact they have very different views, and no one but you yourself can judge if one view is better than the other. Only you as an individual, with your own mental capacity, taste, feelings, and upbringing, can choose the view that works for you. Like an abundant buffet, the variety of approaches offers something for everyone. For example, the Jain message of *ahimsa* is so beautiful that one wonders why this great religion is not flourishing like other religions. And the Christian message of love and salvation has brought peace and harmony to the hearts of millions.

The outward appearance of these religions can seem foreign and illogical to outsiders. Many of us are understandably apprehensive about age-old religions and superstitions that lack apparent reason. For example, many people are puzzled by the maroon robes and shaved heads of Buddhist monks because they seem irrelevant to science, economy, and life in general. I can't help wondering what such people would think if they were transported to a Tibetan monastery and faced with paintings of wrathful deities and naked ladies in sexual positions. They might think that they were seeing some exotic aspects of the *Kama Sutra*, or even worse—evidence of depravity or demon worship.

Outsiders might also be appalled at seeing Jain practitioners walking naked or Hindus worshipping gods that resemble cows and monkeys. Some find it difficult to understand why Muslims use their profound philosophy of forbidding idol worship as justification for demolishing the sacred icons of other religions, while in Mecca, one of Islam's most sacred sites, the Ka'aba, Hajre-Aswad (the sacred black stone), is a physical object of worship and the destination of millions of Muslim pilgrims each year. For those who have no understanding of Christianity, it may be inconceivable why the Christians don't pick a story out of Christ's heyday rather than his most gloomy episode on the cross. They may find it incomprehensible that the central icon, the cross, makes the savior seem so helpless. But these are all appearances. Judging or valuing a path or religion by such appearances is not wise, and it can foster prejudice.

Strict conduct can't be used to define a religion either. Adherence to rules does not make a good person. It is believed that Hitler was a vegetarian and very careful about his grooming. But discipline and smart outfits are not in themselves holy. And who determines what is "good" in the first place? What is wholesome in one religion is unwholesome or inconsequential in another. For example, Sikh men never cut their hair and beards, whereas monks in both Eastern and Western traditions often shave their heads, and Protestants can

do as they please with their hair. Each religion has profound explanations for their symbols and practices—why they don't eat pork or
prawns, why they are required to shave or prohibited from shaving.
But within these infinite dos and don'ts, each religion must have a
fundamental view, and that view is what matters most.

The view is the final reference point to determine whether or
not an action is justifiable. Action is valued by how well it comple-
ments one's view. For example, if you live in Venice Beach, California, and you have the view that it's good to be slim, your motivation
is to lose weight, you meditate on the beach about how nice that
would be, and your action might be to avoid carbohydrates. Now
suppose you are a sumo wrestler in Tokyo. Your view is that it's good
to be enormously fat, your motivation is to gain weight, and you
meditate on how you can't be a skinny sumo wrestler. Your action is
to eat as much rice and doughnuts as possible. The act of eating a
doughnut is therefore good or bad, depending on your view. Thus
we can mistakenly consider someone who abstains from meat to be
a compassionate person, when actually their view is simply that
meat is bad because it raises their cholesterol.

Ultimately no one can judge other people's actions without fully
understanding their view.

All methods of Buddhism can be explained with the four
seals—all compounded phenomena are impermanent, all emotions
are pain, all things have no inherent existence, and enlightenment is
beyond concepts. Every act and deed encouraged by Buddhist scriptures is based on these four truths, or seals.

In the Mahayana sutras, Buddha advised his followers not to eat
meat. Not only is it nonvirtuous to bring direct harm to another
being, but the act of eating meat does not complement the four
seals. This is because when you eat meat, on some level you are doing
it for survival—to sustain yourself. This desire to survive is connected to wanting to be permanent, to live longer at the expense of
the life of another being. If putting an animal into your mouth
would absolutely guarantee an extension of your life, then, from a
selfish point of view, there would be reason to do so. But no matter

how many dead bodies you stuff into your mouth, you are going to die one of these days. Maybe even sooner.

One may also consume meat for bourgeois reasons—savoring caviar because it is extravagant, eating tigers' penises for virility, consuming boiled bird's nests to maintain youthful-appearing skin. One cannot find a more selfish act than that—for your vanity, a life is extinguished. In a reverse situation, we humans cannot even bear a mosquito bite, let alone imagine ourselves confined in crowded cages with our beaks cut off waiting to be slaughtered, along with our family and friends, or being fattened up in a pen to become human burgers.

The attitude that our vanity is worth another's life is clinging to the self. Clinging to the self is ignorance, and as we have seen, ignorance leads to pain. In the case of eating meat, it also causes others to experience pain. For this reason, the Mahayana sutras describe the practice of putting oneself in the place of these creatures and refraining from eating meat out of a sense of compassion. When Buddha prohibited consumption of meat, he meant all meats. He didn't single out beef for sentimental reasons, or pork because it is dirty, nor did he say that it's okay to eat fish because they have no soul.

THE BEAUTIFUL LOGIC OF THE FOUR SEALS

As an example of the first seal—impermanence—consider generosity. When we begin to realize the first truth, we see everything as transitory and without value, as if it belonged in a Salvation Army donation bag. We don't necessarily have to give it all away, but we have no clinging to it. When we see that our possessions are all impermanent, compounded phenomena, that we cannot cling to them forever, generosity is already practically accomplished.

Understanding the second seal, that all emotions are pain, we see that the miser, the self, is the main culprit, providing nothing but a feeling of poverty. Therefore, by not clinging to the self, we find no reason to cling to our possessions, and there is no more pain of miserliness. Generosity becomes an act of joy.

Realizing the third seal, that all things have no inherent existence, we see the futility of clinging because whatever we are clinging to has no truly existing nature. It's like dreaming that you are distributing a billion dollars to strangers on the street. You can give generously because it's dream money, and yet you are able to reap all the fun of the experience. Generosity based on these three views inevitably makes us realize that there is no goal. It is not a sacrifice endured in order to get recognition or to ensure a better rebirth.

Generosity without a price tag, expectations, or strings provides a glimpse into the fourth view, the truth that liberation, enlightenment, is beyond conception.

If we measure the perfection of a virtuous action, such as generosity, by material standards—how much poverty is eliminated—we can never reach perfection. Destitution and the desires of the destitute are endless. Even the desires of the wealthy are endless; in fact, the desires of humans can never be fully satisfied. But according to Siddhartha, generosity should be measured by the level of attachment one has to what is being given and to the self that is giving it. Once you have realized that the self and all its possessions are impermanent and have no truly existing nature, you have nonattachment, and that is perfect generosity. For this reason, the first action encouraged in the Buddhist sutras is the practice of generosity.

A DEEPER UNDERSTANDING OF KARMA, PURITY, AND NONVIOLENCE

The concept of karma, the undeniable trademark of Buddhism, also falls within these four truths. When causes and conditions come together and there are no obstacles, consequences arise. Consequence is karma. This karma is gathered by consciousness—the mind, or the self. If this self acts out of greed or aggression, negative karma is generated. If a thought or action is motivated by love, tolerance, and a wish for others to be happy, positive karma is generated. Yet motivation, action, and the resulting karma are inherently like a dream, an illusion. Transcending karma, both good and bad, is nirvana. Any so-called good action that is not based on these four views is merely righteousness; it is not ultimately Siddhartha's path. Even if you were to feed all the hungry beings in the world, if you acted in complete absence of these four views, then it would be merely a good deed, not the path to enlightenment. In fact it might be a righteous act designed to feed and support the ego.

It is because of these four truths that Buddhists can practice purification. If one thinks that one is stained by negative karma or is weak or "sinful," and is frustrated, thinking that these obstacles are always getting in the way of realization, then one can take comfort in knowing that they are compounded and therefore impermanent and thus purifiable. On the other hand, if one feels lacking in ability or merit, one can take comfort knowing that merit can be accumulated through performing good deeds, because the lack of merit is impermanent and therefore changeable.

The Buddhist practice of nonviolence is not merely submissiveness with a smile or meek thoughtfulness. The fundamental cause of violence is when one is fixated on an extreme idea, such as justice or morality. This fixation usually stems from a habit of buying into dualistic views, such as bad and good, ugly and beautiful, moral and immoral. One's inflexible self-righteousness takes up all the space that would allow empathy for others. Sanity is lost. Understanding that all these views or values are compounded and impermanent, as is the person who holds them, violence is averted. When you have no ego, no clinging to the self, there is never a reason to be violent. When one understands that one's enemies are held under a powerful influence of their own ignorance and aggression, that they are trapped by their habits, it is easier to forgive them for their irritating behavior and actions. Similarly, if someone from the insane asylum insults you, there is no point in getting angry. When we transcend believing in the extremes of dualistic phenomena, we have transcended the causes of violence.

THE FOUR SEALS: A PACKAGE DEAL

In Buddhism, any action that establishes or enhances the four views is a rightful path. Even seemingly ritualistic practices, such as lighting incense or practicing esoteric meditations and mantras, are designed to help focus our attention on one or all of the truths. Anything that contradicts the four views, including some action that may seem loving and compassionate, is not part of the path. Even emptiness meditation becomes pure negation, nothing but a nihilistic path, if it is not in compliance with the four truths. For the sake of communication, we can say that these four views are the spine of Buddhism. We call them "truths" because they are simply facts. They are not manufactured; they are not a mystical revelation of the Buddha. They did not become valid only after the Buddha began to teach. Living by these principles is not a ritual or a technique. They don't qualify as morals or ethics, and they can't be trademarked or owned. There is no such thing as an "infidel" or a "blasphemer" in Buddhism because there is no one to be faithful to, to insult, or to doubt. However, those who are not aware of or do not believe in these four facts are considered by Buddhists to be ignorant. Such ignorance is not cause for moral judgment. If someone doesn't believe that humans have landed on the moon, or thinks that the world is flat, a scientist wouldn't call him a blasphemer, just ignorant. Likewise, if he doesn't believe in these four seals, he is not an infidel. In fact, if someone were to produce proof that the logic of the four seals is faulty, that clinging to the self is actually not pain, or that some element defies impermanence, then Buddhists should willingly follow that path instead. Because what we seek is enlightenment, and enlightenment means realization of the truth. So far, though, in all these centuries no proof has arisen to invalidate the four seals.

If you ignore the four seals but insist on considering yourself a Buddhist merely out of a love affair with the traditions, then that is superficial devotion. The Buddhist masters believe that however you choose to label yourself, unless you have faith in these truths, you will continue to live in an illusory world, believing it to be solid and real. Although such belief temporarily provides the bliss of ignorance, ultimately it always leads to some form of anxiety. You then spend all your time solving problems and trying to get rid of the anxiety. Your constant need to solve problems becomes like an addiction. How many problems have you solved only to watch others arise? If you are happy with this cycle, then you have no reason to complain. But when you see that you will never come to the end of problem solving, that is the beginning of the search for inner truth. While Buddhism is not the answer to all the world's temporal problems and social injustices, if you happen to be searching and if you happen to have chemistry with Siddhartha, then you may find these truths agreeable. If that is the case, you should consider following him seriously.

RICHNESS WITHIN RENUNCIATION

As a follower of Siddhartha, you don't necessarily have to emulate his every action—you don't have to sneak out while your wife is sleeping. Many people think that Buddhism is synonymous with renunciation; leaving home, family, and job behind; and following the path of an ascetic. This image of austerity is partly due to the fact that a great number of Buddhists revere the mendicants in the Buddhist texts and teachings, just as the Christians admire Saint Francis of Assisi. We can't help being struck by the image of the Buddha walking barefoot in Magadha with his begging bowl, or Milarepa in his cave subsisting on nettle soup. The serenity of a simple Burmese monk accepting alms captivates our imagination.

But there is also an entirely different variety of follower of the Buddha: King Ashoka, for example, who dismounted from his royal chariot, adorned with pearls and gold, and proclaimed his wish to spread the buddhadharma throughout the world. He knelt down, seized a fistful of sand, and proclaimed that he would build as many stupas as there were grains of sand in his hand. And in fact he kept his promise. So one can be a king, a merchant, a prostitute, a junkie, a chief executive officer, and still accept the four seals. Fundamentally it is not the act of leaving behind the material world that Buddhists cherish but the ability to see the habitual clinging to this world and ourselves and to renounce the clinging.

As we begin to understand the four views, we don't necessarily discard things; we begin instead to change our attitude toward them, thereby changing their value. Just because you have less than someone else doesn't mean that you are more morally pure or virtuous. In fact humility itself can be a form of hypocrisy. When we understand the essencelessness and impermanence of the material world, renunciation is no longer a form of self-flagellation. It doesn't mean that we're hard on ourselves. The word *sacrifice* takes on a different meaning. Equipped with this understanding, everything becomes about as significant as the saliva we spit on the ground. We don't feel sentimental about saliva. Losing such sentimentality is a path of bliss, *sugata*. When renunciation is understood as bliss, the stories of many other Indian princesses, princes, and warlords who once upon a time renounced their palace life become less outlandish.

This love of truth and veneration for the seekers of truth is an ancient tradition in countries like India. Even today, instead of looking down on renunciants, Indian society venerates them just as respectfully as we venerate professors at Harvard and Yale. Although the tradition is fading in this age when corporate culture reigns, you can still find naked, ash-clad sadhus who have given up successful law practices to become wandering mendicants. It gives me goose bumps to see how Indian society respects these people instead of shooing them away as disgraceful beggars or pests. I can't help but imagine them at the Marriott Hotel in Hong Kong. How would the nouveau riche Chinese, desperately trying to copy Western ways, feel about these ash-clad sadhus? Would the doorman open the door for them? For that matter, how would the concierge at the Hotel Bel-Air in Los Angeles react? Instead of worshipping the truth and venerating sadhus, this is an age that worships billboards and venerates liposuction.

Adopting Wisdom, Dropping Distorted Moralities

As you read this, you may be thinking, I'm generous and I don't have that much attachment to my things. It may be true that you aren't tightfisted, but in the midst of your generous activities, if someone walks off with your favorite pencil, you may get so angry that you want to bite his ear off. Or you may become completely disheartened if someone says, "Is that all you can give?" When we give, we are caught up in the notion of "generosity." We cling to the result—if not a good rebirth, at least recognition in this life, or maybe just a plaque on the wall. I have also met many people who think they are generous simply because they have given money to a certain museum, or even to their own children, from whom they expect a lifetime of allegiance.

If it is not accompanied by the four views, morality can be similarly distorted. Morality feeds the ego, leading us to become puritanical and to judge others whose morality is different from ours. Fixated on our version of morality, we look down on other people and try to impose our ethics on them, even if it means taking away their freedom. The great Indian scholar and saint Shantideva, himself a prince who renounced his kingdom, taught that it is impossible for us to avoid encountering anything and everything unwholesome, but if we can apply just one of these four views, we are protected from all nonvirtue. If you think the entire West is somehow satanic or immoral, it will be impossible to conquer and rehabilitate it, but if you have tolerance within yourself, this is equal to conquering. You can't smooth out the entire earth to make it easier to walk on with your bare feet, but by wearing shoes, you protect yourself from rough, unpleasant surfaces.

If we can understand the four views not only intellectually but also experientially, we begin to free ourselves from fixating on things that are illusory. This freedom is what we call wisdom. Buddhists venerate wisdom above all else. Wisdom surpasses morality, love, common sense, tolerance, and vegetarianism. It is not a divine spirit that we seek from somewhere outside of ourselves. We invoke it by first hearing the teachings on the four seals—not accepting them at face value, but rather analyzing and contemplating them. If you are convinced that this path will clear some of your confusion and bring some relief, then you can actually put wisdom into practice.

In one of the oldest Buddhist teaching methods, the master gives his disciples a bone and instructs them to contemplate its origin. Through this contemplation, the disciples eventually see the bone as the end result of birth, birth as the end result of karmic formation, karmic formation as the end result of craving, and so on. Thoroughly convinced by the logic of cause, condition, and effect, they begin to apply awareness to every situation and every moment. This is what we call meditation. People who can bring us this kind of information and understanding are venerated as masters because, even though they have profound realization and could happily live in the forest, they are willing to stick around to explain the view to those who are still in the dark. Because this information liberates us from all kinds of unnecessary hiccups, we have an automatic appreciation for the explainer. So we Buddhists pay homage to the teacher.

Once you have intellectually accepted the view, you can apply any method that deepens your understanding and realization. In other words, you can use whatever techniques or practices help you to transform your habit of thinking that things are solid into the habit of seeing them as compounded, interdependent, and impermanent. This is true Buddhist meditation and practice, not just sitting still as if you were a paperweight.

Even though we know intellectually that we are going to die, this knowledge can be eclipsed by something as small as a casual compliment. Someone comments on how graceful our knuckles look, and the next thing we know we are trying to find ways to preserve these knuckles. Suddenly we feel that we have something to lose. These days we are constantly bombarded by so many new things to lose and so many things to gain. More than ever we need methods that remind us and help us get accustomed to the view, maybe even hanging a human bone from the rearview mirror, if not shaving your head and retreating to a cave. Combined with these methods, ethics and morality become useful. Ethics and morality may be secondary in Buddhism, but they are important when they bring us closer to the truth. But even if some action appears wholesome and positive, if it takes us away from the four truths, Siddhartha himself cautioned us to leave it be.

THE TEA AND THE TEACUP: WISDOM WITHIN CULTURE

The four seals are like tea, while all other means to actualize these truths—practices, rituals, traditions, and cultural trappings—are like a cup. The skills and methods are observable and tangible, but the truth is not. The challenge is not to get carried away by the cup. People are more inclined to sit straight in a quiet place on a meditation cushion than to contemplate which will come first, tomorrow or the next life. Outward practices are perceivable, so the mind is quick to label them as Buddhism, whereas the concept "all compounded things are impermanent" is not tangible and is difficult to label. It is ironic that evidence of impermanence is all around us yet is not obvious to us.

The essence of Buddhism is beyond culture, but it is practiced by many different cultures, which use their traditions as the cup that holds the teachings. If the elements of these cultural trappings help other beings without causing harm, and if they don't contradict the four truths, then Siddhartha would encourage such practices.

Throughout the centuries, so many brands and styles of cups have been produced, but however good the intention behind them, and however well they may work, they become a hindrance if we forget the tea inside. Even though their purpose is to hold the truth, we tend to focus on the means rather than the outcome. So people walk around with empty cups, or they forget to drink their tea. We human beings can become enchanted, or at least distracted, by the ceremony and color of Buddhist cultural practices. Incense and candles are exotic and attractive; impermanence and selflessness are not.

Siddhartha himself said that the best way to worship is by simply remembering the principle of impermanence, the suffering of emotions, that phenomena have no inherent existence, and that nirvana is beyond concepts.

On a superficial level, Buddhism can seem ritualistic and religious. Buddhist disciplines such as maroon robes, rituals and ritual objects, incense and flowers, even monasteries, have form—they can be observed and photographed. We forget that they are a means to an end. We forget that one does not become a follower of Buddha by performing rituals or adopting disciplines such as becoming a vegetarian or wearing robes. But the human mind loves symbols and rituals so much that they are almost inevitable and indispensable. Tibetan sand mandalas and Japanese Zen gardens are beautiful; they can inspire us and even be a means to understanding the truth. But the truth itself is neither beautiful nor not beautiful.

Although we can probably do without things like red hats, yellow hats, and black hats, there are some rituals and disciplines that are universally advisable. One cannot definitively say that it is wrong to meditate while lying in a hammock and holding a drink garnished with a small umbrella, as long as you are contemplating the truth. But antidotes such as sitting up straight actually have great benefit. Correct posture is not only accessible and economical, it has the power to deprive your emotions of their usual quick reflex that engrosses you and sends you adrift. It gives you a little space to become sober. Other institutionalized rituals, such as group ceremonies and religious hierarchical structures, may have some benefit, but it is important to note that they have been the targets of sarcasm of past masters. I personally think that these rituals must be the reason why many people in the West categorize Buddhism as a cult even though there isn't even the smallest trace of cultishness in the four truths.

Now that Buddhism is flourishing in the West, I have heard of people altering Buddhist teachings to fit the modern way of thinking. If there is anything to be adapted, it would be the rituals and symbols, not the truth itself. Buddha himself said that his discipline and methods should be adapted appropriately to time and place. But the four truths don't need to be updated or modified, and it's impossible to do so anyway. You can change the cup, but the tea remains pure. After surviving 2,500 years and traveling 40,781,035 feet from the Bodhi tree in central India to Times Square in New York City, the concept "all compounded things are impermanent" still applies. Impermanence is still impermanence in Times Square. You cannot bend these four rules; there are no social or cultural exceptions.

Unlike some religions, Buddhism is not a survival kit for living that dictates how many husbands a wife should have, or where to pay taxes, or how to punish thieves. In fact, strictly speaking, Buddhists don't even have a ritual for wedding ceremonies. The purpose of Siddhartha's teaching was not to tell people what they wanted to hear. He taught because of his strong impulse to release others from their misconceptions and endless misunderstandings of the truth. However, in order to explain these truths effectively, Siddhartha taught with different manners and means, according to the needs of his different audiences. These different ways of teaching have now been labeled as different "schools" of Buddhism. But the fundamental view for all schools is the same.

It is normal for religions to have a leader. Some, such as the Roman Catholic Church, have an elaborate hierarchy, led by an all-powerful figure, to make decisions and pass judgments. Contrary to popular belief, Buddhism does not have such a figure or institution. The Dalai Lama is a secular leader for the Tibetan community in exile and a spiritual master to many people all over the world, but not necessarily for all Buddhists. There is no one authority with the power to decide who is a true Buddhist and who is not for all the forms and schools of Buddhism that exist in Tibet, Japan, Laos, China, Korea, Cambodia, Thailand, Vietnam, and the West. No one can declare who is punishable and who is not. This lack of a central power may bring chaos, but it is also a blessing because every source of power in every human institution is corruptible.

Buddha himself said, "You are your own master." Of course, if a learned master makes the effort to present the truth to you, you are a fortunate being. In some cases, such masters should be revered even more than the Buddha, because although thousands of buddhas may have come, this person is the one who brought the truth to your doorstep. Finding a spiritual guide is entirely in your own hands. You are free to analyze him or her. When you are convinced of the master's authenticity, accepting, enduring, and enjoying him or her is part of your practice.

Respect is often confused with religious zeal. Because of unavoidable outward appearances, and also because of the lack of skill of some Buddhists, outsiders may think that we are worshipping Buddha and the lineage masters as though they were gods.

In case you are wondering how to decide which path is the right path, just remember that any path that doesn't contradict the four truths should be a safe path. Ultimately it is not the high-ranking masters who guard Buddhism, but the four truths that are the guardians.

I cannot emphasize enough that understanding the truth is the most important aspect of Buddhism. For centuries, scholars and thinkers have taken full advantage of Siddhartha's invitation to analyze his findings. Hundreds of books scrutinizing and debating his words are evidence of that. In fact, if you are interested in Buddhism, far from the threat of being labeled a blasphemer, you are encouraged to explore every doubt. Countless intelligent people have come to respect Siddhartha's wisdom and vision first. Only then do they offer their trust and devotion. It is for this reason that, once upon a time, princes and ministers didn't give a second thought to abandoning their palaces in the quest for truth.

Practicing Harmony

Profound truths aside, these days even the most practical and obvious truths are ignored. We are like monkeys who dwell in the forest and shit on the very branches from which we hang. Every day we hear people talking about the state of the economy, not recognizing the connection between recession and greed. Because of greed, jealousy, and pride, the economy will never become strong enough to ensure that every person has access to the basic necessities of life. Our dwelling place, the earth, becomes more and more polluted. I have met people who condemn ancient rulers and emperors and ancient religions as the source of all conflict. But the secular and modern world has not done any better; if anything, it has done worse. What is it that the modern world has made better? One of the main effects of science and technology has been to destroy the world more quickly. Many scientists believe that all living systems and all life support systems on earth are in decline.

It's time for modern people like ourselves to give some thought to spiritual matters, even if we have no time to sit on a cushion, even if we are put off by those who wear rosaries around their necks, and even if we are embarrassed to exhibit our religious leanings to our secular friends. Contemplating the impermanent nature of everything that we experience and the painful effect of clinging to the self brings peace and harmony—if not to the entire world, at least within your own sphere. Keep in mind that as a Buddhist, you have a mission to refrain as much as possible from harming others and to help others as much as possible. This is not a huge responsibility, because if you genuinely accept and contemplate the truths, all these deeds flow naturally.

Letting Go

Judith Lief

The basic Buddhist practice is letting go—letting go of our attachments, concepts, neuroses, and reference points. Letting go is nirvana, freedom, but it is also what we fear most, for without our perceptions and preferences, where would we be, what would confirm our existence? Here Judith Lief, following in the tradition of her own teacher, Chögyam Trungpa, the great dissector of spiritual materialism, shows us how we can take the concept of letting go and turn it into just another thing to hold on to.

In our fast-paced society, letting go is often paired with moving on. People encourage friends who have suffered a loss to learn to let go of the past and get on with living. In New Age terminology, "just let go" has become an all-purpose piece of advice. But we humans are very cunning: While we talk a lot about letting go, we usually find a way to have our cake and eat it, too—to let go and still manage to hang on. In fact, it is easy to use the notion of letting go as yet another ego-tool. We can use it to prop ourselves up, to cloud things over, and to uphold our illusion of solidity. We are so clever: we can take a concept like letting go, so threatening to our ego-fixation, and turn it completely on its head, so that instead it becomes a credential, an ego-adornment. We can take pride in our letting go and revel in how pure we are now that we have pared down and simplified and become so much less materialistic. We can mask our laziness by seeing it instead as a letting go of ambition; we can mask our inability to connect with other people with the more spiritual notion of letting go of frivolous attachments. The possibilities are endless. So if we are to deepen our understanding of letting go, it is important to begin with an insight into how easily it can be distorted. Then we may be able to discriminate between a pretense of letting go and the real thing.

To learn to let go, it is necessary to understand how averse we are to change, and how attached we are to our idea of a solid, separate self. At times, of course, we do want change for various and sundry reasons. But when we begin to bump up against the fact that no matter what we want or do not want, change just happens, we begin to feel a little uneasy. We feel protective. Of what? We're not completely sure, but we hang on anyway, struggling to secure our ground. We are reactive and we dig in our heels. The greater the threat, the more tightly we hold on. We try to capture something moving and to make it still, so that an experience that has come and gone seems still to exist. Viewing our life as something we can fix and possess, we become completely attached to our mental snapshot of ourselves and equally threatened by its potential loss. We have taken a tiny speck of the vastness of the universe and staked it out as our territory, and now we are stuck with protecting it from change.

How do we deepen our approach to letting go and undercut some of these distortions? The Buddhist teachings provide a pretty clear answer. The starting point is realizing that letting go is not a dramatic moment we build up to some time in the future. It is happening now, in the present moment—it is not singular but ongoing. Letting go is based on our present realization of the reality of impermanence.

Change is continuous in spite of our efforts to resist it. We begin to realize that we do not have any way to stop it or to slow it down. The more we try, the more we suffer. But there is a way to let go, to break this cycle of suffering. We can slow down and have a closer look at our experience of it. When we have a look, we begin to realize what we have been doing, and the whole enterprise begins to feel more and more dubious. It becomes more difficult to hide from what in our hearts we know to be true—the fact of impermanence. We recognize that we have fabricated a false and fixed identity based on self-deception, delusion, and fear; that we have enslaved ourselves to the never-ending project of shoring it up. And we begin to long for another way of going about things.

The process of letting go begins at the point when we recognize how trapped we are. Being trapped is the bad news, but the fact that something or someone has recognized we're trapped is the good news. It's as if we have spent all our life living in a house with very dirty windows, so dirty we had no idea any windows were there. What at first had seemed quite cozy gradually begins to feel claustrophobic. We begin to question what has been so safe and familiar. That questioning is very powerful. To our surprise, as we gingerly explore our little house, a smidgen of dirt falls off a window and we discover a peephole—we see that there is an entire world outside. That tiny glimpse awakens our desire to be free.

Even the smallest glimpse of freedom heightens our awareness of the pain we have created by our ego-fixation. Seeing the contrast is what inspires us to go forward on the path. In particular, each time we sit on the cushion and meditate, we relax and let go a little bit more. The notion we've held on to—that if we don't keep up our ego-momentum something bad is going to happen—dissolves bit by bit. In a traditional analogy of walking the path, it is said that our ego-attachment is like a pair of shoes. Without such shoes we wouldn't start out on the path, although as we walk along, we find that our shoes begin to break down and wear away. But if someone told you to toss out your shoes right at the start, you would be offended. "How dare you! Do you think there's something wrong with my shoes? I love these shoes!"

As you walk the path, the letting go happens naturally, just as your shoes wear away. You do not need to make a dramatic statement by tossing them out; you just need to continue on. The path that initially seemed so inviting and accommodating slowly and surely begins to be more sandpapery and scrapes away tougher and tougher layers of leather.

From beginning to end, the path of dharma is about letting go. As we let go of one thing along the way, we find ourselves attaching to the next. As we let go of gross attachments, we find our more subtle attachments becoming heightened. For instance, we may let go of clinging to material possessions, but then find ourselves totally attached to our philosophy of simplicity. It is hard to let go of things, harder to let go of ideas, and even harder to let go of spiritual pretensions. Over time, as we familiarize ourselves with the many subtle twists and turns of letting go, we begin to be more savvy about how ego steps in to appropriate the entire process. In the millions of minidecisions we make day by day and moment by moment, we are challenged each time either to let go or to resolidify. To let go cleanly—without resolidifying—we can practice what my teacher Chögyam Trungpa Rinpoche referred to as "disowning":

> Even though the acceptance of what is happening may be confusing, just accept the given situation and do not try to make it something else; do not try to make it into an educational process at all. Just see it, perceive it, and then abandon it. If you experience something and then disown that experience, you provide a space between that knowledge and yourself, which permits it simply to take its course. The letting go itself is not held, but immediately dropped. Then letting go becomes simple and natural, like a snake shedding its skin.

The process of letting go is a tender one. We should notice the poignancy and humor of this very human struggle. It is less of a battle and more a path of acceptance and accommodation to the natural arising and dissolving of our ordinary experience. The two-step process—first letting go, and then letting go of the letting go—allows us to approach the idea of letting go gently, precisely, step-by-step. In doing so we see that even though we so often tend to resolidify our experience, between the letting go and the resolidifying there are real glimpses of openness.

Although letting go is something that happens all along the Buddhist path, it tends to rise to the surface most vividly in relation to death. When dealing with terminal illness, someone else's or, finally, our own, we are bluntly confronted with the ultimate futility of holding on to anything. Our concept of our own mortality, once safely distant and abstract, suddenly gets close and personal in the face of death, exposing powerful emotional undercurrents and deep attachments. At this point, telling someone to simply "let go" may not be very skillful or effective. The problem with the phrase is that there seems to be something solid to let go of and someone solid to do the letting go. Furthermore, trying to force an experience tends to be a stumbling block in terms of practice.

Death has a way of bringing us back to what is most essential. In the presence of death, I have found that many extraneous concerns and preoccupations fall away quite simply and naturally. A lot of letting go just happens, simply and effortlessly. So we can approach death by attuning ourselves to its presence and all that it has to teach us. In that heightened atmosphere, our own sticking points become more obvious. In working with a dying individual, we can begin with our own letting go—especially letting go of how we want that person to be. We can relax our opinions and moral judgments as to how that person is going about dying. We can be a more true support, less cluttered by our own fixations. On that basis, we can encourage the dying person to use her remaining time to continue on her journey—to let go of attachments and distractions, and at the same time to hold what is truly meaningful.

In terms of our own practice, when we ourselves come to die, we can remain in the space between holding on and letting go. In that space, you are not trying to get rid of anything or force anything to happen. Instead, you are being present with experience, whatever it is, as it arises and falls. Things go, accept that, be with what is. Being present is the best way of letting go, and, curiously, as we let go we become more present. It may even be possible, as Trungpa Rinpoche suggested, to die with curiosity and to breathe our last breath without expectation or regret.

Writers and the War against Nature

Gary Snyder

Buddhism, like art, is about magic in the world. Both draw their power from attention to the world—to its details and energies, its vastness and profundity—and both are devoted to healing it. In this powerful auto-biographical essay, the great American poet, sage, and Zen practitioner Gary Snyder describes his lifelong commitment to the environment and calls on the shamans of art to rise in its defense.

I grew up in the maritime Pacific Northwest, on a farm north of Seattle where we kept a hen flock, had a small orchard, and tended dairy cows. My uncles were loggers, merchant seamen, or fishermen.

After college, where I studied anthropology, literature, and East Asian culture, I had no choice but to go back to working in the woods and at sea. In the late fifties I worked in the engine room on an American-flag oil tanker that hired me out of the port of Yokohama. I was a member of the National Maritime Union and had my seaman's papers, and it wasn't hard to pick up a job in almost any port of the world.

That ship kept me at sea for a continuous nine months. Two things touched me deeply on that job: one was the stars, night after night, at every latitude, including way below the equator. With my little star book and red-beam flashlight, I mastered the constellations of the Southern Hemisphere. The other was getting to know the birds of the ocean. I loved watching the albatross—a few of those huge graceful birds would always be cruising along behind our ship, trailing the wake for bits of food. I learned that a wandering albatross (of the Southern Hemisphere) might fly a million miles in one lifetime, and that it takes a pair of them almost a year to raise one chick. Night and day, they always followed us, and if they ever slept it seems it was on the wing.

Last year a study was released describing the sudden decline of albatross numbers worldwide. It even prompted an editorial in the *New York Times*. This sharp decline is attributed to much death by drowning. The long-line fishing boats lay out lines with bait and hooks that go miles back, dragging just below the surface. An albatross will go for the bait, get hooked, and be pulled down to drown. As many as 100,000 a year are estimated to perish in this way, enough to threaten the survival of the species if it keeps up. What have the albatross, "distinguished strangers who have come down to us from another world," ever done to us? The editorial concludes, "The long-line fishing fleet is over-harvesting the air as well as the sea."

Out on the South Pacific in 1958, watching the soaring albatrosses from the stern of a ship, I could never have guessed that their lives would be threatened by industrial societies, turning them into "collateral damage" of the affluent appetite for ahi and maguro tuna species (my own taste too). Yet this is just a tiny, almost insignificant, example of the long reach of the globalized economy and the consumer society into the wild earth's remote places. A recent book on global logging and deforestation is titled *Strangely Like War*. What is happening now to nature worldwide, plant life and wildlife, ocean, grassland, forest, savannah, desert—all spaces and habitats—the nonhuman realm of watersheds and ecosystems with all their members, can be likened to a *war against nature*.

Although human beings have interacted with nature, both cultivated and wild, for millennia, and sometimes destructively so, it was never quite like "war." It has now become disconcertingly so, and the active defense of nature has been joined by a few artists and writers who have entered the fight on "the wild side," along with subsistence peoples, indigenous spiritual leaders, many courageous scientists, and conservationists and environmentalists worldwide.

There is a tame, and also a wild, side to the human mind. The tame side, like a farmer's field, has been disciplined and cultivated to produce a desired yield. It is useful, but limited. The wild side is larger, deeper, more complex, and though it cannot be fully known, it can be explored. The explorers of the wild mind are often writers and artists. The "poetic imagination" of which William Blake so eloquently spoke is the territory of wild mind. It has landscapes and creatures within it that will surprise us; it can refresh us and scare us; it reflects the larger truth of our ancient selves, both animal and spiritual.

The French anthropologist Claude Levi-Strauss once said something like, "Art survives within modern civilization rather like little islands of wilderness saved to show us where we came from." Someone once said that what makes writing good is the wildness in it. The wildness gives heart, courage, love, spirit, danger, compassion, skill, fierceness, and sweetness—all at once—to language. From ancient times storytellers, poets, and dramatists have presented the world in all its fullness: plants, animals, men and women, changing shape, speaking multiple languages, intermarrying, traveling to the sky and under the earth. The great myths and folktales of human magic and nature's power were our school for ten thousand years. Whether they know it or not, even modern writers draw strength from the wild side.

How can artists and writers manage to join in the defense of the planet and wild nature? Writers and artists by their very work "bear witness." They don't wield financial, governmental, or military power. However, at the outset they were given, as in fairy tales, two "magic gifts." One is the "Mirror of Truth." Whatever they hold this mirror up to is shown in its actual form, and the truth must come out. May we use that mirror well!

The second is a "Heart of Compassion," which is to say the ability to feel and know the pains and delights of other people, and to weave that feeling into their art. For some this compassion can extend to all creatures and to the world itself. In a way, nature even borrows the voices of some writers and artists. Anciently this was a shamanistic role where the singer, dancer, or storyteller embodied a force, appearing as a bear dancer or a crane dancer, and became one with a spirit or creature. Today such a role is played by the writer who finds herself a spokesperson for nonhuman entities communicating to the human realm through dance or song. This could be called "speaking on behalf of nature" in the old way.

Song, story, and dance are fundamental to all later "civilized" literature. In archaic times these were unified in dramatic performance, back when drama and religious ceremony were still one. They are reunited today in the highest and greatest of performance arts—the grand scale of European opera, the height of ballet, the spare and disciplined elegance of Japanese Nô theater, the grand and almost timeless dance-and-story of Indonesian gamelan, the wit and hardiness of Bertolt Brecht's plays, or the fierce and stunningly beautiful intensity of Korean P'ansori performance. Performance is of key importance because this phenomenal world and all life is of itself "not a book, but a performance."

For a writer or artist to become an advocate for nature, he or she must first stumble into some connection to that vast world of energies and ecologies. Because I was brought up in a remote rural district, instead of having kids to play with, I had to entertain myself by exploring the forest surrounding our farm, observing the dozens of bird species and occasional deer, fox, or bobcat; sometimes hunting; sometimes gathering plants that I could sell to herb buyers for a few pennies; and camping out alone for several days at a time. Heavy logging was going on in the nearby hills. Even as a boy I was deeply troubled by the destruction of the forests and the careless way that hunting, both of waterfowl and deer, was conducted.

At fifteen I got into the higher mountains of the Cascade Range in Washington State, starting with the ridges and high meadows around the snow-covered volcano called Mount Saint Helens, or *Luwit,* a 3,000-meter peak just north of the Columbia River. Here is what I discovered back then, and finally chose to write about in my recent book, *Danger on Peaks:*

Climbing the Mountain

Reaching the summit, I thought—West Coast snow peaks are too much! They are too far above the surrounding lands, there is a break between, they are in a different world. If you want to get a view of the world you live in, climb a little rocky mountain with a neat small peak. The big snow peaks pierce the realm of clouds and cranes, rest in the zone of five-colored banners and writhing crackling dragons in veils of ragged mist and frost-crystals, of pure transparency in blue.

Mt. St. Helens' summit is smooth and broad, a place to nap, to sit and write, watch what's higher in the sky, or do a little dance. Whatever the numbers say, snow peaks are always far higher than the highest airplanes ever get. I made my petition to the perfect shapely mountain, "Please help this life." When I tried to look over and down to the world below, there was nothing there.

And then we grouped up to descend. The afternoon snow was perfect for glissade, and leaning on our stocks we slid and skid between cracks and thumps into soft snow, dodged lava slabs, got into the open snowfield slopes and almost flew to the soft pumice slopes below. Coming down is so fast. Still high we walked the three-mile dirt road back to the lake.

Atomic Dawn

The day I first climbed Mt. St. Helens was August 13, 1945. Spirit Lake was far from the cities of the valley, and news came slow. Though the first atomic bomb was dropped on Hiroshima August 6, and the second dropped on Nagasaki August 9, photographs didn't appear in the Portland Oregonian until August 12. Those papers must have been driven in to Spirit Lake on the 13th. Early the morning of the 14th I walked over to the lodge to check the bulletin board. There were whole pages of the paper pinned up: photos of a blasted city from the air, the estimate of 150,000 dead in Hiroshima alone, the American scientist quoted saying "nothing will grow there again for seventy years." The morning sun on my shoulders, the fir forest smell and the big tree shadows; my feet in thin moccasins feeling the ground, and my heart still one with the snow peak mountain at my back. Horrified, blaming scientists and politicians and the governments of the world, I swore a vow to myself something like "By the purity and beauty and permanence of Mt. St. Helens, I swear I will fight against this cruel destructive power and those who would seek to use it, for all my life."

The statement in that 1945 newspaper saying that nature would be blighted for decades to come outraged me almost as much as the destruction of innocent human life. I was already a youthful conservationist/environmentalist, and after that I went on to be active in the antiwar movement as a student and struggled against the use and proliferation of nuclear weapons. At the time it seemed as though these efforts were naive and hopeless, but we persevered

During my university years I was studying the philosophies and religions of the world. I learned that the most important single ethical teaching of the Buddhist tradition is nonviolence toward all of nature, *ahimsa*. This seemed absolutely right to me. In the Abrahamic religions, "Thou shalt not kill" applies only to human beings. In socialist thought as well, human beings are all-important, and with the "labor theory of value," it is as though organic nature contributes nothing of worth. Later it came to me that "green plants doing photosynthesis are the ultimate working class." Nature creates the first level of value, labor the second.

Then I read translations of Buddhist texts from India and China. The *Dao De Jing* and the *Zhuang-zi* texts helped broaden my view. I read the *Lun yü*—the Confucian "Analects"—and saw how the Master called for etiquette in regard to nature, as well as human society. These studies brought me to the thought that almost all of later "high civilization" has been a type of social organization that alienates humans from their own biological and spiritual heritage.

While I was laboring in the forests, most of my fellow loggers were Native Americans of the Wasco and Wishram tribes of eastern Oregon. From them I learned that it was possible to be a hunter and a fisherman with a deep spiritual attitude of gratitude and nonviolence.

Eventually I reentered college as a graduate student in East Asian languages at the University of California at Berkeley, and finally got a chance to go to East Asia. I lived for a while in a Zen practice hall in Kyoto and studied with a Zen teacher in the Rinzai (Chinese: *Linji*) tradition. I took the precepts under my teacher, who told me that, "Of all the precepts, the First Precept is most important and contains the others: ahimsa, nonharming, cause the least possible harm." To live with that precept is a challenge. He once said to me, "How do you not harm a fence? How would you save a ghost?"

I lived in Japan for ten years, partly in the monastery but also in my own little house, and supported myself by teaching English conversation to Japanese company people. I asked my adult students, "Why are you so intent on learning English?" They answered, "Because we intend to extend our economic influence worldwide, and English is the international language." I didn't take them seriously. Today that company, Matsushita Electric, is worldwide.

In my spare time I hiked in the local mountains, learned East Asian plants and birds, and started seriously reading scientific books on ecology and biology. All those essays analyzing food chains and food webs—this was a science, I realized, dealing with energy exchange and the natural hierarchies of various living systems. "When energy passes through a system it tends to organize that system," someone wrote. It finally came to me that this was about "eating each other," almost as a sacrament. I wrote my first truly ecological poem, which explores the essential qualities of human foods:

The Song of the Taste

Eating the living germs of grasses
Eating the ova of large birds
    the fleshy sweetness packed around
    the sperm of swaying trees

The muscles of the flanks and thighs of
    soft-voiced cows
    the bounce in the lamb's leap
    the swish in the ox's tail

Eating roots grown swoll
        inside the soil.

Drawing on life of living
clustered points of light spun
        out of space
        hidden in the grape.

Eating each other's seed
        eating
        ah, each other.

Kissing the lover in the mouth of bread:
        lip to lip.

This innocently celebratory poem went straight to the question of conflict between the ethics of ahimsa, nonviolence, respect for all beings, and the necessary lives of indigenous peoples and Native Americans I had known. They still practice ceremonies of gratitude, and they never present themselves as superior to other life forms. Ahimsa taken too literally leaves out the life of the world and makes the rabbit virtuous but the hawk somehow evil. We must see the organic world as a great feast, a *puja*, to which we are the invited guests, and also, sooner or later, part of the meal. We can be grateful for that. We can enter into the process, but with gratitude and care, not an arrogant assumption of human privilege. This cannot come from thinking about nature; it comes from being *within* nature.

There are plenty of people of influence and authority in the churches, in industry, the universities, and high in government, who still like to describe nature as "red in tooth and claw" (a line of Alfred Tennyson's)—a fundamental misunderstanding—and use it as part of the justification for the war against nature.

I would now like to propose some simple definitions: The English word *nature* is from the Latin *natura*, "birth, constitution, character, course of things," and ultimately from *nasci*, "to be born." It connects with the root *nat*, which is connected with birth, so we have nation, natal, and native. The Chinese word for *nature* is *zi-ran*, meaning "self-thus." Although in common English and American usage, *nature* is sometimes used to mean "the outdoors" and set in opposition to the realm of development, the word *nature* is best used in its specific scientific sense, referring to the physical universe and its rules— the "laws of nature." In this use it is equivalent to the Greek *physis*. In other words, *nature* means "everything." The agricultural, the urban, the wild mountains and forests, and the many stars in the sky are all equally phenomena. Nature is our reality.

Cities and agricultural lands, however, are not wild. *Wild* is a valuable word. It is a term for the free and independent process of nature. A *wilderness* is a place where wild process dominates and human impact is minimal. Wilderness need not be a place that was never touched by humans, but simply a place where wild process has ruled for some decades.

The wild is self-creating, self-maintaining, self-propagating, self-reliant, and self-actualizing, and it has no "self." It is perhaps the same as what East Asian philosophers call the Dao. The human mind, imagination, and even natural human language can also thus be called wild. The human body itself, with its circulation, respiration, and digestion, is wild. In these senses, *wild* is a word for the intrinsic, nontheistic, forever-changing, natural order.

Ecology, another key word, has the Greek *oikos* as its main root, with the simple meaning of "household." It referred originally to the study of biological interrelationships and the flow of energy through organisms and inorganic matter. In recent years it has become a popular synonym for "outdoor nature." I prefer to use it closer to the original meaning, with an emphasis on the dynamics of relationship in wild natural process. (I presented these definitions more fully in my 1990 book, *The Practice of the Wild.*)

The field of ecological study embraces questions of population rise and fall, plant and animal succession, predator-prey relationships, competition and cooperation, feeding levels, and the flow of energy through ecosystems—and this is just the beginning. I have learned a great deal in my work on the forest issues of western North America over the last few years from people in the field of "forest ecology" (sometimes with the help of my older son, Kai Snyder, who is in this field). I have come to better understand the dynamism of natural systems, the continuous role of disturbance, and the unremitting effects of climactic fluctuations. The "human ecology" aspect of the ecological sciences helps us understand the role that human beings have played as members of wild nature and how the interconnectedness of the entire planet requires that we take care of this place that we live in and which lives in us. It tells us what *sustainable* means, and that modern humans must again become members of the organic world.

The organic life of the planet has maintained itself, constantly changing, and has gone through and recovered from several enormous catastrophic events over hundreds of millions of years. Now we are realizing that the human impact on air, water, wildlife, soil, and plant life is so extreme that there are species becoming extinct, water dangerous even to touch, mountains with mudslides but no trees, and soil that won't grow food without the continuous subsidy provided by petroleum. As we learned over time to positively work for peace to head off the possibilities of war, so now we must work for sustainable biological practices and a faith that includes wild nature if we are to reverse the prospect of continually dwindling resources and rising human populations.

One can ask what it might take to have an agriculture that does not degrade the soils, a fishery that does not deplete the ocean, a forestry that keeps watersheds and ecosystems intact, population policies that respect human sexuality and personality while holding numbers down, and energy policies that do not set off fierce little wars. These are the key questions.

Many of our leaders assume that the track we're on will go forever and nobody will learn much: politics as usual. It's the same old engineering, business, and bureaucracy message, with its lank rhetoric of data and management. Or when the talk turns to "sustainability," the focus is on a limited ecological-engineering model that might guarantee a specific resource for a while longer (like grass, water, or trees) but lacks the vision to imagine the health of the whole planet. The ethical position that would accord intrinsic value to nonhuman nature, and would see human beings as involved in moral as well as practical choices in regard to the natural world, makes all the difference.

"As . . . a dewdrop, a bubble, a cloud, a flash of lightning, view all created things." Thus ends the *Diamond Sutra,* reminding us of irreducible impermanence. Sustainability cannot mean some kind of permanence. A waggish commentary says, "Sustainability is a physical impossibility. But it is a very nice sentiment." The quest for permanence has always led us astray—whether building stone castles,

Great Walls, pyramids for the kings, great navies, giant cathedrals to ease us toward heaven, or Cold War–scale weapons systems guaranteeing "mutually assured destruction." We must live with change, like a bird on the wing, and doing so, let all the other beings live on too. Not permanence, but "living in harmony with the Way."

The albatross, all sixteen species of them, are companions with us on earth, sailing on their own way, of no use to us humans, and we should be no use to them. They can be friends at a distance, fellow creatures in the stream of evolution. This is fundamental etiquette. Legislation from the governments regarding fisheries in the sea or deforestation in the mountains would help enormously.

So, back to those key questions, what would it take? We know that science and the arts can be allies. We need far more women in politics. We need a religious view that embraces nature and does not fear science; business leaders who know and accept ecological and spiritual limits; political leaders who have spent time working in schools, factories, or farms and who still write poems. We need intellectual and academic leaders who have studied both history and ecology, and like to dance and cook. We need poets and novelists who pay no attention to literary critics. But what we ultimately need most is human beings who love the world.

One time in Alaska, a young Koyukon Indian college student asked me, "If we humans have made such good use of animals, eating them, singing about them, drawing them, riding them, and dreaming about them, what do they get back from us?" I thought it an excellent question, directly on the point of etiquette and propriety, and putting it from the animals' side. I told her, "The Ainu say that the deer, salmon, and bear like our music and are fascinated by our languages. So we sing to the fish or the game, speak words to them, say grace. We do ceremonies and rituals. *Performance is currency in the deep world's gift economy*." The "deep world" is of course the thousand-million-year-old world of rock, soil, water, air, and all living beings, all acting through their roles. "Currency" is what you pay your debt with. We all receive, every day, the gifts of the deep world, from the air we breathe to the food we eat. How do we repay that gift? Performance. "A song for your supper."

I went on to tell her that I felt that nonhuman nature is basically well inclined toward humanity and only wishes modern people were more reciprocal, not so bloody. The animals are drawn to us, they see us as good musicians, and they think we have cute ears. The human contribution to the planetary ecology might be our entertaining eccentricity, our skills as musicians and performers, our awe-inspiring dignity as ritualists and solemn ceremonialists— because that is what seems to delight the watching wild world.

"Gift economy," what's that? That might be another perspective on the meaning of ecology. We are living so to speak in the midst of a great potluck feast to which we are all the invited guests, and we also are eventually the meal. The Ainu of Hokkaido, when they had venison for dinner, sang songs aloud to the deer spirits who were hanging about waiting for the performance. The deer visit human beings so that they might hear some songs. In Buddhist spiritual ecology, the first thing to give up is your ego. The ancient Vedic philosophers said that the gods like sacrifices, but of all sacrifices that which they most appreciate is your ego. This critical little point is the foundation of yogic and Buddhist *askesis*. Zen philosopher Dogen famously said, "We study the self to forget the self. When you forget the self you become one with the ten thousand things." (There is only one offering that is greater than the ego, and that is enlightenment itself.)

The being who is willing to give away her enlightenment is called a bodhisattva. In some of the Polynesian societies the Big Person, the most respected and powerful figure in the village, was the one who had *nothing*—whatever gift came to him or her was promptly given away again. This is the real heart of a gift economy, the economy that would save, not devour, the world. (Gandhi once said, "For greed, all of nature is insufficient.") Art takes nothing from the world; it is a gift and an exchange. It leaves the world nourished.

Poems, novels, and plays, with their great deep minds of story, awaken the Heart of Compassion. And so they confound the economic markets, rattle the empires, and open us up to the actually existing human and nonhuman world. *Performance* is art in motion, in the moment, both enactment and embodiment. This is exactly what nature herself is.

> Soaring just over the sea-foam
> riding the wind of the endless waves
> albatross, out there, way
>
> away,　　a far cry
> down from the sky

Creating a Culture of Love

bell hooks

The practice of love, says the feminist critic bell hooks, is the most powerful antidote to the politics of domination. She traces her thirty-year meditation on love, power, and Buddhism, and concludes it is only love that transforms our personal relationships and heals the wounds of oppression.

At a conference on women and Buddhism that took place recently, I was upset because most of the speakers were giving their talks in this serene, beautiful chapel, a place evoking a sense of the divine, a sacred place for the word to be spoken and heard, yet my talk was to take place on a Friday night in an unappealing, cavernous auditorium. Lamenting my exclusion from the realm of the sacred, I complained that I was exiled because I was not seen as a "real" Buddhist—no long time with a teacher, no journey to India or Tibet, never present at important retreats—definitely someone engaged in buddhadharma without credentials. The two companions who had joined me at the conference listened with compassion to my whining. Why did I have to speak in a huge auditorium? Why did I have to speak on a Friday night? Yes, I told them, lots of people might want to hear bell hooks speak on feminist theory and cultural criticism, but that's not the same as a talk about Buddhism.

Yet when the time came, the seats were filled. And it was all about Buddhism. It was a truly awesome night. Sacred presence was there, a spirit of love and compassion like spring mist covered us, and loving-kindness embraced me and my words. This is always the measure of mindful practice—whether we can create the conditions for love and peace in circumstances that are difficult, whether we can stop resisting and surrender, working with what we have, where we are.

Fundamentally, the practice of love begins with acceptance—the recognition that wherever we are is the appropriate place to practice, that the present moment is the appropriate time. But for so many of us, our longing to love and be loved has always been about a time to come, a space in the future when it will just happen, when our hungry hearts will finally be fed, when we will find love.

More than thirty years ago, when I first began to think about Buddhism, there was little or no talk about Buddhism and love. Being a Buddhist was akin to being a leftist; it was all about the intellect, the philosophical mind. It was faith for the thinking "man," and love was nowhere to be found in the popular Buddhist literature at that time. D. T. Suzuki's collection on Buddhism published in the late forties and throughout the fifties had nothing to say about love. Shunryu Suzuki's *Zen Mind, Beginner's Mind* was the Buddhist manifesto of the early seventies, and it did not speak to us of love.

Even though Christmas Humphreys would tell readers in his fifties publication *Buddhism: An Introduction and Guide* that "Buddhism is as much a religion of love as any on earth," Westerners looking to Buddhism in those days were not looking for love. In fact Humphreys was talking back to folks who had designated Buddhism a "cold religion." To prove that love was important to Buddhists, he quoted from the *Itivuttaka:* "All the means that can be used as bases for right action are not worth the sixteenth part of the emancipation of the heart through love. This takes all others up into itself, outshining them in glory." Yet twenty years after this publication, there was still little talk of Buddhism and love. In circles where an individual would dare to speak of love, they would be told that Buddhists were more concerned with the issue of compassion. It was as though love was just not a relevant, serious subject for Buddhists.

During the turbulent sixties and seventies the topic of love made its way to the political forefront. Peace activists were telling us to "make love not war." And the great preacher Martin Luther King, Jr., elevated the call to love from the hidden longing of the solitary heart to a public cry. He proclaimed love to be the only effective way to end injustice and bring peace, declaring that "Sooner or later all the people of the world will have to discover a way to live together in peace. . . . If this is to be achieved, man must evolve for all human conflict a method which rejects revenge, aggression, and retaliation. The foundation of such a method is love."

There could not have been a more perfect historical dharma moment for spiritual leaders to speak out on the issue of love. No doubt divine providence was at work in the universe when Martin Luther King, Jr., and a little-known Vietnamese Buddhist monk named Thich Nhat Hanh found themselves walking the same path—walking toward one another—engaged in a practice of love. Young men whose hearts were awakening, they created in mystical moments of sacred encounter a symbolic sangha.

They affirmed one another's work. In the loneliness of the midnight hour, King would fall on his knees and ask himself the question, "How can I say I worship a god of love and support war?" Thich Nhat Hanh, knowing by heart all the bonds of human connection that war severs, challenged the world to think peace, declaring in the wake of the Vietnam War that he "thought it was quite plain that if you have to choose between Buddhism and peace, then you must choose peace." Linking Buddhism with social engagement, Thich Nhat Hanh's work attracted Westerners (myself included) precisely because he offered a spiritual vision of the universe that promoted working for peace and justice.

In *Essential Buddhism: A Complete Guide to Beliefs and Practices,* Jack Maguire sees Buddhism's emphasis on nonviolence as one of the central features that attracts Westerners. He writes: "Already large numbers of people concerned about such violence have been drawn to Buddhism as a spiritual path that addresses the problem directly. Besides offering them a means of committing themselves more actively to the cause of universal peace, it gives them a context for becoming more intimate with others who are like-minded. It therefore helps restore their hope that people can live together in harmony."

Significantly, Buddhism began to attract many more Western followers because it linked the struggle for world peace with the desire of each individual to be engaged in meaningful spiritual practice. Coming out of a time when it had been cool for smart people to be agnostic or atheist, people wanted permission to seek spiritual connection.

Introducing the collection of essays entitled *Engaged Buddhism in the West,* editor Christopher Queen calls attention to the fact that socially engaged Buddhism "has emerged in the context of a global conversation on human rights, distributive justice, and social progress. . . . As a style of ethical practice engaged Buddhism may be seen as a new paradigm of Buddhist liberation." In the late eighties and nineties, Thich Nhat Hanh's teachings on engaged Buddhist practice spoke directly to concerned citizens in the United States who had been working on behalf of peace and justice, especially for an end to domination based on racial, gender, and sexual practice, but who had begun to feel hopelessness and despair. The assassination of visionary leaders, the inability to end racism and create a just society, the failure of contemporary feminism, which, rather than healing the split between men and women, actually led to further gender warfare—all of this engendered a collective feeling of hopelessness. Buddhist teachers addressed this suffering directly.

Chögyam Trungpa Rinpoche was one of the first Buddhist teachers in the West offering the insight that this profound hopelessness could be the groundwork for spiritual practice. Certainly I came to Buddhism searching for a way out of suffering and despair. Thich Nhat Hanh spoke to my struggle to connect spiritual practice with social engagement. Yet at the time, his Buddhism often seemed rigid, and like many other seekers I turned to the teachings of Trungpa Rinpoche to confront the longings of my heart and find a way to embrace a passionate life. For many Western seekers, the feeling that we had failed to create a culture of peace and justice led us back to an introspective search of our intimate relations, which more often than not were messy and full of strife, suffering, and pain. How could any of us truly believe that we could create world peace when we could not make peace in our intimate relationships with family, partners, friends, and neighbors?

Responding to this collective anguish of spirit, visionary teachers (like King, Thich Nhat Hanh, the Dalai Lama, Sharon Salzberg) were moved by spiritual necessity to speak more directly about the practice of love. Proclaiming transformation in his consciousness engendered by a focus on love, Thich Nhat Hanh declared in the poem "The Fruit of Awareness Is Ripe": *When I knew how to love the doors of my heart opened wide before the wind. / Reality was calling out for revolution. That spirit of revolution, that call to practice transformative love captured my critical imagination and merged with my longing to find a loving partner.*

When lecturing on ending domination around the world, listening to the despair and hopelessness, I asked individuals who were hopeful to talk about what force in their life pushed them to make a profound transformation, moving them from a will to dominate toward a will to be compassionate. The stories I heard were all about love. That sense of love as a transformative power was also present in the narratives of individuals working to create loving personal relationships. Writing about *metta,* "love" or "loving-kindness," as the first of the *brahmaviharas,* the heavenly abodes, Sharon Salzberg reminds us in her insightful book, *Loving-kindness: The Revolutionary Art of Happiness,* that "in cultivating love, we remember one of the most powerful truths the Buddha taught . . . that the forces in the mind that bring suffering are able to temporarily hold down the positive forces such as love or wisdom, but they can never destroy them. . . . Love can uproot fear or anger or guilt, because it is a greater power.

Love can go anywhere. Nothing can obstruct it." Clearly, at the end of the nineties, an awakening of heart was taking place in our nation, our concern with the issue of love evident in the growing body of literature on the subject.

Because of the awareness that love and domination cannot co-exist, there is a collective call for everyone to place learning how to love on their emotional and/or spiritual agenda. We have witnessed the way in which movements for justice that denounce dominator culture, yet have an underlying commitment to corrupt uses of power, do not really create fundamental changes in our societal structure. When radical activists have not made a core break with dominator thinking (imperialist, white supremacist, capitalist patriarchy), there is no union of theory and practice, and real change is not sustained. That's why cultivating the mind of love is so crucial. When love is the ground of our being, a love ethic shapes our participation in politics.

To work for peace and justice, we begin with the individual practice of love, because it is there that we can experience firsthand love's transformative power. Attending to the damaging impact of abuse in many of our childhoods helps us cultivate the mind of love. Abuse is always about lovelessness, and if we grow into our adult years without knowing how to love, how then can we create social movements that will end domination, exploitation, and oppression? John Welwood shares the insight in *Perfect Love, Imperfect Relationships* that many of us carry a "wound of the heart" that emerged in childhood conditioning, creating "a disconnection from the loving openness that is our nature." He explains, "This universal wound shows up in the body as emptiness, anxiety, trauma, or depression, and in relationships as the mood of unlove. . . . On the collective level, this deep wound in the human psyche leads to a world wracked by struggle, stress, and dissension. . . . The greatest ills on the planet—war, poverty, economic injustice, ecological degradation—all stem from our inability to trust one another, honor differences, engage in respectful dialogue, and reach mutual understanding." Welwood links individual failure to learn how to love in childhood with larger social ills; however, even those who are fortunate to love and be loved in childhood grow to maturity in a culture of domination that devalues love.

Being loving can actually lead one to be more at odds with mainstream culture. Even though, as Riane Eisler explains in *The Power of Partnership*, our "first lessons about human relations are not learned in workplaces, businesses, or even schools, but in parent-child and other relations," those habits of being are not formed in isolation. The larger culture in our nation shapes how we relate. Any child born in a hospital first experiences life in a place where private and public merge. The interplay of these two realities will be constant in our lives. It is precisely because the dictates of dominator culture structure our lives that it is so difficult for love to prevail.

When I began, years ago now, to focus on the power of love as a healing force, no one really disagreed with me. Yet what they continue to accept in their daily life is lovelessness, because doing the work of love requires resisting the status quo. In Thich Nhat Hanh's most recent treatise on the subject, *True Love: A Practice for Awakening the Heart*, he reminds us that "to love, in the context of Buddhism, is above all to be there." He then raises the question of whether or not we have time for love. Right now there is such a profound collective cultural awareness that we need to practice love if we are to heal ourselves and the planet. The task awaiting us is to move from awareness to action. The practice of love requires that we make time, that we embrace change.

Fundamentally, to begin the practice of love we must slow down and be still enough to bear witness in the present moment. If we accept that love is a combination of care, commitment, knowledge, responsibility, respect, and trust, we can then be guided by this understanding. We can use these skillful means as a map in our daily life to determine right action. When we cultivate the mind of love, we are, as Sharon Salzberg says, "cultivating the good," and that means "recovering the incandescent power of love that is present as a potential in all of us" and using "the tools of spiritual practice to sustain our real, moment-to-moment experience of that vision." To be transformed by the practice of love is to be born again, to experience spiritual renewal. What I witness daily is the longing for that renewal and the fear that our lives will be changed utterly if we choose love. That fear paralyzes. It leaves us stuck in the place of suffering. When we commit to love in our daily life, habits are shattered. We are necessarily working to end domination. Because we no longer are playing by the safe rules of the status quo, rules that if we obey guarantee us a specific outcome, love moves us to a new ground of being. This movement is what most people fear. If we are to galvanize the collective longing for spiritual well-being that is found in the practice of love, we must be more willing to identify the forms that longing will take in daily life. Folks need to know the ways we change and are changed when we love. It is only by bearing concrete witness to love's transformative power in our daily lives that we can assure those who are fearful that commitment to love will be redemptive, a way to experience salvation.

Lots of people listen and affirm the words of visionary teachers who speak on the necessity of love. Yet they feel in their everyday lives that they simply do not know how to link theory and practice. When Thich Nhat Hanh tells us in *Transformation and Healing* that "understanding is the very foundation of love and compassion," that "if love and compassion are in our hearts, every thought, word, and deed can bring about a miracle," we are moved. We may even feel a powerful surge of awareness and possibility.

Then we go home and find ourselves uncertain about how to realize true love. I remember talking deeply with Thich Nhat Hanh about a love relationship in which I felt I was suffering. In his presence, I was ashamed to confess the depths of my anguish and the intensity of my anger toward the man in my life. Speaking with such tenderness, he told me, "Hold on to your anger and use it as compost for your garden." Listening to these wise words, I felt as though a thousand rays of light were shining throughout my being. I was certain I could go home, let my light shine, and everything would be better; I would find the promised happy ending. The reality was that communication was still difficult. Finding ways to express true love required vigilance, patience, a will to let go, and the creative use of the imagination to invent new ways of relating. Thich Nhat Hanh had told me to see the practice of love in this tumultuous relationship as spiritual practice, to find in the mind of love a way to understanding, forgiveness, and peace. Of course, this was all work. Just as cultivating a garden requires turning over the ground, pulling weeds, planting, and watering, doing the work of love is all about taking action.

Whenever anyone asks me how they can begin the practice of love, I tell them giving is the place to start. In *The Return of the Prodigal Son,* Henri Nouwen offers this testimony: "Every time I take a step in the direction of generosity I know that I am moving from fear to love." Salzberg sees giving as a way to purify the mind: "Giving is an inward state, a generosity of the spirit that extends to ourselves as well as to others." Through giving we develop the mind of gratitude. Giving enables us to experience the fullness of abundance—not only the abundance we have, but the abundance in sharing. In sharing all that we have, we become more. We awaken the heart of love.

Dominator thinking and practice relies for its maintenance on the constant production of a feeling of lack, of the need to grasp. Giving love offers us a way to end this suffering—loving ourselves, extending that love to everything beyond the self, we experience wholeness. We are healed. The Buddha taught that we can create a love so strong that, as Salzberg states, our "minds become like a pure, flowing river that cannot be burned." Such love is the foundation of spiritual awakening.

If we are to create a worldwide culture of love, then we need enlightened teachers to guide us. We need concrete strategies for practicing love in the midst of domination. Imagine all that would change for the better if every community in our nation had a center (a sangha) that would focus on the practice of love, of loving-kindness. All the great religious traditions share the belief that love is our reason for being. This shared understanding of love helps connect Buddhist traditions with Christian practice. Those coming to Buddhism from Christian traditions appreciate the work that Thich Nhat Hanh has done to create a bridge connecting these spiritual paths. In *Living Buddha, Living Christ,* he offers a vision of inclusiveness, reminding us that both Jesus and Buddha are doors we can walk through to find true love. He explains, "In Buddhism such a special door is deeply appreciated because that door allows us to enter the realm of mindfulness, loving-kindness, peace, and joy." Sharing the truism that there are many doors of teaching, he states, "Each of us, by our practice and our loving-kindness, is capable of opening new dharma doors."

All of us who work toward creating a culture of love seek to share a real body of teaching that can reach everyone where we are. That was the lesson I learned at the conference on women and Buddhism—to be broad, to extend the circle of love beyond boundaries, bringing together people from different backgrounds and traditions, and feeling together the way love connects us.

THE WORK OF LOVE IS ALL ABOUT TAKING ACTION.

TAKING A STEP IN THE DIRECTION OF GENEROSITY, MOVING FROM FEAR TO LOVE!

GIVING EXTENDS TO OURSELVES ASWELL AS OTHERS.

"LOVE IS OUR REASON FOR BEING"

He Had Me at Hello ☽

Perry Garfinkel

Journalist Perry Garfinkel's interview with the Dalai Lama was to be the culmination of his twenty-week study of Buddhism in the West. Full of preconceptions about meeting such a renowned spiritual leader, he found himself unexpectedly—and delightfully—disarmed.

His Holiness is ready for you now," an assistant announced.

I have done thousands of interviews in thirty-five years as a journalist. This one was scaring the shit out of me. The night before, I had reviewed my questions and my strategy. I cued up the tape to the message from his nephew that I had recorded in Tibet and practiced how I would suggest the Dalai Lama attach the headset to his ears. I tried to make myself pure, knowing full well if I had one impure thought he would be able to see right through me and terminate the interview then and there. I nibbled simply on fruits and nuts, no alcohol.

Now, as I stood and gathered up my paraphernalia, I went into a panic. I had not studied—or even bothered to ask anyone—the protocols involved when meeting a Tibetan lama, much less the highest-ranking lama. The one rule, which seems to be appropriate upon meeting any Buddhist priest of any rank throughout Asia, is "Look but don't touch." I decided I would bow with palms together but not extend my hand, as is the almost involuntary gesture Western men make with each other.

We walked out the door of the waiting room that leads to a veranda overlooking a garden and lawns. I was expecting a long walk to yet another holding area and then, perhaps, to be ushered into His Holiness's interview area. As we turned the corner, I was looking down because when I am nervous I have a tendency to be klutzy. When I looked up, I almost walked into His Holiness. I stepped back quickly, placed my palms together and modestly dipped my body from the waist up. As I began to bow again (I remembered you are supposed to bow three times, one for each of the three jewels of Buddhist wisdom: the Buddha, the dharma, and the sangha), out of the corner of my eye I saw him stepping toward me, hand extended presumably to shake mine, Western style. I looked to Mr. Lhakdur, the translator, inquisitively. He read my mind, smiling and nodding ahead, which I took to mean it was okay to make physical contact.

The Dalai Lama—the fourteenth reincarnation of the Buddha of Compassion, Nobel Prize winner, revered as an enlightened being—took my hand and shook it robustly. Awkwardly at first and then enthusiastically, I returned the shake—and added a bit of my own robustness. Still trying to maintain decorum and out of great respect (and the fear that my sweaty palms would belie my exterior cool), I tried to withdraw my hand, working on the assumption that there must also be some protocol that defines the length of time it is appropriate to shake a Dalai Lama's hand. But much to my surprise and delight, he tightened his grip.

Sure, I thought, keep my hand—forever. His grip softened slightly but he did not let go. Rather, he led me like that—his right hand holding my right hand, walking side by side—from the veranda all the way into and across the length of a large room until we came to a stop in front of his seat. Finally he let go, at this point to my relief. If he did not let go—and halfway across the room I decided I would hold on until he let go and no sooner—I was already strategizing how I would maneuver the tape recorder with one hand.

We must have held hands for close to a minute. I have never shared an experience like that with another man, and I have hugged more men than the average guy. It completely disarmed me—as a man, as a journalist, as a human being—and at the same time it made me feel completely embraced. It was asexual but very sensual. His gentleness was palpable. And somehow his calm made me feel calm. It was like he gave me a tranquillity transfusion from his hand through mine.

The man had me at hello.

So much for your journalistic objectivity, I thought. I was putty in his hands and any idea of a no-holds-barred interview vanished. He took his seat, a high-backed, stiff-looking wooden chair covered with the thick tapestries that are characteristic of Tibetan furniture. I sat beside him on a high, oversized couch that made me feel about nine years old, my legs dangling over the sides.

Seeing him so close up, about two feet from me, I was riveted. He has a huge face, dominated by his glasses, and it is an expressive face. He shifts from earnest man to wise man to the jokester in the same sentence. He has very few age wrinkles, just laugh wrinkles.

I immediately went into the spiel I had been rehearsing for about six weeks.

"Holiness, I know I sent some questions and I'll get to as many as you let me ask. But I want to depart from that and ask your indulgence first."

I briefly explained about my journey to Taktser. "So I brought you back something from where you were born," I said, and with that I brought out the photos I'd had printed back in D.C. and showed them to him. Among them was a shot of the white stupa in the next rise from Taktser. He stopped at that one and said, "Has anyone told you or not . . . ?" he started. I knew the story I thought he was going to launch into but I shook my head. I wanted to hear his version, already prepared to ask a question about it.

"It was in this place that Thirteenth Dalai Lama . . . I don't know exactly but I was told the Thirteenth Dalai Lama was passing through this way. Then here he stopped and took some rest, and looked toward my village. Then he exclaims, 'Ah, this village is very beautiful.' People said the Thirteenth Dalai Lama determined his next reincarnation will come in that place."

He told it simply, careful to add that qualifier of "I was told." I waited a second to see if he would go on, ready to ask my first potentially upsetting question, which would have been, "Do you believe that story?" Before I could, however, he paused with perfect Borscht Belt timing and added, "Who knows?" Then he let out his signature laugh, a rippling giggle that went on so long it seemed to have a life of its own. Though obviously a believer in reincarnation, he looked at such divinations with a certain realism.

Then I pulled out my tape recorder. "Now I have a message for you from someone you know in Taktser," I said and handed him the earphones, which he took and adjusted on his head without hesitation, apparently happy to play along. For no particular reason, it was an odd sight: the Dalai Lama wearing a headset. Very un–Dalai Lama–like.

I put on the tape of his fifty-eight-year-old nephew, Gongbu Tashi, whose message in Tibetan had been translated to me this way: "Every day we are waiting and hoping and expecting you. You are my uncle and you are getting older and it's time for you to come back. The statues of Buddha and pictures you gave me in India, we put up and every day a lot people come to this place to worship. Not a few—a lot. Here especially we are free to believe in Buddhism or whatever religion. It's pretty good now. This is from the bottom of my heart. Now the government is doing a really good job and gave us all freedoms."

The segment lasted about three minutes. During that time he listened intently, his face softening, his brows furrowing at one point. He smiled and nodded.

"Every day they are thinking that way," he said. Then he went silent.

"Walking up to that village," I said, "I thought, 'How amazing that from such humble beginnings a man could rise to such world renown.' Does it ever amaze you too?"

"Yes, if you look back, a person from a very small village eventually reaches Lhasa with the name of Dalai Lama. So then in the last few decades the Tibetan nation's interest is somehow very connected with that village boy." He laughed, as though the implausibility of it just struck him.

It made me think of Abraham Lincoln, who every American kid knows was born in a one-room log cabin to poor Kentucky farmers and from whom every American kid of humble roots takes hope that he or she too could rise to be president of the United States. I mentioned this to His Holiness, then recalled Lincoln's nickname, the Great Emancipator, being widely regarded as a champion of freedom for American slaves of African descent. Now I was sitting with a man of similar humble background who may someday be recognized as his nation's emancipator. Of course, I did not forget the major difference between the two: Lincoln was elected by the American people, and the Dalai Lama was elected thousands of lifetimes ago and happened to take his incarnation at the time Tibet was overrun by China.

"We believe we have not one but many lives," he continued. "So we can explain something as very certain or coincidence . . . Of course, generally speaking, all human beings have the same potential, each individual, no matter where that person or little boy was born. I don't know if it's facility or opportunity or circumstance. From a Buddhist viewpoint, we have limitless past lives. So then during the last, say, hundred or several thousand years or lifetimes, we make different karmas, or links, so that eventually creates different destinations. . . . Something like that."

Something like what? It sounded like Buddha-babble to me. I tried to interpolate it to something I could understand: "So maybe humans start out headed for one destination but then, like Ping-Pong balls, they are hit and move in other directions? Something like that?"

"That's right," he confirmed. "Also, from a Buddhism viewpoint, from those thousand lifetimes or years, certain shapes eventually develop, but until the last moment other factors are possible and can make changes. Many factors. Like from a seed growing into a flower, until the last moment anything is possible."

"Like the wind takes it in another direction and you could be a farmer in Taktser?" I asked.

"Ohhh, that's right," His Holiness laughed.

"Though somehow I don't think you'd still be a farmer in that village," I put in. He laughed more loudly. "Well, I'm glad to bring you these things from Taktser."

"Thank you, thank you," he said.

Now I was ready to launch into the questions I had prepared. But, as his front men had predicted, he took so long to answer the first question I barely got to the rest. The Dalai Lama is a systematic thinker. I had recalled that among his hobbies was taking apart and putting together watches. It was evident in the way he organized his answers. When I asked why he thought Buddhism was growing in popularity in the West, the sixty-four-thousand-dollar question I'd been asking around the world, he began creating "categories," as he called them. They came fast and furious.

"In the West, people have a view that Tibet is a mysterious land. And then also I think there is a generation who enter the establishment now, so they want something new. During the happies . . ."

Here Lhakdur corrected him, "That's hippies." We all laughed.

"I like your pronunciation," I said. "*Happies* is better than *hippies.*"

"Ha, ha, ha." His Holiness got it. "I think they are quite free, quite happy. So that's one category. Another factor, another category maybe, genuine Buddhism concept is self-reliance, and self-transformation. Why do I put 'genuine'? On a popular level many people worship something like prayer flags or . . . these people are usually satisfied with these things but that's not genuine Buddhism concept. 'Genuine' means he looks inward to self-transformation. Not only true prayer or recitation but meditation, analyze, thinking. I believe genuine Buddhist technique is just increased awareness: what's the reality on the basis of the law of causality?

"Another category: Then some describe Buddhism as a kind of humanism, just emphasis on the human good quality.

"Next, some people not much concerned about next life or nirvana. They want some kind of transformation on an emotional level. Result: more happier, more calm.

"Then another category, thinking, reality. Buddhism's explanation about mind is quite sophisticated. Now some scientists are carrying some experiments."

"Yes," I butt in, dying to impress him with my contacts and knowledge. "You might be talking about some of my friends, Richie Davidson, Dan Goleman, all good old friends of mine." Luckily he did not call me on my egotism, nice guy that he is.

"Yes," he went on, "they found some effect, new findings, new fact. So, including some scientists, it appeals to intellectuals and philosophers who are showing deeper and more and more interest in Buddhist explanation.

"Another category: Buddhism has different gods and goddesses, of wealth and long life and curing illness. Something like that. Protection cords. Pray to gods to cure illness and or for more successful business." Here he let out a chuckle. "That's superficial. Not the main thing."

Now I offered my own theory: "In my interviews around the world, I've noticed people and even countries historically find Buddhism when they are fed up with money, success, political power. Even religion: they question the faith-based religions. Buddhism does not ask you to take a 'leap of faith,' as we say. It's all empirical, as you said. Do you think there is validity to this idea? That people shift to Buddhism when they are full and not satisfied? And then, therefore, the West is at that same point—full, but empty."

"Yes," he said. "This is a new category. Firstly, the material. There are limits. At the beginning we felt, 'Ah, once we have prosperity, then all problems can be solved.' We put every hope on money or power. Then when you have these things, through your own experience you notice their limitations, you could be billionaire then still something missing."

"We call this diminishing returns," I suggested.

"So, through deeper awareness, through one's own experience, they turn to inner value. Inner value is not necessarily Buddhism's alone but other traditions' too. Then I have Christian friends who adopt Buddhist techniques for meditation or to reduce anger and increase patience. Perfectly fine, without losing one's own main faith, to increase some of the basic human values. This should be alright for an open-minded Christian.

"This leads to another category: kind of people curiosity. Once people get to deeper levels, they ask: 'What's reality? What is I? What's God? What's the beginning? What is the ultimate reality of nature?'"

"You describe me," I said.

"So finally, I usually describe Buddhism as a combination of science, philosophy, and religion. Combined. As a science, we look for external signs of mind or emotions. From Buddhist viewpoint, I think this is a science. What is reality? It's a subtle energy. We call it wind. Wind means movement, energy. In scripture it mentions wind, means energy. The description of reality is a science. On that basis, the reality itself should change. By nature there are contradictions. So first things always changing, then second contradictory movement. Therefore transformation is possible. That is basis of buddhadharma. We take the values of good and bad out of the opposites. Now I can take action. Karma. But we cannot make distinction on the action itself—the demarcation of right action or wrong action or positive action or negative action—but on the motivation. Motivation is so important. So motivation means hatred, jealousy, compassion, forgiveness, fear, all those emotions. Some action comes from serving without self-interest, genuine service and helping, not due to money or fame but genuine altruistic motivation. That really brings positive, useful, beneficial actions. Therefore when we realize that, then try to transform or reduce negative and try to increase positive. How? Understanding the contradiction of forces."

"And wrestling with them," I said, but what I thought was, "Whew, that was a mouthful."

He tried to reduce it to simple terms: "Like once you recognize anger is bad—for myself, my body, my peace of mind, for my friend and the whole world on a global level—then you consider what is the opposite force? Compassion, love. Try to increase love and compassion. And why do I need loving-kindness toward others? Because it brings increased benefit to me. Not in the next life, but even in the moment. The more compassionate mind becomes something fuller. Self-confidence. Fearless determination."

This was something I could grasp. Though he talked in circles and fragmented sentences, with imperfect grammar, he nonetheless conveyed his meaning. The man is brilliant, there is no doubt. Part of his brilliance is his way of explaining Buddhist concepts, and the complexities of Tibetan Buddhism in particular, in a way that Westerners can comprehend. It was hard not to idolize him.

"How do you keep people from hero-worshipping you?" I finally asked.

"In the realistic way," he replied and explained by a small example. "Yesterday I met one sick girl. They brought her to me with some expectation. I said, 'I can't help you, but I can give some advice.' That is my limitation. I just share their worry, same worry. I can't do anything, I accept the reality. So when I describe myself as a simple Buddhist monk, that is reality. That is realistic. I don't care what other people say or feel. Important is mindfulness myself. I should not exaggerate from reality. I am human being, I am Buddhist. But in the name of humility, you can belittle yourself too much and then that is also not realistic. One of the important purposes of education is to try to reduce the gap between appearance and reality."

I got to witness his skillfulness with this "reality" after my interview ended, when some dozen Westerners, fresh from a three-month retreat nearby, filed in, bowing almost obnoxiously. Their leader pulled out a sheet of questions each had composed for His Holiness. They preceded their questions with elaborate intros like, "Holiness, in your infinite wisdom and with greatest respect for your thousands of lifetimes and bowing to the gods of compassion and..." Then they would launch into questions that, I am sure, were causing each of them great suffering. They were the most inane, selfish questions, of such a personal nature that there would be no way for His Holiness to offer guidance without spending hours (in some of their cases, years) in personal psychoanalysis with them. One woman wanted to know what Buddhist tradition of retreat she should do next? A man was struggling with his relationship with his mother and his stepfather, and some business he was being asked to join with them even though he did not get along with the stepfather. It went on. With each question, the Dalai Lama listened patiently, scratched his jaw, even asked a question or two. Then, with great delicacy and discretion, he made simple recommendations. Mostly his suggestions could be reduced to two words: keep sitting. But I saw how these people, vulnerable in that way people are when they come out of long retreats, hung on his every word. I knew they would do whatever he said. They would go home, and for months his off-the-cuff suggestion would be their guiding mantra, their compass in life. What a burden. What a responsibility. What ridiculousness to carry on this charade. But he too knew that they would do whatever he said, so he was careful and conservative in his responses. It only made me respect him more.

In sum, I would like to report, first, that the forty-five-minute interview turned into ninety minutes. Later I was told that that was quite exceptional. "He really warmed up to you," Lhakdur said. He liked me; he *really* liked me. For months afterward, when people asked about the encounter, I joked, "We really bonded."

I would also like to report on all the details of the encounter, but in truth the whole thing went by in a blur. Later when I transcribed the taped conversation—and I waited six months to do so, like a kid who saves the cherry on the sundae until the end—I discovered that much of what he said was just barely interpretable. Sometimes in interviews people express what they mean more through inflection and pauses and meaningful looks, or even through physical gestures and mannerisms, or through the trappings of their clothes or the room furnishings. But this was in the extreme. I pieced together fragmented sentences to make it all make sense.

In an attempt to glean deeper meaning from it all, I noticed how many times he used certain words, thinking that he might have been talking cryptically. Indeed, the words he used most frequently—

reality, realistic, reason, intelligence, intellectual—spoke volumes about the deeper point he was making.

I came away believing His Holiness the Dalai Lama is a man of science, a man of intellect, a man of reason, a man of ethics, who himself is part of the reason Buddhism has grown in popularity. Had he not become the Fourteenth Dalai Lama, I think he would have become a valued citizen of the planet. He is a man of deep compassion, embedded in all the best religions, and, finally, he is a religious man. He is the leader of a nation not through instinct or desire, but because history required it of him. He had told me that he does not proselytize Buddhism, that he rather promotes "human values." Nonetheless, without ever intending it, he is Buddhism's best advertising agency.

How to See Yourself as You Really Are

His Holiness the Dalai Lama

Buddhism doesn't begin with lofty concepts like God, sin, or transcendence. It starts with the simple, undeniable fact of suffering. Then it looks for the cause of suffering—because how else can we find a remedy?—and finds it in ignorance, our failure to understand the true nature of ourselves and what we experience. Here is the Dalai Lama in his guise as renowned logician, helping us to see the errors in our thinking so we can finally see ourselves as we really are.

What makes all this trouble in the world? Our own counterproductive emotions. Once they are generated, they harm us both superficially and deeply. These afflictive emotions accomplish nothing but trouble from beginning to end. If we tried to counteract each and every one individually, we could find ourselves in an endless struggle. So what is the root cause of afflictive emotions that we can address more fruitfully?

In the many scriptures of the Buddha, we find descriptions of practices to counter lust, such as meditating on what lies beneath the skin—flesh, bone, organs, blood, solid waste, and urine. These reflections do indeed temporarily suppress lust, but they do not accomplish the same for hatred. And the reverse is also true: those practices taught for the sake of undermining hatred, such as cultivating love, do not act as cures for lust. Like medicines used to counteract a specific illness, they do not treat other illnesses. However, because all counterproductive emotions are based on ignorance of the true nature of things, practices that teach us how to overcome that ignorance undercut all afflictive emotions. The antidote to ignorance addresses all troubles. This is the extraordinary gift of insight.

As preparation for developing insight into how you, other persons, and things actually exist, it is crucial to study spiritual teachings closely, thinking about them again and again. This is important because in order to generate a state that allows us to penetrate clear through to reality, we must first correct our mistaken ideas about existence.

Identifying Ignorance

To succeed at developing insight, first you need to identify ignorance. Ignorance in this context is not just a lack of knowledge—it is an active misapprehension of the nature of things. It mistakenly assumes that people and things exist in and of themselves, by way of their own nature. This is not an easy concept to grasp, but it is very important to identify this faulty perception, for it is the source of destructive emotions such as lust and hatred. In Buddhism we repeatedly speak of emptiness, but if you do not see how people mistakenly attribute to things their own inherent existence, it is impossible to understand emptiness. You have to recognize, at least in a rough way, what you are falsely superimposing on phenomena before you can understand the emptiness that exists in its stead.

All of the Buddha's many teachings are aimed at attaining liberation from cyclic existence—with its endless movement from one life to another—and achieving omniscience. Ignorance is the root of everything that stands in the way of these attainments. Ignorance binds us to suffering; therefore ignorance has to be clearly identified.

To do so we must consider how this false quality of inherent existence appears to the mind, how the mind assents to it, and how the mind bases so many ideas on this fundamental mistake.

Ignorance is not just other than knowledge; it is the contradiction of knowledge. Scientists tell us that the more closely we examine things the more likely we are to find empty space. Ignorance, by relying on appearances, superimposes onto persons and things a sense of concreteness that, in fact, is not there. Ignorance would have us believe that these phenomena exist in some fundamental way. Through ignorance what we see around us seems to exist independently, without depending on other factors for its existence, but this is not the case. By giving people and things around us this exaggerated status, we are drawn into all sorts of overblown and ultimately hurtful emotions.

Identifying this false appearance of things and acknowledging our tacit assent to this illusion are the first steps toward realizing that you and other beings, as well as all other objects, do not exist the way they appear to; they do not exist so concretely and autonomously. In the process of developing an accurate assessment of who you actually are, you need to appreciate the disparity between how you appear to your own mind and how you indeed exist. The same holds true for other people and all the other phenomena of the world.

DISCOVERING THE SOURCE OF PROBLEMS

Our senses contribute to our ignorance. To our faculties of seeing, hearing, smelling, tasting, and feeling, objects seem to exist in their own right. Presented with this distorted information, the mind assents to this exaggerated status of things. Buddhists call such a mind "ignorant" for accepting this false appearance instead of resisting it. The ignorant mind does not question appearances to determine if they are correct; it merely accepts that things are as they appear.

Next we become committed to the seeming truth of the concreteness of objects, thinking, "If this is not true, what could possibly be true?" As we do so, our ignorant misapprehension gets stronger. For instance, when we first encounter something or someone new, we briefly take notice of the object of our attention, merely recognizing its presence. The mind at this point is pretty much neutral. But when circumstances cause us to pay more attention to the object, it appears to be attractive in a way that is integral to the object. When the mind adheres to the object this way—thinking that it exists as it appears—lust for the object and hatred for what interferes with getting it can set in.

When our own self is involved, we emphasize that connection: now it is "*my* body," "*my* stuff," "*my* friend," or "*my* car." We exaggerate the object's attractiveness, obscuring its faults and disadvantages, and become attached to it as helpful in acquiring pleasure, whereby we are forcibly led into lust, as if by a ring in our nose. We might also exaggerate the object's attractiveness, making something minor into a big defect, ignoring its better qualities, and now we view the object as interfering with our pleasure, being led into hatred, again as if by a ring in our nose. Even if the object does not seem to be either agreeable or disagreeable but just an ordinary thing in the middle, ignorance continues to prevail, although in this case it does not generate desire or hatred. As the Indian scholar-yogi Nagarjuna says in his *Sixty Stanzas of Reasoning*:

> How could great poisonous afflictive emotions not arise
> In those whose minds are based on inherent existence?
> Even when an object is ordinary, their minds
> Are grasped by the snake of destructive emotions.

Cruder conceptions of "I" and "mine" evoke grosser destructive emotions, such as arrogance and belligerence, making trouble for yourself, your community, and even your nation. These misconceptions need to be identified by watching your own mind.

As the Indian thinker and yogi Dharmakirti says in his exposition of Buddhist thinking:

> In one who exaggerates self
> There is always adherence to "I."

Through that adherence there is attachment to pleasure.
Through attachment disadvantages are obscured
And advantages seen, whereby there is strong attachment,
And objects that are "mine" are taken up as means of achieving
   pleasure.
Hence, as long as there is attraction to self,
So long do you revolve in cyclic existence.

It is crucial to identify and recognize different thought processes. Some thoughts merely make us aware of an object, such as seeing a watch as just a watch without any afflictive emotions like lust. Other thoughts determine correctly that an object is good or bad but still do not introduce any afflictive emotions; these thoughts just recognize good as good and bad as bad. However, when the idea that objects inherently exist takes hold, fundamental ignorance has been introduced. As the mistaken assumption of inherent existence becomes stronger, lust or hatred becomes involved.

The turning point from mere awareness to misconception comes when ignorance exaggerates the status of the goodness or badness of the object so that it comes to be seen as *inherently* good or bad, *inherently* attractive or unattractive, *inherently* beautiful or ugly. Ignorantly misjudging this false appearance to be fact opens the way for lust, hatred, and myriad other counterproductive emotions. These destructive emotions, in turn, lead to actions based on lust and hatred. These actions establish karmic predispositions in the mind that drive the process of cyclic existence from life to life.

THE ROOT OF CYCLIC EXISTENCE

The process I just described is how we are ruined by our own ignorance and fixed to this round of suffering in life after life that we call "cyclic existence"; some levels of mind which we normally identify as correct are actually exaggerations of the status of persons and things that create trouble for ourselves and others. Ignorance keeps us from seeing the truth, the fact that people and other phenomena are subject to the laws of cause and effect but do not have essential being that is independent in and of themselves.

You need to identify this process as well as you can, gradually developing greater and greater understanding of the sequence of events beginning with dispassionate observation and culminating in counterproductive emotions and actions. Without ignorance, counterproductive emotions are impossible: they cannot occur. Ignorance is their support. This is why Nagarjuna's student, the Indian scholar-yogi Aryadeva, says:

> Just as the capacity to feel is present throughout the body,
> Ignorance dwells in all afflictive emotions.
> Therefore all afflictive emotions are overcome
> Through overcoming ignorance.

Love without Limit: An Interview with Thich Nhat Hanh

Thich Nhat Hanh

I had the honor of interviewing the great Vietnamese Zen teacher Thich Nhat Hanh at Deer Park Monastery near San Diego. He is best known for his courageous opposition to the Vietnam War and as the founder of Engaged Buddhism, but I found him to be so much more—a profound Buddhist teacher, a global thinker, a poet, a man of deep love. I asked him questions important to my own life and practice, and his answers meant a lot to me. I hope they do to you too.

Shambhala Sun: Around us at this monastery are many signs and slogans reminding people to be mindful, to return to their body and breath, and to recollect their nature as human beings. At mealtimes, everyone stops eating when the clock chimes to practice a few moments of mindfulness. Why is it so important for us to return to this basic ground of breath and body and being?

Thich Nhat Hanh: To meditate means to go home to yourself. Then you know how to take care of the things that are happening inside you, and you know how to take care of the things that happen around you. All meditation exercises are aimed at bringing you back to your true home, to yourself. Without restoring your peace and calm and helping the world to restore peace and calm, you cannot go very far in the practice.

SS: What is the difference between this true self, the self you come home to, and how we normally think of ourselves?

TNH: True self is nonself, the awareness that the self is made only of nonself elements. There's no separation between self and other, and everything is interconnected. Once you are aware of that, you are no longer caught in the idea that you are a separate entity.

SS: What happens to you when you realize that the true nature of the self is nonself?

TNH: It brings you insight. You know that your happiness and suffering depend on the happiness and suffering of others. That insight helps you not to do wrong things that will bring suffering to yourself and to other people. If you try to help your father to suffer less, you have a chance to suffer less. If you are able to help your son suffer less, then you, as a father, will suffer less. Thanks to the realization that there is no separate self, you realize that happiness and suffering are not individual matters. You see the nature of interconnectedness, and you know that to protect yourself, you have to protect the human beings around you.

That is the goal of the practice—to realize nonself and interconnectedness. This is not just an idea or something you understand intellectually. You have to apply it to your daily life. Therefore you need concentration to maintain this insight of nonself so it can guide you in every moment. Nowadays, scientists are able to see the nature of nonself in the brain, in the body, in everything. But what they have found doesn't help them, because they cannot apply that insight to their daily lives. So they continue to suffer. That is why in Buddhism we speak of concentration. If you have the insight of nonself, if you have the insight of impermanence, you should make that insight into a concentration that you keep alive throughout the day. Then what you say, what you think, and what you do will be in the light of that wisdom and you will avoid making mistakes and creating suffering.

SS: So the practice of mindfulness is to try to maintain the insight of nonself and interconnectedness at all times.

TNH: Yes, exactly.

SS: We human beings say that above all else we want love. We want to give love; we want to be loved. We know that love is the medicine that cures all ills. But how do we find love in our heart, because often we can't?

TNH: Love is the capacity to take care, to protect, to nourish. If you are not capable of generating that kind of energy toward yourself—if you are not capable of taking care of yourself, of nourishing yourself, of protecting yourself—it is very difficult to take care of another person. In the Buddhist teaching, it's clear that to love oneself is the foundation of the love of other people. Love is a practice. Love is truly a practice.

SS: Why don't we love ourselves?

TNH: We may have a habit within ourselves of looking for happiness elsewhere than in the here and the now. We may lack the capacity to realize that happiness is possible in the here and now, that we already have enough conditions to be happy right now. The habit energy is to believe that happiness is not possible now, and that we have to run to the future in order to get some more conditions for happiness. That prevents us from being established in the present moment, from getting in touch with the wonders of life that are available in the here and now. That is why happiness is not possible.

To go home to the present moment, to take care of oneself, to get in touch with the wonders of life that are really available—that is already love. Love is to be kind to yourself, to be compassionate to yourself, to generate images of joy, and to look at everyone with eyes of equanimity and nondiscrimination.

That is something to be cultivated. Nonself can be achieved. It can be touched slowly. The truth can be cultivated. When you discover something, in the beginning you discover only part of it. If you continue, you have a chance to discover more. And finally you discover the whole thing. When you love, if your love is true, you begin to see that the other person is a part of you and you are a part of her or him. In that realization there is already nonself. If you think that your happiness is different from their happiness, you have not seen anything of nonself, and happiness cannot be obtained.

So as you progress on the path of insight into nonself, the happiness brought to you by love will increase. When people love each other, the distinction, the limits, the frontier between them begins to dissolve, and they become one with the person they love. There's no longer any jealousy or anger, because if they are angry at the other person, they are angry at themselves. That is why nonself is not a theory, a doctrine, or an ideology, but a realization that can bring about a lot of happiness.

SS: And peace.

TNH: Sure. Peace is the absence of separation, of discrimination.

SS: You are renowned for teachings on community, which in Buddhism is called sangha. Through practices such as the Fourteen Mindfulness Trainings of the Order of Interbeing, you define mindfulness in ways that are social, even political. You teach about communication techniques and the power of deep listening and loving speech. Why do you emphasize the community, interpersonal aspect?

TNH: You have experiences in the practice—peace, joy, transformation, and healing—and on that foundation, you help other people. You don't practice just as an individual, because you realize very soon on the path of practice that you should practice with community if you want the transformation and healing to take place more quickly. This is taking refuge in the sangha.

In sharing the practice with others, the energy of mindfulness, concentration, and joy is much more powerful. That is what the

Buddha liked to do. Everywhere he went, many monastics accompanied him, and that way the monastics could learn from his way of walking and sitting and interacting with people. Soon the community began to behave like an organism, with everyone engaged in the same energy of peace, joy, calm, and brotherhood.

At the same time, everyone in the sangha speaks for the Buddha, speaking for him not just by their words but by the way they act and the way they treat people. That is why King Prasanjit told the Buddha, "Dear teacher, every time I see your community of monks and nuns, I have great faith in you." He meant that the sangha is capable of representing the Buddha. The Buddha with the sangha can achieve a lot of things. I don't think a teacher can do much without a community. It's like a musician, who cannot perform without a musical instrument. The sangha is very important—the insight and the practice of the teacher can be seen in the sangha. It has a much stronger effect when you share in the practice and the teaching as a sangha.

SS: So for the dharma to really be powerful, we must transform not just ourselves but, in effect, society.

TNH: Yes, that is Mahayana. That is going together in a larger vehicle. That is why Buddhism should always be engaged. It's not by cutting yourself off from society that you can realize that. That is why Mahayana, the great vehicle, is already seen in what they call the Hinayana, the lesser vehicle.

SS: Do you think that one reason you emphasize community and society as a practice is the terrible conflict that you saw in your home country of Vietnam? Did seeing a society destroyed by war, seeing the terrible stakes involved, heighten your concern for our community life?

TNH: I think that's true. It is the insight you get when you are in touch with the real situation. But it is also emphasized in the tradition. We say, "I take refuge in sangha," but sangha is made of individual practitioners. So you have to take care of yourself. Otherwise you don't have much to contribute to the community because you do not have enough calm, peace, solidity, and freedom in your heart. That is why in order to build a community, you have to build yourself at the same time. The community is in you, and you are in the community. You interpenetrate each other. That is why I emphasize sangha-building. That doesn't mean that you neglect your own practice. It is by taking good care of your breath, of your body, of your feelings, that you can build a good community, you see.

SS: You've been in the West now for a long time. What do you think are the best ways to present Buddhism to meet the needs of Western students?

TNH: I think Buddhism should open the door of psychology and healing to penetrate more easily into the Western world. As far as religion is concerned, the West already has plenty of belief in a supernatural being. It's not by the law of faith that you should enter the spiritual territory of the West, because the West has plenty of this.

So the door of psychology is good. The Abhidharma literature of Buddhism represents a very rich understanding of the mind, which has been developed by many generations of Buddhists. If you approach the Western mind through the door of psychology, you may have better success helping people to understand their mind, helping people to practice in such a way that they can heal the mind and the body.

The mind and body are very much linked to each other, and we can say that the practice of Buddhist meditation has the power to heal the body and the mind. You see this very clearly when you study the basic texts of Buddhist meditation, like the *Anapannasati Sutra*, on the practice of mindful breathing, and the *Sutra of the Four Foundations of Mindfulness*. The practice of meditation helps us to release the tension—within the body, within the mind, within the emotions—so that healing can take place. Even if you take a lot of medicine, it won't work very well if the tension is still strong in your body and your mind. So the Buddha offers very practical methods, such as, "Breathing in, I'm aware of my body; breathing out, I release the tension in my body. Breathing in, I'm aware of the emotion in me; breathing out, I release the tension in the emotion. I embrace my body and my feelings with the energy of mindfulness."

The practice of releasing tension in the body and mind is the foundation of healing. In the beginning it helps to bring you relief. Then, with more mindfulness and concentration, you practice looking more deeply into the pain and the tension, and you find its roots, the cause of the ill-being. You discover the second noble truth. You can identify the source of that tension, that depression, that ill-being. And when you identify the roots of the suffering, namely the second noble truth, then you begin to see the fourth noble truth, the way that leads to the cessation of the ill-being, the tension, and the pain. That is the most important thing to see—the path. If you follow the path, very soon ill-being will disappear and give way to well-being, which is the third noble truth. So the Buddhist principle is the principle of medicine.

Another door that we should open is the door of ecology, because in Buddhism there is a deep respect toward animals, vegetables, and even minerals. In Mahayana Buddhism we say that everyone has buddhanature—not only humans but animals, vegetables, and even minerals. When you study the *Diamond Sutra,* you can see that the *Diamond Sutra* is the oldest text on the protection of environment. The idea of self is removed, because self is made of nonself elements, and the idea of man is removed, because man is made of nonman elements, mainly animals, vegetables, minerals, and so on. That means that in order to protect man, you have to protect the nonman elements. It's very clear.

So the door of ecology is a very wonderful door to open. And the door of peace, because Buddhism is about peace. The true Buddhist cannot refuse working for peace. And I think the door of feminism, the nondiscrimination between genders. The Buddha opened the door for women to enter the holy order, and that was a very revolutionary act on his part.

I think all these dharma doors should be opened wide so the West can receive the true teaching of the Buddha. These dharma doors all exist within the roots of Buddhism, but many generations of Buddhists have lost these values. Buddhists should practice in such a way as to restore these values to the tradition so they can offer them to other people.

SS: Conversely, do you see things in Western thought or knowledge that can contribute to Buddhism?

TNH: I think that democracy and science can help Buddhism, but not in the way people might think. You know, the practice of democracy already exists in the Buddhist tradition. But if you compare it to democracy in the West, you see that Buddhist democracy is more grounded in the truth, because if you are a teacher and you have much more experience and insight, your vote has more value than the vote of a novice who has not got much insight and experience. So in Buddhism, voting should combine the way of democracy with the way of seniority. That is possible. We have done that with a lot of success in our community, because the younger and less experienced people always have faith and respect toward the elder ones. But, you know, many Buddhist communities don't follow that approach; the teacher decides everything and they have lost the democracy. Now we have to restore the democracy, but not as it is practiced in the West. We have to combine it with the spirit of seniority.

Personally, learning about science has helped me to understand Buddhism more deeply. I agree with Einstein that if there is a religion that can go along with science, it is Buddhism. That is because Buddhism has the spirit of nonattachment to rules. You may have a view that you consider to be the truth, but if you cling to it, then that is the end of your free inquiring. You have to be aware that with the practice of looking deeply, you may see things more clearly. That is why you should not be so dogmatic about what you have found; you have to be ready to release your view in order to get a higher insight. That is very exciting.

In the sutra given to the young people of the Kalama tribe, the Kalama Sutra, the Buddha said, "Don't just believe in something because it has been repeated by many people. Don't just believe in something because it has been uttered by a famous teacher. Don't just believe in something even if it is found in holy scripture." You have to look at it, you have to try it and put it into the practice, and if it works, if it can help you transform your suffering and bring you peace and liberty, you can believe it in a very scientific way.

So I think Buddhists should not be afraid of science. Science can help Buddhism to discover more deeply the teaching of the Buddha. For example, the *Avatamsaka Sutra* says that the one is made of the many, and the many can be found in the one. This is something that can be proven by science. Out of a cell, they can duplicate a whole body. In one cell, the whole genetic heritage can be found, and you can make a replica of the whole body. In the one, you see the many. These kinds of things help us to understand the teaching of Buddha more deeply.

So there is no reason why Buddhists have to be afraid of science, especially when Buddhists have the capacity to release their view in order to get a higher view. And in Buddhism, the highest view is no view at all. No view at all! You say that permanence is the wrong view. So you use the view of impermanence to correct the view of permanence. But you are not stuck to the view of impermanence. When you have realized the truth, you abandon not only the view of permanence, but you also abandon the view of impermanence. It's like when you strike a match: the fire that is produced by the match will consume the match. When you practice looking deeply and you find the insight of impermanence, then the insight of permanence will burn away that notion of impermanence.

That is what is very wonderful about the teaching of nonattachment to view. Nonself can be a view, impermanence might be a view, and if you are caught in a view, you are not really free. The ultimate has no view. That is why nirvana is the extinction of all views, because views can bring unhappiness—even the views of nirvana, impermanence, and no-self—if we fight each other over these views.

SS: I very much like the way you describe what other Buddhist traditions call relative and absolute truth. You describe these as the historical and ultimate dimensions. Much of your teaching focuses on the relative or historical dimension, or on the principle of interdependence, which you call interbeing. Is that a complete or final description of reality, or is there a truth beyond the insight that nothing exists independently and all things are interrelated?

TNH: There are two approaches in Buddhism: the phenomenal approach and the true nature approach. In the school of Madhyamaka, in the school of Zen, they help you to strike directly into your true nature. In the school of Abhidharma, mind-only, they help you to see the phenomena, and if you touch the phenomena deeper and deeper, you touch the ultimate. The ultimate is not something separated from the phenomena. If you touch the ultimate, you touch also the phenomena. And if you touch deeply the phenomena, you touch also the ultimate.

It is like a wave. You can see the beginning and the end of a wave. Coming up, it goes down. The wave can be smaller or bigger, or higher or lower. But a wave is at the same time the water. A wave can live her life as a wave, of course, but it is possible for a wave to live the life of a wave and the life of water at the same time. If she can bend down and touch the water in her, she loses all her fear. Beginning, ending, coming up, going down—these don't make her afraid anymore, because she realizes she's water. So there are two dimensions in the wave. The historical dimension is coming up and going down. But in the ultimate dimension of water, there is no up, no down, no being, no nonbeing.

The two dimensions are together and when you touch one dimension deeply enough, you touch the other dimension. There's no separation at all between the two dimensions. Everything is skillful means in order to help you touch the ultimate.

SS: Some people I have spoken to seem to interpret the concept of interbeing as a statement that all things are one. That sounds like one of those views we're not supposed to hold on to.

TNH: Yes. One is a notion, and many is also a notion. It's like being and nonbeing. You say that God is the foundation of being, and then people ask, "Who is the foundation of nonbeing?" [Laughter.] That is why that notion of being and nonbeing cannot be applied to reality. They're only notions. The notion of two different things, or just one, are also notions. Sameness and otherness are notions. Nirvana is the removal of all notions, including the notions of sameness and otherness. So interbeing does not mean that everything is one or that everything is different. It will help you to remove both, so you are not holding a view.

SS: You said that the Buddha was a human being. But the Mahayana says that there are countless buddhas and bodhisattvas at many levels of existence who are sending their compassion to us. How are we rationalist Westerners to understand these beings? How can we open ourselves to them when we can't perceive them with our five senses?

TNH: In Buddhism, the Buddha is considered as a teacher, a human being, and not a god. It is very important to tell people that. I don't need the Buddha to be a god. He is a teacher, and that is good enough for me! I think we have to tell people in the West about that. And because the Buddha was a human being, that is why countless buddhas become possible.

SS: Did the Buddha die?

TNH: Sure. As a human being, you should be born and you should die. That is the historical dimension. Then you have to touch the Buddha deeply in order to touch his or her ultimate dimension. You can also look deeply at an ordinary human being—not a buddha, just a nonbuddha like myself or yourself. If you look deeply at yourself, you see that you have this historical dimension—you have birth and death. But if you look at yourself more deeply, you see that your true nature is the nature of no birth and no death. You are also like a buddha: you have never been born; you'll never die. So in you I see a buddha; in everyone I see buddha in the ultimate dimension.

That's why we can talk about countless buddhas. It is exactly because the Buddha is a human being that countless buddhas are possible.

We have to remember that inside of the historical dimension there is the ultimate dimension. We are not really subjected to birth and death. It is like a cloud. A cloud can never die; a cloud only becomes rain or snow or ice, but a cloud can never be nothing. That is the true nature of the cloud. No birth and no death. A buddha shares the same nature of no birth and no death, and you share the same nature of no birth and no death.

We know that on Earth there are human beings who possess great wisdom and great compassion. They are buddhas. Don't think that the buddhas are very far away up in the sky. You touch the buddha in yourself; you touch the buddha in people around you. It's wonderful that it's possible in the here and the now.

The buddhaland is here. If you know how to practice mindful walking, then you enjoy walking in the pure land of Buddha in the here and the now. This is not something to talk about; it's something to taste. In our tradition, you should walk in such a way that each step helps you to touch the buddhaland. The buddhaland is available to you in the here and now. The question is whether you are available to the pure land. Are you caught by your jealousy, your fear, your anger? Then the pure land is not available. With mindfulness and concentration you have the capacity to touch the celestial realm of the buddhas and the bodhisattvas in the here and the now. That is not theory at all. That is what we live each day. What we practice each day. It's possible.

Many of us are capable of this. When I talk to Christians I say that the Kingdom of God is now or never. You are free, and then the kingdom is there for you. If you are not free, well, the kingdom does not exist, even in the future. So the same teaching and practice can be shared between many traditions.

SS: You've lived a long life during a century that was as terrible as any, in a country that suffered as much as any. I think there are many people who now look at this new century and see, again, the seeds of tragedy, both at the human level and the natural level. Where do you feel the world is headed now?

TNH: I think the twentieth century was characterized by individualism, and more than 100 million people perished because of wars. Too much violence, too much destruction of life and environment. If we want the twenty-first century to be different, if we want healing and transformation, the realization is crucial that we are all one organism, that the well-being of others, the safety of others, is our own safety, our own security. That kind of realization is very crucial. Modern biology has realized that the human being is really a community of billions of cells. No cell is a leader; every cell is collaborating with every other cell in order to produce the kind of energy that helps the organism to be protected and to grow. Only that kind of awakening, that kind of insight—that our danger, our security, our well-being, and our suffering are not something individual but something common to us all—can prevent the destruction that has arisen from individualism in the twentieth century.

This insight of no-self, this insight of togetherness, is very crucial for our survival and for the survival of our planet. It should not be just a notion that we can read in books; this insight should be something that animates our daily life. In school, in business, in the Congress, in the town hall, in the family, we should practice in order to nurture the insight that we are together as an organism, and something happening to the other cells is happening to us at the same time. This insight goes perfectly with science, and it goes perfectly with the spirit of Buddhism. We should learn how to live as an organism.

I have spent much of my time building communities, and I have learned a lot from it. In Plum Village we try to live like an organism. No one has a private car, no one has a private bank account, no one has a private telephone—everything belongs to the community. And yet, happiness is possible. Our basic practice is seeing each one as a cell in the body, and that is why fraternity, brotherhood, sisterhood become possible. When you are nourished by brotherhood, happiness is possible, and that is why we are able to do a lot of things to help other people to suffer less.

This can be seen, it can be felt. It's not something you just talk about. It is a practice, it is a training, and every breath and every step that you take aims at realizing that togetherness. It's wonderful to live in a community like that, because the well-being of the other person is also our well-being. By bringing joy and happiness to one person, we bring joy and happiness to every one of us. That is why I think that community-building, sangha-building, is the most important, most noble work that we can do.

SS: And to extend that to the greater society.

TNH: Yes. It's like in a classroom at school. If the teacher knows how to organize the kids in her class into a family, they will suffer much less and they will have a lot of joy. It's the same in the town hall or in a business. Business leaders can organize their enterprise as a family where everyone can look at each other as a cell of the organism.

We know that in our own body there are many kinds of cells: liver cells, lung cells, neurons. And every cell is doing her best. There's no envy about the position of the other cells, because there's no discrimination at all. It's by being the best kind of liver cell that you can nourish other cells. Every cell is doing her best in order to bring about the well-being of the whole body. There is no discrimination, no fight among the cells, and that is what we can learn from modern biology. We can organize ourselves in this way as a family, as a school, as a town hall, as a Congress. It is possible, because if our cells are able to do that, we humans can do that also.

SS: I hope you don't mind my asking this question, and you don't have to answer. But I have always been very touched by what you've written about a love that you had, someone you clearly loved very deeply, whom you left. How do you feel about that now? Is that, at this point in your life, a regret?

TNH: That love has never been lost. It has continued to grow. The object of my love grows every day, every day, every day, until I can embrace everyone. To love someone is a very wonderful opportunity for you to love everyone. If it is true love. In the insight of nonself, you see that the object of your love is always there and the love continues to grow. Nothing is lost and you don't regret anything, because if you have true love in you, then you and your true love are going in the same direction, and each day you are able to embrace, more and more. So to love one person is a great opportunity for you to love many more.

SS: Yet monasticism—and you are very encouraging toward those who would like to become monks or nuns—renounces this love. Why is it a good thing to forego this opportunity to love?

TNH: In the life of a monastic, you make the vow to develop your love and your understanding. You develop the capacity to embrace everyone into your love. So loving one person, as I said, is an opportunity for you to love many more people. Especially when that person shares the same aspiration as you, there is no suffering at all. As a monastic you lead a life of monastic celibacy and community, and if the one you love realizes that, she will not suffer and you will not suffer, because love is much more than having a sexual relationship. Because of great love you can sacrifice that aspect of love, and your love becomes much greater. That nourishes you, that nourishes the other person, and finally your love will have no limit. That is the Buddha's love.

Our True Home

Thich Nhat Hanh

Our true home is nowhere but in this present moment. Our true being is no one but who we are right now. That we find this so difficult to accept is the greatest of all mysteries. Perhaps the key is trust in the great teachers like Thich Nhat Hanh who tell us this is so.

Do you remember anything from your stay in your mother's womb? All of us spent about nine months there. That's quite a long time. I believe that all of us had a chance to smile during that time. But who were we smiling at? When we're happy, there's a natural tendency to smile. I have seen people, especially children, smiling during their sleep.

Our time in our mothers' wombs was a wonderful time. We did not have to worry about food or drink. We were protected from heat and cold. We didn't have to do homework or housework. Protected in our mothers' wombs, we felt quite safe. We didn't have to worry about anything at all. No worry is wonderful. I believe many of us still remember that time spent in our mothers' wombs. Many people have the impression that they were once in a safe and wonderful paradise and now they have lost that paradise. We think somewhere out there is a beautiful place without worry or fear, and we long to get back there. In the Vietnamese language, the word for *uterus* is "the palace of the child." Paradise was inside of our mothers.

In the womb, your mother took care of you. She ate and drank for you. She breathed air for you, in and out. And I guess that she dreamed for you as well. I imagine you dreamed your mother's dreams. And if your mother smiled, I think you smiled too. If your mother dreamed about something difficult, and she cried in her dream, I guess that you probably cried with her. You shared her dreams and her nightmares, because you and your mother weren't two separate people. You were physically attached to your mother through the umbilical cord. And your mother channeled to you through that umbilical cord food and drink, oxygen, everything, including her love. Your mother probably took care of her body differently when you were in it. She may have been more careful while walking. She may have stopped drinking or quit smoking. These are very concrete expressions of love and care. You were there, you had not been born, and yet you were the object of love.

Your mother nourished you before you were born, but if you look deeply, you will see that you also nourished your parents. Because of your presence in her body, they may have smiled more and loved life even more. You hadn't done anything to your parents yet, and yet they were nourished by your presence. And their life changed from the moment of your conception in your mother's womb. Perhaps your mother talked to you before you were born. And I believe, I am convinced, that you heard her talking with you and you responded. Perhaps it happened that occasionally she forgot you were there. So perhaps you gave her a kick to remind her. Your kick was a bell of mindfulness, and when she felt that, she may have said, "Darling, I know you are there and I am very happy." This is the first mantra.

When you were first born, someone cut your umbilical cord. And quite likely you cried aloud for the first time. Now you had to breathe for yourself. Now you had to get used to all the light surrounding you. Now you had to experience hunger for the first time. You were outside of your mother, but still somehow inside her. She embraced you with her love. And you embraced her at the same time. You were still dependent on her. You may have nursed at her breast. She took care of you day and night. And although the cord was no longer whole between you, you were linked to your mother in a very concrete, intimate way.

As an adult, you may fight very hard to convince yourself that you and your mother are two different people. But it's not really so. You are a continuation of both your parents. When I meditate, I can still see the cord connecting me to my mother. When I look deeply, I see there are umbilical cords linking me to phenomena as well. The sun rises every morning. And thanks to the sun, we have heat and light. Without these things, we can't survive.

So an umbilical cord links you to the sun. Another umbilical cord links you to the clouds in the sky. If the clouds were not there, there would be no rain and no water to drink. Without clouds, there is no milk, no tea, no coffee, no ice cream, nothing. There is an umbilical cord linking you to the river; there is one linking you to the forest. If you continue meditating like this, you can see that you are linked to everything and everyone in the cosmos. Your life depends on everything else that exists—on other living beings, but also on plants, minerals, air, water, and earth.

Suppose you plant a kernel of corn and seven days later it sprouts and begins to take the form of a corn stalk. When the stalk grows high, you may not recognize it as the kernel you planted. But it wouldn't be true to say the kernel had died. With Buddha's eyes, you can still see the corn seed in the corn stalk. The stalk is the continuation of the kernel in the direction of the future, and the kernel is the continuation of the stalk in the direction of the past. They are not the same thing, but they are not completely separate either. You and your mother are not exactly the same person, but you aren't two different people either. This is the truth of interdependence. No one can be one's self alone. We have to *inter-be* to be.

When we are inside our mothers, there is no tension in our bodies. We are soft and flexible. But once we are out in the world, tension creeps in, sometimes from our first breath. Before we can release the tension in our bodies, though, we have to release the tension in our breath. If our bodies are not peaceful, then our breath is not peaceful. When we generate the energy of mindfulness and embrace our breath, the quality of our in-breath and out-breath will improve. As we breathe in mindfulness, our breathing becomes calmer and more profound. The tension in our breathing dissipates. And when our breathing is relaxed, we can embrace our bodies and we can relax. The exact word that the Buddha used translates as "calm."

There is a Pali text called the *Kayagatasati Sutta,* the *Sutra on the Contemplation of the Body in the Body.* In it, the Buddha proposed an exercise for releasing the tension in each particular part of the body, and in the body as a whole. He used the image of a farmer who went up to the attic and brought down a bag of beans. The farmer opened one end of the bag, and he allowed all the beans to flow out. With his good eyesight, he was able to distinguish the particular kind of beans and see which were kidney beans, which were mung beans, and so forth. The Buddha recommended that, like this farmer, we learn to pay attention.

To begin, you can lie in a comfortable position and scan your whole body, and then focus on different parts of the body. Begin with the head, or the hair on the head, and finish with the toes. You can say, "Breathing in, I am aware of my brain. Breathing out, I smile to my brain." Continue with the rest of your body. Like the farmer with his seeds, scan the body—not with x-rays but with the ray of mindfulness. Even fifteen minutes is enough time to scan your body slowly with the energy of mindfulness.

When the fully conscious mind recognizes a part of the body and embraces it with the energy of mindfulness, that part of the body is finally allowed to relax and release its tension. This is why smiling is such a good way to help your body relax. Your first smiles in the womb were completely relaxed smiles. There are hundreds of muscles in your face, and when you get angry or fearful, they get very tense. But if you know to breathe in and to be aware of them and to breathe out and smile to them, you can help these muscles release the tension. With one in-breath and out-breath, your face can transform. One smile can bring a miracle.

If, during your scan, you come to a part of your body that is sore or ill, stay focused on that part longer. We tend to hurry past pain. But this hurrying causes more tension instead of healing. If we spend more time with what hurts, using the energy of mindfulness, we can smile at our pain and release some of the tension. If we know how to help release the tension in that part of the body, the healing will take place much more quickly.

You may be in real physical pain. Mindfulness will tell you that it is only a physical pain. The Buddha spoke about the second arrow. He tells the story of a person struck by an arrow who is in a lot of pain. Suppose a second arrow hit the man in exactly the same spot. The pain would be a hundred times more intense because he was already wounded. Worry, fear, exaggeration, and anger about an injury act as a second arrow, aggravating a part of the body that is already wounded. So if you are struck by one arrow, you can practice mindfulness so that another arrow of fear or worry doesn't hit you in that same spot.

In the *Sutra on the Contemplation of the Body in the Body,* the Buddha advises us to become aware of the four natural elements within the body. In the womb, these elements of water, fire, air, and earth are completely balanced. The mother balances the womb for the baby, sending in oxygen and nutrients as the baby rests in water. Once we are born, if we have a balance within the four elements, then we are in good health. But often these elements are out of balance; we cannot get warm, or we find it difficult to take a full breath. Often, our mindful breath can naturally bring these elements into balance.

The Buddha also recommended that we become aware of our body's positions and actions. In sitting meditation, the first thing is to be aware that you are in a sitting position. Then you can sit in a way that brings you calm, solidity, and well-being. In each moment we can notice the position of our body, whether we are sitting, walking, standing, or lying down. We can be aware of our actions, whether we are getting up, bending down, or putting on a jacket. Awareness brings us back to ourselves, and when we are fully mindful of our body, and living in the here and now, we are in our true home.

Did you know you had a true home? This question touches everybody. Even if you have the feeling that you don't belong to any land, to any country, to any geographical spot, to any cultural heritage, or to any particular ethnic group, you have a true home. When you were in your mother's body, you felt at home. Perhaps you long for a return to that place of peace and safety. But now, inside of your own body, you can come home.

Your true home is in the here and the now. It is not limited by time, space, nationality, or race. Your true home is not an abstract idea. It is something you can touch and live in every moment. With mindfulness and concentration, the energies of the Buddha, you can find your true home in the full relaxation of your mind and body in the present moment. No one can take it away from you. Other people can occupy your country, they can even put you in prison, but they cannot take away your true home and your freedom.

When we stop speaking and thinking and enjoy deeply our in- and out-breath, we are enjoying being in our true home and we can touch deeply the wonders of life. This is the path shown to us by the Buddha. When you breathe in, you bring all yourself together, body and mind; you become one. And equipped with that energy of mindfulness and concentration, you may take a step. You have the insight that this is your true home—you are alive, you are fully present, you are touching life as a reality. Your true home is a solid reality that you can touch with your feet, with your hands, and with your mind.

It is fundamental that you touch your true home and realize your true home in the here and the now. All of us have the seed of mindfulness and concentration in us. By taking a mindful breath or making a mindful step, you can bring your mind back to your body. In your daily life, your body and mind often go in two different directions. You are in a state of distraction; mind in one place, body in another. Your body is putting on a coat, but your mind is preoccupied, caught in the past or the future. But between your mind and your body, there is something: your breath. And as soon as you go home to your breath and you breathe with awareness, your body and mind come together very quickly. While breathing in, you don't think of anything; you just focus your attention on your in-breath. You focus, you invest 100 percent of yourself in your in-breath. You become your in-breath. There is a concentration on your in-breath that will make body and mind come together in just one moment. And suddenly you find yourself fully present, fully alive. There is no more longing to return to the womb, to your perfect paradise. You are already there, already home.

There's No "I" in Happy

Matthieu Ricard

Here, the French monk and former scientist Matthieu Ricard expands on the analysis offered to us by the Dalai Lama. The diagnosis for unhappiness is called the Second Noble Truth, the truth that our continuing struggle to maintain the illusion of an independent and permanent self is the cause of our suffering. To put it another way, our search for happiness is the very reason we're unhappy.

An American friend of mine, a successful photography editor, once told me about a conversation she'd had with a group of friends after they'd finished their final college exams and were wondering what to do with their lives. When she'd said, "I want to be happy," there was an embarrassed silence, and then one of her friends had asked, "How could someone as smart as you want nothing more than to be happy?" My friend answered, "I didn't say how I want to be happy. There are so many ways to find happiness: start a family, have kids, build a career, seek adventure, help others, find inner peace. Whatever I end up doing, I want my life to be a truly happy one."

The word *happiness*, writes Henri Bergson, "is commonly used to designate something intricate and ambiguous, one of those ideas which humanity has intentionally left vague, so that each individual might interpret it in his own way." From a practical point of view, leaving the definition of *happiness* vague wouldn't matter if we were talking about some inconsequential feeling. But the truth is altogether different, since we're actually talking about a way of being that defines the quality of every moment of our lives. So what exactly is happiness?

Sociologists define *happiness* as "the degree to which a person evaluates the overall quality of his present life-as-a-whole positively. In other words, how much the person likes the life he or she leads." This definition, however, does not distinguish between profound satisfaction and the mere appreciation of the outer conditions of our lives. For some, happiness is just "a momentary, fleeting impression, whose intensity and duration vary according to the availability of the resources that make it possible." Such happiness must by nature be elusive and dependent on circumstances that are quite often beyond our control. For the philosopher Robert Misrahi, on the other hand, happiness is "the radiation of joy over one's entire existence or over the most vibrant part of one's active past, one's actual present, and one's conceivable future." Maybe it is a more enduring condition. According to André Comte-Sponville, "By 'happiness' we mean any span of time in which joy would seem immediately possible."

Is happiness a skill that, once acquired, endures through the ups and downs of life? There are a thousand ways of thinking about happiness, and countless philosophers have offered their own. For Saint Augustine, happiness is "a rejoicing in the truth." For Immanuel Kant, happiness must be rational and devoid of any personal taint, while for Marx, it is about growth through work. "What constitutes happiness is a matter of dispute," Aristotle wrote, "and the popular account of it is not the same as that given by the philosophers."

Has the word *happiness* itself been so overused that people have given up on it, turned off by the illusions and platitudes it evokes? For some people, talking about the search for happiness seems almost in bad taste. Protected by their armor of intellectual complacency, they sneer at it as they would at a sentimental novel.

How did such a devaluation come about? Is it a reflection of the artificial happiness offered by the media? Is it a result of the failed efforts we use to find genuine happiness? Are we supposed to come to terms with unhappiness rather than make a genuine and intelligent attempt to untangle happiness from suffering?

What about the simple happiness we get from a child's smile or a nice cup of tea after a walk in the woods? As rich and comforting as such genuine glimpses of happiness might be, they are too circumstantial to shed light on our lives as a whole. Happiness can't be limited to a few pleasant sensations, to some intense pleasure, to an eruption of joy or a fleeting sense of serenity, to a cheery day or a magic moment that sneaks up on us in the labyrinth of our existence. Such diverse facets are not enough in themselves to build an accurate image of the profound and lasting fulfillment that characterizes true happiness.

By *happiness,* I mean here a deep sense of flourishing that arises from an exceptionally healthy mind. This is not a mere pleasurable feeling, a fleeting emotion, or a mood, but an optimal state of being. Happiness is also a way of interpreting the world, since while it may be difficult to change the world, it is always possible to change the way we look at it.

Changing the way we see the world does not imply naive optimism or some artificial euphoria designed to counterbalance adversity. So long as we are slaves to the dissatisfaction and frustration that arise from the confusion that rules our minds, it will be just as futile to tell ourselves, "I'm happy! I'm happy!" over and over again as it would be to repaint a wall in ruins. The search for happiness is not about looking at life through rose-colored glasses or blinding oneself to the pain and imperfections of the world. Nor is happiness a state of exultation to be perpetuated at all costs; it is the purging of mental toxins, such as hatred and obsession, that literally poison the mind. It is also about learning how to put things in perspective and reduce the gap between appearances and reality. To that end we must acquire a better knowledge of how the mind works and a more accurate insight into the nature of things, for in its deepest sense, suffering is intimately linked to a misapprehension of the nature of reality.

REALITY AND INSIGHT

What do we mean by *reality*? In Buddhism the word connotes the true nature of things, unmodified by the mental constructs we superimpose upon them. Such concepts open up a gap between our perception and reality, and create a never-ending conflict with the world. "We read the world wrong and say that it deceives us," wrote Rabindranath Tagore. We take for permanent that which is ephemeral and for happiness that which is but a source of suffering: the desire for wealth, for power, for fame, and for nagging pleasures.

By *knowledge*, we mean not the mastery of masses of information and learning but an understanding of the true nature of things. Out of habit, we perceive the exterior world as a series of distinct, autonomous entities to which we attribute characteristics that we believe belong inherently to them. Our day-to-day experience tells us that things are "good" or "bad." The "I" that perceives them seems to us to be equally concrete and real. This error, which Buddhism calls ignorance, gives rise to powerful reflexes of attachment and aversion that generally lead to suffering. As Etty Hillesum says so tersely, "That great obstacle is always the representation and never the reality." The world of ignorance and suffering—called *samsara* in Sanskrit—is not a fundamental condition of existence but a mental universe based on our mistaken conception of reality.

The world of appearances is created by the coming together of an infinite number of ever-changing causes and conditions. Like a rainbow that forms when the sun shines across a curtain of rain and then vanishes when any factor contributing to its formation disappears, phenomena exist in an essentially interdependent mode and have no autonomous and enduring existence. Everything is relation; nothing exists in and of itself, immune to the forces of cause and effect. Once this essential concept is understood and internalized, the erroneous perception of the world gives way to a correct understanding of the nature of things and beings: this is insight. Insight is not a mere philosophical construct; it emerges from a basic approach that allows us gradually to shed our mental blindness and the disturbing emotions it produces and hence the principal causes of our suffering.

Every being has the potential for perfection, just as every sesame seed is permeated with oil. Ignorance, in this context, means being unaware of that potential, like the beggar who is unaware of the treasure buried beneath his shack. Actualizing our true nature, coming into possession of that hidden wealth, allows us to live a life full of meaning. It is the surest way to find serenity and let genuine altruism flourish.

There exists a way of being that underlies and suffuses all emotional states, that embraces all the joys and sorrows that come to us. A happiness so deep that, as Georges Bernanos wrote, "Nothing can change it, like the vast reserve of calm water beneath a storm." The Sanskrit word for this state of being is *sukha*.

Sukha is the state of lasting well-being that manifests itself when we have freed ourselves of mental blindness and afflictive emotions. It is also the wisdom that allows us to see the world as it is, without veils or distortions. It is, finally, the joy of moving toward inner freedom and the loving-kindness that radiates toward others.

First we conceive the "I" and grasp onto it.
Then we conceive the "mine" and cling to the material world.
Like water trapped on a waterwheel, we spin in circles,
    powerless.
I praise the compassion that embraces all beings.
—CHANDRAKIRTI

Mental confusion is a veil that prevents us from seeing reality clearly and clouds our understanding of the true nature of things. Practically speaking, it is also the inability to identify the behavior that would allow us to find happiness and avoid suffering. When we look outward, we solidify the world by projecting onto it attributes that are in no way inherent to it. Looking inward, we freeze the flow of consciousness when we conceive of an "I" enthroned between a past that no longer exists and a future that does not yet exist. We take it for granted that we see things as they are and rarely question that opinion. We spontaneously assign intrinsic qualities to things and people, thinking "this is beautiful, that is ugly," without realizing that our mind superimposes these attributes upon what we perceive. We divide the entire world between "desirable" and "undesirable," we ascribe permanence to ephemera and see independent entities in what is actually a network of ceaselessly changing relations. We tend to isolate particular aspects of events, situations, and people, and to focus entirely upon these particularities. This is how we end up labeling others as "enemies," "good," "evil," etc., and clinging strongly to those attributions. However, if we consider reality carefully, its complexity becomes obvious.

If one thing were truly beautiful and pleasant, if those qualities genuinely belonged to it, we could consider it desirable at all times and in all places. But is anything on earth universally and unanimously recognized as beautiful? As the canonical Buddhist verse has it: "For the lover, a beautiful woman is an object of desire; for the hermit, a distraction; for the wolf, a good meal." Likewise, if an object were inherently repulsive, everyone would have good reason to avoid it. But it changes everything to recognize that we are merely attributing these qualities to things and people. There is no intrinsic quality in a beautiful object that makes it beneficial to the mind, and nothing in an ugly object to harm it.

In the same way, a person whom we consider today to be an enemy is most certainly somebody else's object of affection, and we may one day forge bonds of friendship with that selfsame enemy. We react as if characteristics were inseparable from the object we assign them to. Thus we distance ourselves from reality and are dragged into the machinery of attraction and repulsion that is kept relentlessly in motion by our mental projections. Our concepts freeze things into artificial entities and we lose our inner freedom, just as water loses its fluidity when it turns to ice.

The Crystallization of the Ego

Among the many aspects of our confusion, the most radically disruptive is the insistence on the concept of a personal identity: the ego. Buddhism distinguishes between an innate, instinctive "I"—when we think, for instance, "I'm awake" or "I'm cold"—and a conceptual "self" shaped by the force of habit. We attribute various qualities to it and posit it as the core of our being, autonomous and enduring.

At every moment between birth and death, the body undergoes ceaseless transformations and the mind becomes the theater of countless emotional and conceptual experiences. And yet we obstinately assign qualities of permanence, uniqueness, and autonomy to the self. Furthermore, as we begin to feel that this self is highly vulnerable and must be protected and satisfied, aversion and attraction soon come into play—aversion for anything that threatens the self, attraction to all that pleases it, comforts it, boosts its confidence, or puts it at ease. These two basic feelings, attraction and repulsion, are the fonts of a whole sea of conflicting emotions.

The ego, writes Buddhist philosopher Han de Wit, "is also an affective reaction to our field of experience, a mental withdrawal based on fear." Out of fear of the world and of others, out of dread of suffering, out of anxiety about living and dying, we imagine that by hiding inside a bubble—the ego—we will be protected. We create the illusion of being separate from the world, hoping thereby to avert suffering. In fact, what happens is just the opposite, since ego-grasping and self-importance are the best magnets to attract suffering.

Genuine fearlessness arises with the confidence that we will be able to gather the inner resources necessary to deal with any situation that comes our way. This is altogether different from withdrawing into self-absorption, a fearful reaction that perpetuates deep feelings of insecurity.

Each of us is indeed a unique person, and it is fine to recognize and appreciate who we are. But in reinforcing the separate identity of the self, we fall out of sync with reality. The truth is, we are fundamentally interdependent with other people and our environment.

Our experience is simply the content of the mental flow, the continuum of consciousness, and there is no justification for seeing the self as an entirely distinct entity within that flow. Imagine a spreading wave that affects its environment and is affected by it but is not the medium of transmission for any particular entity. We are so accustomed to affixing the "I" label to that mental flow, however, that we come to identify with it and to fear its disappearance. There follows a powerful attachment to the self and thus to the notion of "mine"— my body, my name, my mind, my possessions, my friends, and so on—which leads either to the desire to possess or to the feeling of repulsion for the "other." This is how the concepts of the self and of the other crystallize in our minds. The erroneous sense of duality becomes inevitable, forming the basis of all mental affliction, be it alienating desire, hatred, jealousy, pride, or selfishness. From that point on, we see the world through the distorting mirror of our illusions. We find ourselves in disharmony with the true nature of things, which inevitably leads to frustration and suffering.

We can see this crystallization of "I" and "mine" in many situations of daily life. You are napping peacefully in a boat in the middle of a lake. Another craft bumps into yours and wakes you with a start. Thinking that a clumsy or prankish boater has crashed into you, you leap up furious, ready to curse him out, only to find that the boat in question is empty. You laugh at your own mistake and return peaceably to your nap. The only difference between the two reactions is that in the first case, you'd thought yourself the target of someone's malice, while in the second you realized that your "I" was not a target.

Here is another example to illustrate our attachment to the idea of "mine." You are looking at a beautiful porcelain vase in a shop window when a clumsy salesman knocks it over. "What a shame! Such a lovely vase!" you sigh, and continue calmly on your way. On the other hand, if you had just bought that vase and had placed it proudly on the mantle, only to see it fall and smash to smithereens, you would cry out in horror, "My vase is broken!" and be deeply affected by the accident. The sole difference is the label "my" that you had stuck to the vase.

This erroneous sense of a real and independent self is, of course, based on egocentricity, which persuades us that our own fate is of greater value than that of others. If your boss scolds a colleague you hate, berates another you have no feelings about, or reprimands you bitterly, you will feel pleased or delighted in the first case, indifferent in the second, and deeply hurt in the third. But in reality, what could possibly make the well-being of any one of these three people more valuable than that of the others? The egocentricity that places the self at the center of the world has an entirely relative point of view. Our mistake is in fixing our own point of view and hoping, or worse yet, insisting, that "our" world prevail over that of others.

THE DECEPTIVE EGO

In our day-to-day lives, we experience the self through its vulnerability. A simple smile gives it instant pleasure and a scowl achieves the contrary. The self is always "there," ready to be wounded or gratified. Rather than seeing it as multiple and elusive, we make it a unitary, central, and permanent bastion. But let's consider what it is we suppose contributes to our identity. Our body? An assemblage of bones and flesh. Our consciousness? A continuous stream of instants. Our history? The memory of what is no more. Our name? We attach all sorts of concepts to it—our heritage, our reputation, and our social status—but ultimately it's nothing more than a grouping of letters. When we see the word *John*, our spirits leap; we think, "That's me!" But we only need to separate the letters, *J-o-h-n*, to lose all interest. The idea of "our" name is just a mental fabrication.

It is the deep sense of self lying at the heart of our being that we have to examine honestly. When we explore the body, the speech, and the mind, we come to see that this self is nothing but a word, a label, a convention, a designation. The problem is, this label thinks it's the real deal. To unmask the ego's deception, we have to pursue our inquiry to the very end. When you suspect the presence of a thief in your house, you have to inspect every room, every corner, every potential hiding place, just to make sure there's really no one there.

Only then can you rest easy. We need introspective investigation to find out what's hiding behind the illusion of the self that we think defines our being.

Rigorous analysis leads us to conclude that the self does not reside in any part of the body, nor is it some diffuse entity permeating the entire body. We willingly believe that the self is associated with consciousness, but consciousness too is an elusive current: in terms of living experience, the past moment of consciousness is dead (only its impact remains), the future is not yet, and the present doesn't last. How could a distinct self exist, suspended like a flower in the sky, between something that no longer exists and something that does not yet exist? It cannot be detected in either the body or the mind; it is neither a distinct entity in a combination of the two, nor one outside of them. No serious analysis or direct introspective experience can lead to a strong conviction that we possess a self. Someone may believe himself to be tall, young, and intelligent, but neither height nor youth nor intelligence is the self. Buddhism therefore concludes that the self is just a name we give to a continuum, just as we name a river the Ganges or the Mississippi. Such a continuum certainly exists, but only as a convention based upon the interdependence of the consciousness, the body, and the environment. It is entirely without autonomous existence.

The Deconstruction of the Self

To get a better handle on this, let's resume our analysis in greater detail. The concept of personal identity has three aspects: the "I," the "person," and the "self." These three aspects are not fundamentally different from one another but reflect the different ways we cling to our perception of personal identity.

The "I" lives in the present; it is the "I" that thinks, "I'm hungry" or "I exist." It is the locus of consciousness, thoughts, judgment, and will. It is the experience of our current state.

As the neuropsychiatrist David Galin clearly summarizes, the notion of the "person" is broader. It is a dynamic continuum extending through time and incorporating various aspects of our corporeal, mental, and social existence. Its boundaries are more fluid. The person can refer to the body ("personal fitness"), intimate thoughts ("a very personal feeling"), character ("a nice person"), social relations ("separating one's personal from one's professional life"), or the human being in general ("respect for one's person"). Its continuity through time allows us to link the representations of ourselves from the past to projections into the future. It denotes how each of us differs from others and reflects our unique qualities. The notion of the person is valid and healthy so long as we consider it simply as connoting the overall relationship between the consciousness, the body, and the environment. It becomes inappropriate and unhealthy when we consider it to be an autonomous entity.

As to the "self," we've already seen how it is believed to be the very core of our being. We imagine it as an invisible and permanent thing that characterizes us from birth to death. The self is not merely the sum of my limbs, my organs, my skin, my name, my consciousness, but their exclusive owner. We speak of "my arm" and not of an "elongated extension of my self." If our arm is cut off, the self has simply lost an arm but remains intact. A person without limbs feels his physical integrity to be diminished, but clearly believes he has preserved his self. If the body is cut into cross sections, at what point does the self begin to vanish? We perceive a self so long as we retain the power of thought. This leads us to Descartes's celebrated phrase underlying the entire Western concept of the self: "I think, therefore I am." But the fact of thought proves absolutely nothing about the existence of the self, because the "I" is nothing more than the current contents of our mental flow, which changes from moment to moment. It is not enough for something to be perceived or conceived of for that thing to exist. We clearly see a mirage or an illusion, neither of which has any reality.

The idea that the self might be nothing but a concept runs counter to the intuition of most Western thinkers. Descartes, again, is categorical on the subject: "When I consider my mind—that is, myself, given that I am merely a thing that thinks—I can identify no distinct parts to it, but conceive of myself as a single and complete thing." The neurologist Charles Scott Sherrington adds, "The self is a unity. . . . It regards itself as one, others treat it as one. It is addressed as one, by a name to which it answers." Indisputably, we instinctively see the self as unitary, but as soon as we try to pin it down, we have a hard time coming to grips with it.

THE FRAGILE FACES OF IDENTITY

The notion of the "person" includes the image we keep of ourselves. The idea of our identity, our status in life, is deeply rooted in our mind and continuously influences our relations with others. The least word that threatens our image of ourselves is unbearable, although we have no trouble with the same qualifier applied to someone else in different circumstances. If you shout insults or flattery at a cliff and the words are echoed back to you, you remain unaffected. But if someone else shouts the very same insults at you, you feel deeply upset. If we have a strong image of ourselves, we will constantly be trying to assure ourselves that it is recognized and accepted. Nothing is more painful than to see it opened up to doubt.

But what is this identity worth? The word *personality* comes from the Latin *persona,* for an actor's mask—the mask through which (*per*) the actor's voice resounds (*sonat*). While the actor is aware of wearing a mask, we often forget to distinguish between the role we play in society and an honest appreciation of our state of being.

We are generally afraid to tackle the world without reference points and are seized with vertigo whenever masks and epithets come down. If I am no longer a musician, a writer, sophisticated, handsome, or strong, what am I? And yet flouting all labels is the best guarantee of freedom and the most flexible, lighthearted, and joyful way of moving through the world. Refusing to be deceived by the ego in no way prevents us from nurturing a firm resolve to achieve the goals we've set for ourselves and at every instant to relish the richness of our relations with the world and with others. The effect, in fact, is quite the contrary.

Through the Invisible Wall

How can I expect this understanding of the illusory nature of the ego to change my relationships with my family and the world around me? Wouldn't such a U-turn be unsettling? Experience shows that it will do you nothing but good. Indeed, when the ego is predominant, the mind is like a bird constantly slamming into a glass wall—belief in the ego—that shrinks our world and encloses it within narrow confines. Perplexed and stunned by the wall, the mind cannot pass through it. But the wall is invisible because it does not really exist. It is an invention of the mind. Nevertheless, it functions as a wall by partitioning our inner world and damming the flow of our selflessness and joie de vivre. Our attachment to the ego is fundamentally linked to the suffering we feel and the suffering we inflict on others. Renouncing our fixation on our own intimate image and stripping the ego of all its importance is tantamount to winning incredible inner freedom. It allows us to approach every person and every situation with natural ease, benevolence, fortitude, and serenity. With no expectation of gain and no fear of loss, we are free to give and to receive. We no longer have the need to think, speak, or act in an affected and selfish way.

In clinging to the cramped universe of the ego, we have a tendency to be concerned exclusively with ourselves. The least setback upsets and discourages us. We are obsessed with our success, our failure, our hopes, and our anxieties, and thereby give happiness every opportunity to elude us. The narrow world of the self is like a glass of water into which a handful of salt is thrown—the water becomes undrinkable. If, on the other hand, we breach the barriers of the self and the mind becomes a vast lake, that same handful of salt will have no effect on its taste.

When the self ceases to be the most important thing in the

world, we find it easier to focus our concern on others. The sight of their suffering bolsters our courage and resolve to work on their behalf, instead of crippling us with our own emotional distress.

If the ego were really our deepest essence, it would be easy to understand our apprehension about dropping it. But if it is merely an illusion, ridding ourselves of it is not ripping the heart out of our being, but simply opening our eyes.

So it's worthwhile to devote a few moments of our life to letting the mind rest in inner calm and to understanding, through analysis and direct experience, the place of the ego in our lives. So long as the sense of the ego's importance has control over our being, we will never know lasting peace.

On the Shores
of Lake Biwa

Natalie Goldberg

"Dogen?" her Japanese friend says. "No one understands him." "Zen train-ing?" she is warned, "too hard for a human being." Natalie Goldberg goes to Japan in search of the real Zen and finds it on the shores of Lake Biwa. Her days at the monastery are as tough as advertised, but at the end, she finds Almond Joy.

I wanted to go to Japan to see the country that produced my teacher. But Japan was far away. I'm terrible with languages. When I tried to learn short Japanese phrases, it sounded like I was shredding coleslaw with my tongue and not budging one inch from Brooklyn. And all the words of that island country are written in kanji. I wouldn't even be able to decipher signs.

People assured me that everyone in Japan learned English in school. "No problem," they said. I didn't believe them. Hadn't I stud-ied French for eight years? And all I could do was conjugate the verb "to be." Better to just spend my days on Coney Island—I knew where the hot dogs were.

But I had a writing student who had lived in Japan for several years and generously contacted a Japanese couple; they agreed to take me around Kyoto. They spoke good English, so I could ask questions. I talked my partner, Michele, into coming along.

We'd been there a week when Kenji and Tomoko picked us up at the hotel. I already felt isolated, walking down crowded streets, peering into unknown temples. I found myself several times towering over a young man or woman, asking something and receiving giggles behind polite hands. The Japanese might have learned English in school, but they were too shy to speak it.

"They grind their own beans here," Kenji said, as he drove us to a coffee shop.

Just the smell cleared my sinuses. I never drink coffee—I have enough trouble sleeping and fear chugging that dark brew would send me running at 100 m.p.h. But at this moment, I was so elated to speak to a native, not to feel so alone, that I too ordered a shot.

The four of us sat at a small square table, elbow to elbow. "So how do you know English so well?" I asked.

The white cups were placed in front of us. I took a sip. The black blend cut off the top of my head, hair and all. My eyes darted around the room. No tea, cookies, buns, rolls, rice cakes. Zen purity had been translated into a single-taste caffeine shop.

"We lived in England for four years. I was getting a Ph.D. in philosophy," Kenji explained.

"Really? Who did you study over there?" I'd done my master's in Western philosophy in my early twenties. But soon after I'd discovered Zen, I never thought of Bergson or Heidegger again.

"Immanuel Kant."

"You're kidding." My mouth fell open. "I did my thesis on him. You went all the way over to Europe for Kant?" I was incredulous. "In America we want to study Dogen."

It was Kenji's turn to be dumbstruck. "Ugh, no one understands Dogen. He's much too difficult." His nose crunched up.

Then I let the bomb drop. "I've been a Zen student for over two decades."

Now Tomoko grimaced. "That's awful. No one here likes Zen."

I had suddenly become peculiar to this Japanese couple.

Kenji injected, "Zen monks all die young."

I already knew, but asked, anyway, "Why?" I swallowed another gulp of coffee. I was never able to admit the answer through years of knee-aching, backbreaking sitting on little sleep.

"The training's too hard for a human being," he said.

My teacher had died in his early sixties. I could name several other Zen masters who had died too early. I had hoped it was the difficult shift they had made to America.

The conversation slid into pleasantries. Yes, I was a writer. Yes, my first book had been translated into Japanese.

Michele offered to meet them in New York the next time they visited. She described her family's apartment in that favorite of cities. I was watchful for my next opportunity to gather another crumb of information, a morsel of understanding, to slip in another question about my old practice.

My cup was almost empty. If I took one more sip, I'd buzz out the window. I threw care to the neon lights above the entrance and put liquid to mouth. I leaned in close. "Can I ask you a question?" They both nodded simultaneously. Michele rolled her eyes. She knew where this was going. That morning in bed I had had a realization. Maybe I did know a little Japanese after all. In the *zendo* we chanted from cards that translated Japanese sounds into English syllables.

"Does this sound familiar?" I asked and then belted out the first line of the early morning chant that preceded putting on our *rakusus*. At this moment in the zendo our hands would be clasped in front of us with the lay ordination cloth on top of our heads. I saw the whole scene unfold as I chanted *Dai Sai Ge Da Pu Ku* in the coffee shop.

"Never heard of it." Both Kenji and Tomoko shook their heads. They must have learned that head shake in England. When I shook my head No here, everyone looked at me blankly.

"You're kidding." What had I been studying all these years?

"What does it mean?" Tomoko asked.

I was too disappointed to be embarrassed. "Great robe of liberation." They both stared at me.

"This coffee is delicious," Michele quickly interjected and downed her cup.

They explained where they were going to take us. All I caught was "famous temples." I was templed out. Everyplace Michele and I went no one was meditating—just beautiful buildings, ornate altars, highly waxed, fine wood floors. I hadn't realized it, but what I'd come for was sixteenth-century Japan. I was looking for the descendants of Linji and Hakuin. Where were the kick-ass practitioners, like the wild Americans back in the States who were imitating the monks we thought were over here? We woke at four a.m., meditated all day, sewed robes, ate in formal style with three enamel bowls, even had miso soup for breakfast.

I let Michele do the socializing as I sat looking out the car window in the backseat next to Tomoko. Michele shifted the conversation from the dot-com explosion to a list of Japanese authors we'd been reading since we arrived. I perked up. "Yeah, we're reading these prize-winning novels, and it's a surprise how often the plot is around a homosexual or a lesbian. I thought the Japanese were more uptight than that?"

Kenji lifted a hand off the steering wheel. "Oh, no, we're used to it—from the monasteries. The boys go in young."

I gulped. Is that what goes on in monasteries?

They drove us from one ancient shrine to another, all with indiscernible names. I was young again, dragged to one art museum after another. The afternoon was a blur, and my eyes teared. I wanted to lie down and take a deep nap.

"I'm sorry," Kenji said. "We only have one more, but this one is important. You have to see it. Very famous."

Two young girls in navy-blue school uniforms explained the significance of the temple. All of the other visitors were Japanese. Michele and I politely stood with our hands shading our eyes. We didn't understand a word.

My mind was zinging out in the stratosphere, rejoicing that this was the last temple, when one word snapped through my daydream.

Hold everything! Did that ingénue on the left say a familiar name?

"Excuse me, Tomoko," I whispered. "Who lived here in ancient days? What's his name?"

She shrugged. Even though she spoke the language, this world was foreign to her.

"Please, help me." I took her hand. "I have to find out."

The student didn't know what I was talking about even through translation. She handed me the sheet she read from.

"Is the name *Ikkyu* here?" I turned the paper over to Tomoko. "What's the name of this temple?"

Tomoko slowly pronounced, "Daitokuji."

My eyebrows jumped off my face. "Daitokuji. Did this temple burn down in the fifteenth century? Who rebuilt it? Does it say?"

Tomoko looked back at the paper and translated to the young hosts what I was asking. "Hai, hai." In unison they nodded.

"Oh, my god." I threw my hand over my mouth.

The thinner girl pointed to a square white building over the high stuccoed wall we were standing near. This time Kenji translated. "She says Ikkyu is in there."

"Ikkyu in there." My eyes widened, the eccentric Zen monk with a wild spirit whose poetry I loved. I imagined him preserved in *zazen* position in his ragged, brown monk's robe, the one he wore when hanging out with drunks under the bridge.

My hands curled into fists. I wanted to leap the wall, burst into the tomb, bow at his feet, tell him how I'd spent a cold winter and dark spring reading his poems. They never failed me.

When a friend having a hard time would call, I'd say, "Hold on a minute," and grab *Crow with No Mouth*. "Listen to this," and I'd read them Ikkyu.

People were horrified by Ikkyu's unconventional life—he alternated between practicing hard, then frequenting brothels and bars with prostitutes and hoboes. But when he was eighty-two, he was asked to be head of Daitokuji. It was a great honor. He did not refuse. With his tremendous energy, he rebuilt the temple.

The intensity of having Ikkyu nearby was overwhelming. I was afraid I disappointed this great practitioner. He would have leaped over the barrier. He was waiting for me. I think he is still waiting.

I left Michele in Kyoto to travel north by train to Bukkokuji, one of the few Japanese monasteries that were willing to take Westerners and women. I thought, if I was going to be in this country, I had to experience their monasteries, even if for a short time. Michele and I went over my route many times in the hotel before I departed. The train moved fast and I was alert to hear the Obama stop announced, even though I knew it wouldn't be for quite a while.

To my right out the window was a great gray lake, reflecting the overcast sky. I heard, "Biwa."

"Biwa?" I poked the man next to me. This was very un-Japanese, but the train moved so quickly I had to act fast.

He nodded briskly, not glancing my way. "Hai."

At twenty-seven, Ikkyu, meditating alone at midnight out in a rowboat on this very lake, heard the *caw caw caw* of a crow overhead and was turned inside out, becoming totally realized.

He was a poet. It made sense that awakening would enter his body through sound. For a cook the ax might fall while tasting a particularly pungent lemon: she would drop to the ground, savoring bitter lemon in all things.

My stop was finally called and I jumped off, clutching my knapsack. I followed a path through weeds and empty lots into the monastery cemetery. Often at night monks sat at the gravestones and meditated. It was midafternoon. I was nervous. I kept repeating, "You'll be okay. You've sat six three-month difficult practice periods and this time it's just a few days."

The small building complex was a hundred yards away, built right up against a hill. I stepped into the courtyard. No one was there. A beefily built monk appeared and spoke to me in Japanese.

I shook my head. I understood not a word.

He continued to talk and motion with his hands. At this point, Tangen—I recognized his face from a photo—the Zen master of the monastery, who was in his seventies and had rarely left in the last thirty-five years, glided into the courtyard and he and the head monk (I figured out who the beefily built man was) grunted at each other. The head monk then grabbed my pack and I followed him.

Near twin sinks, he stopped and pointed, holding out my sack. I took it and walked alone through a set of doors. Ten thin mattresses were on the floor, and five Japanese nuns with shaved heads were lying on them. Near the entrance was a small, spare woman—the only other Western female at the monastery—who introduced herself and pointed to a rolled bed. I nervously set out my few things, unrolled the mattress, and laid down. I didn't know what the routine would be, but I knew it would be in silence. I tried to rest. How did the saying go? Rest when you rest, sleep when you sleep, cry when you cry. Et cetera, et cetera. I could have made the list go on: be nervous when you're nervous, feel your tight chest when you feel your tight chest, want to go home when you want to go home. I noticed how hot and humid it was. My straight hair was curling. No one else around me had any hair. I remembered my friend who'd been to Japan saying, there is nothing like the humidity. For emphasis he repeated himself: "Trust me, Natalie, in all the world, your clothes will not get wetter than in Japan." Obama was on the sea. I was in for it.

Bells rang. All seven of us in the dormitory sprang up. They put on their robes; I put on my black long-sleeved T-shirt and black long pants, and we sat through two periods of zazen in the upstairs zendo across the court. I had no idea how long each sitting was. It could have been twenty-five minutes or forty. I was just happy to know how to do something and proud at the end to recognize the *Heart Sutra* as it was shot through at a speed no American could follow.

At dinner we ate cross-legged in the dining room in a ritualized style, with three *oryoki* bowls, chopsticks, napkin, and drying cloth. The actual meal was a mush of colors. What hadn't been eaten from breakfast and lunch was consumed at night. What hadn't been eaten from the meals of the days before were also in there. If mold was forming from a week ago, a high boil took care of it all.

At the end of the meal, we fingered thin slices of pickles to clean our bowls, ate the pickle slices, and drank the washing water. The bowls were then wrapped again in the lap cloth with a formal knot. I could do all this, and the Japanese nuns clucked in surprise. We sat zazen again and went to bed. I hadn't spoken a word to anyone. I didn't know what time we would wake the next morning, but I could rely on the tight structure. "Don't think," I told myself. "Take care of your life—connected to all life—moment by moment."

I did not sleep for one moment the entire night. I was drenched in sweat. I think it was three a.m. when the bells rang and everyone popped out of bed. I ran the brush one time over my teeth. We were in the zendo fifteen minutes later.

The zendo was a comfort, but not for long. The bell quickly rang again and people ran down the stairs. Where were they going? I turned around and everyone was gone. I bolted after them and saw the monks running out the gate. I put on my shoes and dashed after them.

The streets of Obama were quiet. I heard only the swish of my rubber soles. Thank god, I hadn't worn flip-flops. I chugged along, but way behind. Suddenly they turned a corner, and I lost them. We were the Japanese Marx Brothers. I headed east on one block, I saw them passing west on another; I darted north at the lamppost, I caught sight of them sprinting south at the turn. I was panting hard. I hadn't run like this in ten years. The sea was to my right as I galloped up an incline. Just as they neared the gate, I caught up. My lungs were burning. My breath was heaving. I was soaked, hair dripping, pants and shirt stuck to my body.

I followed the monks into an empty room, where less than twenty-four hours ago the head monk had grunted at me. Another monk called out a command and everyone hit the ground flat-out; another shout and everyone was on their feet. Then we were slammed on the floor again, doing push-ups. I was already one command behind. They were down; I was up. They were up; I was down. Finally, the exercise stopped. I was a dishrag.

People stood around. Sunlight was creeping across the grave-stones. I sidled over to the Irishwoman and whispered so softly, the sound could have fit under a saltine cracker, "Can we take showers now?"

She replied with a single line: "There are no showers here."

Uh huh, I nodded. I'd heard a rumor years ago back in the comfort of the Minneapolis zendo that baths in Japanese monasteries were taken once a week at public bathhouses.

I sat on a stone step and waited for the next activity. Exhaustion allowed surrender.

The bell rang. We piled up to the zendo and sat for one period. Another bell rang and off everyone dashed down the stairs again. This time I walked. I didn't care if the fires of hell leaped at me. I found the monks in *seiza,* kneeling with their legs tucked under them, on the hard, wooden floor in a single row. A bell rang in another room and the first person in line jumped up and disappeared. The row of people on their knees slid up to the next place.

I knelt at the end, the last person, the longest wait. My knees felt as though they were about to snap, but I didn't change positions. I crawled behind everyone else each time the first person left. I knew what was happening. This was our chance to talk to the roshi, face to face, in his small interview room. I had heard he was clear, that just to watch him walk across a room was inspiring, that he took joy in the smallest things.

What was I doing here with this resounding pain? No one said I had to stay in this position, but everyone else was doing it and I was a stubborn person. Dedication no longer mattered, only animal will. What could I say to this man from another world? I had already had my true teacher. He'd died eight years ago.

My turn came. I did the three prostrations and sat in front of Tangen Roshi. He tilted his head to peer at me. I was hopeless. I knew it. He said three English words: "Not long enough."

I thought, thank god. I was fifty years old. Too old. Too tired. Too dirty.

The gesture was made for me to leave. The meeting was over. I had the urge to put my hand on his knee, to assure him I would be okay. After all, here was a man who was dedicated to waking us up. I didn't want to disappoint him but right then I wanted to go to sleep.

That afternoon after a work period when we beat mattresses and rolled blankets and towels, we had tea—and doughnuts, wrapped in cellophane, bought at a local store. I could tell this was a real treat and I abstained so the monks could have more.

Each day was long. I had no illusions that something big or deep would happen. I just wanted to make it through each day running, walking, sitting, eating in that single pair of black pants and shirt.

Young monks pounded big bells that hung from eaves and ran in the halls. Even the army knows to take boys early. Only me, only I don't know I'm not young. That is what these days taught me: I was no longer young. How easy it was for me at twenty-six, at thirty-one—but even then I complained. Now I had only a few days left in a Japanese monastery and I was thankful I would get to leave.

That day did come and there was no formality. No one said, "Oh, Natalie, we loved having you." I rolled up my mattress, deposited my scant towel and bedding in the laundry room, and slung my pack on my back.

I was thinking how I couldn't wait to return to Kyoto and take a shower when I passed the altar room. I noticed a big Buddha statue and a small inconspicuous donation box, but it wasn't necessary to pay anything for your stay.

I turned to head out. "C'mon, Nat, you can give a little something, even though these days were no fun."

I counted out yen. I was not good at figuring out the equivalent in dollars, a hundred and ten to one, too many zeros. I left what I thought was twenty-five dollars. I followed the path through weeds back to the railroad station. I was a bit early for the next train. I wandered over to the concession stand and eyed the bags of M&M's. A great compulsion overcame me. I bought two. I ripped one open; they were already melted. I shoved the colored chocolates into my mouth and they smeared over my right hand and around my lips. I had nothing to wipe them with but my dirty black sleeve.

Suddenly I looked up: one of the monks from the monastery had just entered the station, recognized me, and was walking over. He was dressed immaculately in formal traveling attire. I tried to hide my chocolate-covered hand, having already wiped my mouth. He stood in front of me in his platform sandals. He noticed my hand and flashed a warm smile. I felt the color come to my face. He reached into the front of his robe. He pulled out some kind of bar and held it up. My eyes focused. Almond Joy. We both burst out laughing.

My train pulled up. I threw myself into a seat near the window and waved. The scenery zoomed by.

All at once, yens popped into my head. I hadn't left 2,750; I'd left 27,500. Two hundred and fifty American dollars. I gasped, my stomach tightened. Then completely let go. It was fine, just fine. I was glad I'd contributed that much. And right there was everything I knew, and I could not say what that was.

Wanting Enlightenment Is a Big Mistake

Seung Sahn

Bodhidharma, founder of the Zen lineage, is said to have described Zen this way: "A special transmission outside the scriptures / Not depending on words and letters / Pointing directly to the human mind / Seeing into one's nature and attaining buddhahood." There's no better example of Zen's direct, penetrating spirit than these exchanges between the late Seung Sahn, one of the great Zen masters to have lived and taught in the United States, and his students.

Someone asked Zen Master Seung Sahn, "What do you think about the beginning of this world?"

"The beginning of this world came from your mouth. Ha, ha, ha, ha! Do you understand?"

The student was silent.

"Then I will explain: what is this world? You must understand that point first. You make time, space, cause, and effect. In three seconds, when you asked that question, you made this whole world. Physics used to teach that time and space, and cause and effect, are absolutes. But modern physics teaches that time, space, and cause and effect are subjective. So you make this whole world, and you make your time and space."

The student said, "I still don't understand."

Zen Master Seung Sahn replied, "OK, so first you must understand, what is time? One unit of time is an hour. But my thinking sometimes makes this hour very long or very short. You go to the airport to pick up your girlfriend. You haven't seen her in a long time. You wait at the airport, and the airplane is very late. Five, ten, twenty, thirty minutes—waiting, waiting, waiting. Even another half hour passes. Ten minutes seems like a whole day. So this one hour feels like a very, very long time because you want to see her very much, and you sit there saying, 'Where is the plane? Why hasn't it arrived yet?' But yet some other time, you go dancing with friends and dance all night, and even one hour seems to pass by very quickly. Now that same amount of time measured as 'one hour' seems very short. 'A whole hour has already passed? It seems like only a minute!' So mind makes one hour very long or very short. Time depends on thinking, because time is created by thinking. The Buddha taught this, and we can test it in our everyday life. 'Everything is created by mind alone.'

"It is the same with space: Spain is here, and New York is there; Korea is over there, and Japan is over here. People in Spain say, 'This way is north, that's south, east, and west.' But on the opposite side of the earth, Korean people say that north is here, south is over there, and east and west are here and here. If I stay here, my north, south, east, and west are like this. If I am not here, my north, south, east, and west disappear. Cause and effect are also the same: if I do some good action, I go to heaven; bad action, go to hell. That's cause and effect. But if I don't make anything, where do I go?

"So I make time and space, and cause and effect. I make my world; you make your world. A cat makes a cat's world. The dog makes the dog's world. God makes God's world. Buddha makes Buddha's world. If you believe in God 100 percent, then when you die, and your world disappears, you go to God's world. If you believe in Buddha 100 percent, then when your world disappears, you will go to Buddha's world. But if you believe in your true self 100 percent, then you make your world, and that's complete freedom: heaven or hell, coming and going anywhere with no hindrance."

Zen Master Seung Sahn looked at the questioner. "So I ask you, which one do you like?"

The student was silent.

"Anytime you open your mouth, your world appears."

The student asked, "So, who was the first person to open his mouth?"

"You already understand!"

Amid general laughter, the student was silent for a few moments. Then he bowed deeply.

A student had the following exchange with Zen Master Seung Sahn. "What is enlightenment?"

"Enlightenment is only a name," he replied. "If you make enlightenment, then enlightenment exists. But if enlightenment exists, then ignorance exists too. And that already makes an opposites-world. Good and bad, right and wrong, enlightened and ignorant—all of these are opposites. All opposites are just your own thinking. But truth is absolute and is before any thinking or opposites appear. So if you make something, you will get something, and that something will be a hindrance. But if you don't make anything, you will get everything, OK?"

The student continued, "But is enlightenment really just a name? Doesn't a Zen master have to attain the experience of enlightenment in order to become a Zen master?"

"The *Heart Sutra* says that there is 'no attainment, with nothing to attain.' If enlightenment is attained, it is not true enlightenment. Having enlightenment is already a big mistake."

"Then is everyone already enlightened?"

Zen Master Seung Sahn laughed and said, "Do you understand 'no attainment'?"

"No."

"'No attainment' is true attainment. So I already told you about the *Heart Sutra*. It says, 'There is no attainment, with nothing to attain.' You must attain 'no attainment.'"

The student rubbed his head. "I think I understand . . ."

"You understand? So I ask you, What is attainment? What is there to attain?"

"Emptiness," the man replied.

"Emptiness?" Zen Master Seung Sahn asked. "But in true emptiness, there is no name and no form. So there is also no attainment. Even opening your mouth to express it, you are already mistaken. If you say, 'I have attained true emptiness,' you are wrong."

"Hmmm," the student said. "I'm beginning to understand. At least I think I am."

"The universe is always true emptiness, OK? Now you are living in a dream. Wake up! Then you will soon understand."

"How can I wake up?"

"I hit you! [Laughter from the audience.] Very easy, yah?"

The student was silent for a few moments, while Zen Master Seung Sahn eyed him intently. "I still don't get it. Would you please explain a bit more?"

"OK. Can you see your eyes?"

"Yes, I can."

"Oh? How?"

"By looking in a mirror."

"That's not your eyes! That is only a reflection of your eyes. So your eyes cannot see your eyes. If you try to see your eyes, it's already a big mistake. Talking about enlightenment is also like that. It's like your eyes trying to see your eyes."

"But my question is, when you were a young monk, you had the actual experience of enlightenment. What was this experience?"

"I hit you! Ha, ha, ha, ha!"

The student was silent.

"OK, one more try. Suppose we have before us some honey, some sugar, and a banana. All of them are sweet. Can you explain the difference between honey's sweetness, sugar's sweetness, and banana's sweetness?"

"Hmmm . . ."

"But each has a different sweetness, yah? How can you explain it to me?"

The student looked suddenly even more perplexed. "I don't know . . ."

The Zen master continued, "Well, you could say to me, 'Open your mouth. This is honey, this is sugar, and this is banana!' Ha, ha, ha, ha! So, if you want to understand enlightenment, it's already making something. Don't make anything. Moment to moment, just do it. That's already enlightenment. So, first understand your true self. To understand your true self, you must understand the meaning of my hitting you. I have already put enlightenment into your mind. Ha, ha, ha, ha!" [Extended laughter from the audience.]

After a dharma talk at the Cambridge Zen Center, a young woman said to Zen Master Seung Sahn, "Tomorrow is my son's birthday, and he told me he wants either a toy gun or money. But I have a problem: as a Zen student, I want to teach him not to hurt or crave things. So I don't want to give him a toy gun or money."

Seung Sahn replied, "A toy gun is necessary! [Laughter from the audience.] If you give him money, he will only go out and buy a toy gun. [Laughter.] Today a few of us went to see a movie called *Cobra*, starring Sylvester Stallone. Do you know this movie? A very simple story: good guy versus bad guys. Other movies are very complicated, you know? But this movie had only two things: bad and good. Bad. Good. A very simple story.

"Your son wants a toy gun. You think that that is not so good. But instead, you should view the problem as: How do you use this correctly? Don't make good or bad. How do you teach the correct function of this gun, OK? That's very important—more important than just having a gun or not. If you use this gun correctly, you can help many people, but if it is not used correctly, then maybe you will kill yourself, kill your country, kill other people. So the gun itself is originally not good, not bad. More important is: what is the correct function of this gun?

"So you must teach your son: If Buddha appears, kill! If the eminent teachers appear, kill! If a Zen master appears, you must kill! If demons appear, kill! If anything appears, you must kill anything,

OK? [Laughter.] Then you will become Buddha! [Much laughter.] So you must teach your son in this way. The gun itself is not good or bad, good or bad. These are only names. Most important is, why do you do something: only for 'me,' or for all beings? That is the most important point to consider."

After a dharma talk at the Cambridge Zen Center, a student asked Zen Master Seung Sahn, "Is there such a thing as a clean mind?"

"If you have mind, then you must clean your mind. If you have no mind, cleaning is not necessary. So I ask you, do you have a mind?"

"Do I?"

"Do you?"

"Yes, I do."

"Where is it?"

The student looked puzzled for a moment. "Where is it?"

"Yes, where is it? How big is your mind?"

"Uhhh . . ."

"This much [holding arms open wide] or this much [narrowing them together]?"

The student tilted his head back and stretched his arms open wide. "This much right now."

"Ooohh, only that? That's very small! [Much laughter from the assembly.] That's not your original mind. Originally, your mind is the whole universe; the whole universe and your mind are the same. Why do you make just 'this much'? So, that is a problem. Since you make 'this-much' mind, now you must dry-clean your mind. Use don't-know soap. If you clean, clean, clean your mind, it will become bigger, bigger, and bigger—as big as the whole universe. But if there is any taint, it becomes smaller, smaller, smaller. But actually, you have no mind, I think."

"You think I have no mind?"

"Yes, no mind."

The student was silent.

"You don't understand, yah? Do you have mind?"

"Well, I don't understand a lot of . . . I don't understand a lot . . . umm . . . I . . ." [Laughter.]

"The Sixth Patriarch said, 'Originally nothing: where can dust alight?' So maybe you have no mind."

After a long silence, the student brightened a bit. "OK, you talk about right livelihood, you talk about having monk karma and wanting to practice Zen . . . umm . . . and my question is . . . not to live in a Zen center . . . to live in the world it's very difficult to practice, umm . . . to coincide practice and livelihood, umm. . . . So, the mind that meets the mind that's conflicted is the mind I'm speaking with . . . fro . . . umm . . ."

"Yah, your mind is a strange mind," Seung Sahn said.

"A strange mind?"

"Yah, strange mind. Nowadays everybody has a strange mind, because inside it's not correct, not meticulous, not clear. This strange mind is like an animal's mind, not really a human being's mind. It is maybe 80 percent animal mind, 20 percent human mind. So that is strange, that's crazy. Nowadays there are many, many crazy people. But everybody is crazy, so this crazy is not special. Even a Zen master's speech is crazy. Yesterday I said in a dharma speech, 'The sun rises in the east and sets in the west.' Those are crazy words. The sun never rises in the east nor sets in the west. The sun never moves! Only the earth moves, around and around the sun, so why make this speech about the sun rising in the east and setting in the west? That's crazy! [Laughter.] So that means: Crazy is not crazy. Not crazy is crazy. [He looks at the questioner's face.] Do you understand that? Crazy is not crazy; not crazy is crazy."

The student started to say something but stopped.

"Ha, ha, ha! Now complicated! That's no problem. Zen teaches that if you have mind, you have a problem. If you don't have mind, then everything is no hindrance. But everybody makes mind, so there are many problems in this world. Say you own a hotel. Mind is like this hotel's manager, who should be working for you. Usually, everything is OK in the hotel, but this manager is always causing problems: 'I want this, I want that.' 'I like this, I don't like that.' 'I want to be free, go here, do that . . .' That is mind, OK? The Buddha taught, 'When mind appears, dharma appears. When dharma appears, form appears. When form appears, then like/dislike, coming/going, life and death, everything appears.' So, if you have mind, you have a problem; no mind, no problem. Here are some very popular words: 'Everything is created by mind alone.' These are good words; they have a good taste. Your mind makes something, and something hinders you. So, don't make anything! Take your mind and throw it into the garbage. Only don't know!"

The student sat, expressionless.

"So Zen practice means you fire this low-class hotel manager, because he's doing a bad job in your high-class hotel. You must take control of your hotel, which means you control your eyes, ears, nose, tongue, body, and mind. The owner must be strong. If the manager doesn't do his job correctly, the owner must say, 'You are no good! Why didn't you fix these things?! That's your job! Why did you take all the money?! I'm going to fire you!' Then this manager will be afraid. 'Oh, please don't fire me! Please!' Then the owner must say, 'You listen to me, OK?' 'OK, OK, I'll only follow you from now on!'

"You must hit your mind, OK? Tell your mind, 'You must listen to me!' If your mind says, 'OK,' then no problem. If not, you must cut this mind. How? You must use your don't-know sword. Always hold on to this don't-know sword: mind is very afraid of it. If you keep this don't-know sword, then everything is no problem."

Brightening up considerably, the student bowed and said, "Thank you very much for your teaching."

After a dharma talk at the Cambridge Zen Center, someone asked Zen Master Seung Sahn, "Why does Zen seem so difficult?"

"Difficult?"

"Yes," the man said. "Why does it seem so difficult? I didn't say it was, but why does it seem so difficult?"

"Seem difficult? Zen is very easy; why make difficult?"

The man persisted, "All right, I'll ask you as a psychologist: why do I make it difficult?"

"A psychologist said that? Who said what?"

"Why do I or anybody make Zen difficult?"

"You say 'difficult,' so it's difficult. A long time ago in China there lived a famous man named Layman Pang. His whole family was a Zen family. Layman Pang used to be rich, but then he realized that many people didn't have enough food to eat. So he gave all of his land to the farmers. He had many precious jewels and other possessions, but he thought, 'If I give things away, they'll only create desire-mind in other people.' So he took a boat out to the middle of a very deep lake and dumped all his priceless possessions overboard. Then he and his daughter went and lived in a cave; meanwhile, his wife and son moved into a very small house. Sometimes the Pangs would visit Zen temples to have dharma combat with the monks. They had a very simple life and practiced very hard.

"One day, someone asked Layman Pang, 'Is Zen difficult or easy?'

"He replied, 'It's like trying to hit the moon with a stick. Very difficult!'

"Then this man thought, 'Oh, Zen is very difficult.' So, he asked Layman Pang's wife, 'Your husband said Zen is difficult. I ask you, then, is Zen difficult or easy?'

"She said, 'Oh, Zen is very easy! It's like touching your nose when you wash your face in the morning!'

"The man could not understand. He thought to himself, 'Hmmm ... Layman Pang says Zen is difficult; his wife says it is very easy. Which one is correct?' So, he went to their son and said, 'Your father said Zen is very difficult; your mother said it is very easy. Which one is correct?'

"The son replied, 'If you think it's difficult, then it's difficult. If you think it's easy, then it's easy. Don't make difficult and easy!'

"But the man was still not satisfied, so he went to the daughter. 'Everyone in your whole family has a different answer to my question. Your mother said Zen is easy. Your father said Zen is difficult. And your brother said don't make difficult and easy. So I ask you, is Zen difficult or easy?'

"'Go drink tea.'"

Seung Sahn Sunim looked at the student who asked the question and said, "So, go drink tea, OK? Don't make 'difficult.' Don't make 'easy.' Don't make anything. From moment to moment, just do it!"

One afternoon, Zen Master Seung Sahn and several of his students were driving down Route I-95, from Providence, Rhode Island, to New York City. They chatted from time to time as they drove, with the students asking him questions about various things. At one point they stopped at a tollbooth. The driver handed the tollbooth operator some money and was waiting for his change. One of the students said to her through the open window, "Nice day, isn't it?"

"Yes," she replied. "But, my goodness, where did all this wind come from?" After she gave them their change, they drove off.

The car was quiet for several miles. Then Zen Master Seung Sahn turned to his students and said, "That was no ordinary woman at the tollbooth. That was Kwan Seum Bosal [the bodhisattva of compassion] asking you a great question: 'Where did all this wind come from?' What a wonderful koan! You must always be alert to the teaching that comes your way, all the time. Let go of your mind and then you can see what's actually in front of you. So I ask you, where did all this wind come from?"

No one could answer.

"OK. I'll give you a hint. Zen Master Man Gong wrote a poem that will help you:

Everything is born by following the wind;
   everything dies by following the wind.
When you find out where the wind comes
   from,
there is no life, no death.

When you have an answer 'like-this,'
You see nature through spiritual eyes."

Discovering the True Nature of Mind

Thrangu Rinpoche

In contrast to the allusive, paradoxical style of Zen, the Vajrayana teachings of Tibet are explicit and descriptive, yet no less profound and difficult to realize. Here, the renowned Tibetan teacher Thrangu Rinpoche offers a commentary on some key verses from "A Song for the King," an early text in poetic style by the Indian sage Saraha, a founder of the Mahamudra tradition. It explains how we can realize the true nature of our minds at this moment and, in doing so, discover the very ground of reality.

REALIZATION WILL REMOVE FAULTS

> Just as the ocean's salty water
> Taken into the clouds turns sweet,
> The stable mind works to benefit others;
> The poison of objects turns into healing nectar.

If we realize the true nature of the mind, this realization itself will remove all defects and problems. These could be of various types—disturbing thoughts or emotions, experiences of intense sadness or regret. They can all be removed through the recognition of mind's nature in mahamudra practice. How this is possible is explained in this verse through an analogy of ocean water. We cannot drink seawater because it is too salty. Nevertheless, after the ocean's water evaporates, gathers into clouds, and returns to the earth as rain, it has become pure. No longer salty, it is fit to drink.

The meaning of this analogy is as follows. We continually give rise to various forms of disturbing emotions. For example, when we encounter an external object that makes us angry, this experience of anger causes us to be unhappy. If we act on this anger, others can suffer as well. To give another example: when we are frustrated by the failure of our endeavors, we can become highly anxious and miserable, and this may last for our whole life.

In each of these situations, it seems to us that the disturbing emotion or suffering that arises in our mind is very solid and powerful. Since it is so intense, it appears to be more powerful than we feel we are. However, if we actually look and meditate on the mind's nature, we discover that all the things arising in our mind—thoughts, disturbing emotions, sadness, and misery—are mere appearances. If we scrutinize them, looking to see what they really are and where they really are, we will discover they are empty of substance and location. When we look directly at the thoughts, disturbing emotions, and misery that arise in our mind, we cannot find where they are located, or where they came from, or whether they have a shape or color. We never find any of these qualities that all the objects seem to have.

Examining here means looking at the thought within the mind, not examining the object that inspired the thought or the condition that led to the disturbing emotion. It is scrutiny of the thought itself; we directly observe the emptiness of the thought. Whether we do this in the context of benefiting others—as the verse states, "the stable mind works to benefit others"—or simply in the context of benefiting ourselves, what happens when we see the nature of thoughts is that the previously poisonous quality of the thought, the disturbing emotion, or the suffering is transformed into a situation of great benefit. And so as the verse states, "the poison of objects turns into healing nectar." We believe that disturbing emotions are terrible, that thoughts are bad, and that sadness is a shame. But the nature of these conditions that arise in our mind is actually flawless bliss. Since we do not recognize their nature, we are afflicted by them. Actually, in and of themselves, thoughts and emotions are not bad, because their nature is peace. Nevertheless, as long as disturbing emotions arise as afflictions, they are, of course, a problem. When we recognize the nature of thoughts, disturbing emotions, or sadness, it is like experiencing a healing nectar. The poison of thoughts and disturbing emotions is transformed into medicine.

In the context of the gradual instruction of mahamudra, this process of scrutinizing thoughts is called "looking at the mind within occurrence," or "looking at the moving mind." It is normally preceded by the practice of looking at the mind within stillness. This latter practice means that when we are in a stable state of meditation, we look directly at our own mind. Specifically, we look to see where and what the mind is. Through this investigation, we eventually discover that there is no location and no substance of mind to be found. In this way, we resolve experientially that the mind is empty.

This verse presents looking at the mind in motion. Occurrence, or movement, means that a thought occurs within the mind. The thought could be any kind of thought—an angry thought, a jealous thought, an arrogant thought, a desirous thought, a sad thought, a happy thought, or a compassionate thought. Whatever the content of the thought may be, when we recognize that a thought has arisen, we look directly at it. In looking at the thought, we see its nature and discover that it is like the nature of the mind itself: it has no location and no substance. It is empty. So through the practice of looking at the mind within the occurrence of thought, we transform the mind's apparent poison into healing nectar, which is its true nature.

Despite Fear, Realization Turns into Bliss

When you realize the ineffable, it is neither suffering nor bliss.
When there is nothing to meditate upon, wisdom itself is bliss.
Likewise, though thunder may evoke fear,
The falling of rain makes harvests ripen.

This verse is concerned with the benefit of realizing the inexpressible or ineffable, which here refers to emptiness. When we use the word *emptiness* or *empty*, it can sound very threatening. Its literal meaning is "nothing," making it sound like annihilation, but the nature of emptiness is great peace or great bliss. We may incorrectly fear the realization of emptiness, believing that this realization will produce the annihilation of experience; however, the realization of emptiness is the realization of great peace and great tranquility. When the realization of emptiness occurs, it is different from what we fear it will be, because there is nothing within emptiness that inherently justifies the fear. Emptiness is not, in and of itself, negative or threatening.

The word *emptiness*, of course, connotes nothingness and makes us think of something like empty space, a mere absence, such as the absence of any qualities or content. But the emptiness of the mind is what is called "emptiness endowed with the best of all aspects." This means that while the mind is empty, it is not a voidness; rather, it is cognitive lucidity. This means, for example, that when you look at your mind, you do not find the mind, nor do you see thoughts in terms of their having a location or possessing substantial characteristics. The mind and the thoughts within the mind are empty, but they are not nothing because there is an unceasing display of mind's cognition. This shows that the absence of substantial existence does not mean that the mind is dead like a stone. For this reason, the realization of this absence of true existence does not cause the cessation of experience.

While being empty of any kind of substantial existence, the mind remains an unceasing awareness. Yet when you look for it, you cannot find it anywhere; you cannot find anything substantial because the mind is empty. It is also unchanging. If the mind were not empty, if the mind had solidity or substantial existence, it would definitely change. Often called "the inexpressible" or "that which is beyond intellect," the mind's emptiness is the reason that the mind is unchanging. And because the mind is unchanging, its nature is great bliss.

The analogy in this verse is the sound of thunder, which represents emptiness, or more precisely, our concept of emptiness. A child, for example, may be frightened by the sound of thunder and may perceive it as threatening. But when you think about it, thunder is a good thing, because thunder is a sign of rain, which ripens the crops. In the same way, while we might think of emptiness as threatening and negative, in fact its nature is great bliss, and therefore the realization of emptiness is very positive.

Appearance and Emptiness Are Nondual

First a thing and in the end a nonthing—neither is established;
likewise, there is nothing other than these two.
There is no place to abide in the beginning, middle, or end.
For those whose minds are obscured by continual concepts,
Emptiness and compassion are expressed in words.

This next verse is concerned with the lack of an inherent substance in the arising, abiding, and cessation of thoughts. Or we could say that it deals with the unity of appearance and emptiness, which then brings forth the realization of the unity of emptiness and compassion.

When we consider the nature of mind or the essential nature of the thoughts that arise in the mind, we assume that these things must have begun somehow and somewhere. They must dwell somewhere, and at some point they must cease. But when we actually look at how a thought arises and what actually happens, we don't find anything creating the thought, nor do we find the location of this arising. When we look for the characteristics that a thought might possess, such as color and shape, we do not find them. When we look to see where the thought is, even though it is vividly present within the mind, we cannot find it anywhere. The thought is not specifically located in any place within the body nor outside the body nor in some area in between. We must conclude that not only does the thought not truly arise, but it also does not abide or rest anywhere.

Finally, when a thought disappears, we look to see what really happens. Where does it go? We do not find anything. In this way, we are brought to the conclusion that thoughts do not truly arise, do not truly abide, and do not truly cease. Whether recognized or not, the nature of our mind has always been just this. It is not that the discovery of this nature makes the mind empty, because the mind has always been so. The problem is that we have never looked into our mind. We have always turned and looked outward, or away from it. This is the meaning of the verse.

This verse also answers this question: What qualities are produced by meditation on emptiness? The purpose of dharma is to help others, and the root of this is compassion. But if all things are empty and if the emptiness of things is realized, is there then no object and therefore no root of compassion? This verse answers that question in the negative. As the Third Karmapa, Rangjung Dorje, pointed out in his *Aspiration Prayer of Mahamudra:* "The very recognition of emptiness itself is the root of compassion." This is because the realization of mind's empty nature and the realization of phenomena's empty nature produces a state of well-being and tranquility in the mind. Disturbing emotions and suffering are pacified, and this causes all manner of positive qualities to develop within the mind. When we realize the true nature of mind, we gain the understanding that all beings without exception possess this same nature, this same potential to achieve all of the positive qualities through realization. At the same time, we realize that only those few fortunate individuals who recognize the nature of mind have all their suffering pacified, and so compassion arises for those who have not attained this realization.

In general, we do not look at our mind and therefore do not recognize the nature of the mind and the nature of the thoughts. Rather, we are caught up by these thoughts, which then generate disturbing emotions, which lead to suffering. Since the basic nature of ordinary beings is the same as the nature of those who have realized mind's nature, we come to see that all of this suffering is really unnecessary: since beings possess this nature, they do not need to suffer at all. This recognition is why the realization of emptiness is the root of compassion. The Third Karmapa wrote: "May intolerable compassion be born in my mind through the realization of emptiness." The compassion that is born through realization is not merely words but intolerably intense.

How Habits Reify Concepts

When a wintry wind strikes and stirs up water,
Though soft, it takes the form of stone.
When concepts attempt to disturb mind's nature, where
    ignorance cannot take form,
Appearances become very dense and solid.

This verse illustrates that all appearances are the appearances of the mind. Earth, stones, mountains, rocks, and so forth all seem very solid to us, so it is quite hard to understand how these things could be merely the appearances of our mind. *The Ocean of Definitive Meaning* points this out in stages: First, it shows that appearances are mind; then, that mind is emptiness; further, that emptiness is spontaneously present; and finally, that spontaneous presence is liberated in and of itself. The subject of this verse is this same point. While earth, mountains, and rocks in their true nature are no different from our mind, in terms of how they appear, they seem vast, huge, and very solid. We might wonder, How can our mind encompass and perceive what is so big and so apparently solid? The analogy here is of water and ice. When it is not frozen, water is a liquid; but when a body of water is subjected to a very cold wind, it freezes and becomes ice, which is hard like stone. Normally we don't think of water as being hard, and yet ice is water and it is hard.

In this same way, when our mind is disturbed by ignorance and disturbing emotions, which resemble the cold wind, it produces coarse thoughts. The gradual production of coarser and coarser thoughts, which entail coarser and coarser modes of appearance, corresponds to the gradual freezing of the water. These coarse thoughts cause the solid appearance of earth and mountains, even though the thoughts themselves began as mere insubstantial things.

Mind Is Not Affected by Stains

The true nature of any state of mind is free of flaws
And unaffected by the mire of existence and nirvana.
Even so, if a supreme gem is placed in a swamp,
Its radiance will not be clear.

The analogy presented here is of a jewel that has somehow fallen into a swamp. The jewel itself has excellent color and shape and is completely pure in being a jewel. It does not degenerate at all while mired in the swamp; it remains exactly what it was. On the other hand, it can't be used. The jewel's qualities are not apparent because it is concealed. If the jewel is removed from the swamp and the mud is cleaned away, the jewel will be a perfect jewel and can be used appropriately. In the same way, as long as our mind is immersed in bewildered appearances, we cannot gain access to and make use of the mind's innate qualities. Through meditation, however, if we can separate the mind from ignorance, we will be able to make use of the innate qualities of the mind to engage in effortless and spontaneous benefit for ourselves and others.

Although the mind is empty, it is not empty in the sense of being a voidness. The mind's basic nature is simultaneously emptiness and cognitive lucidity. This nature has never been damaged or even affected by all the appearances, confusion, and ignorance within the three realms of *samsara*, the wheel of cyclic existence. So we have to ask, Is liberation from samsara actually effecting a change in the mind at all? It is not. From the very beginning, the mind has been empty and lucid.

In meditation, therefore, we are not trying to change what the mind is; we are not trying to make what is not empty into something that is empty or to make something that is not lucid into something that is lucid. All we are doing in the practice of meditation is experiencing the mind as it is and as it always has been. When the mind is experienced and finally realized, that is liberation. There is no need to change the mind's nature, because the nature of the mind has never been affected by any confusion.

Often the nature of the mind is called buddha nature, or *sugatagarbha* ("the essential nature of those gone to bliss"). When the term *sugatagarbha* is used, even though it refers to the nature of our own mind, it is thought of as a high state, as something very distant from us and unapproachable. It is therefore important to understand what sugatagarbha really means. *Sugata* means "those gone to bliss." The syllable *su* here is "bliss," which means that if you recognize and realize the nature of mind, you eliminate the suffering of samsara: the result of realizing the mind's nature is bliss. *Gata*, or "gone," means that innumerable buddhas have appeared, and all of them have achieved enlightenment through realizing the nature of their mind and thereby attaining the bliss of full awakening.

All of the buddhas began as confused, bewildered sentient beings. They transcended the ignorance and suffering of samsara and entered into bliss. It is up to us now to follow the example of the buddhas and realize the nature of our mind and discover this indwelling bliss. Do we have the ability to do so? Yes, we have the innate capacity to follow and emulate those who have gone to bliss. If we lacked some qualities or abilities that they had, we might not be able to do it, but in the nature of our mind, we have everything that they ever had or have. Since we have what they have and they accomplished full awakening, we can do it also. This is why the nature of the mind is called the essential nature of those gone to bliss.

The *Uttaratantra* states, "Like a jewel, like space, and like pure water, it is continually free of disturbance." When a jewel is purified and the dirt that surrounds it is removed, the nature of the jewel itself does not change. The jewel was always a jewel in its nature or composition. Likewise, when clouds disappear from the sky, the space of the sky does not undergo any change. The space was not inherently affected or polluted in its nature by the presence of the clouds. The third example is water. Water in itself is just pure water; it only becomes polluted when sediment is mixed with it. But even so, the water itself remains just water. Muddy water is water combined with something else, but the water is not, in itself, changed or damaged by the presence of the sediment.

In the same way, while our mind is afflicted and obscured by ignorance, disturbing emotions, and thoughts, the nature of the mind is not touched by their presence. However, when these obscurations are present, the qualities of the mind's nature will not be evident. So it says in the verse, "Even so, if a supreme gem is placed in a swamp, its radiance will not be clear."

THE BASIS FOR SAMSARA AND NIRVANA

When stupidity is clear, wisdom is unclear.
When stupidity is clear, suffering is clear.
Like this, from a seed, a seedling arises;
With this seedling as a cause, offshoots appear.

This verse describes why we wander in samsara and how the confused appearances of samsara increase and spread. All samsara begins with ignorance, and in this verse, ignorance is referred to as a state of stupidity. By its nature, stupidity is unclear. It is an absence of knowledge, a lack of recognizing ultimate truth, which could be called a mere lack of clarity. However, simultaneous with that lack of recognition, there is a great clarity of ignorance in the projection of relative truth. As samsara increases, it becomes clearer and clearer.

The basic nature that lies within every living being can be called the sugatagarbha, or the *dharmadhatu*. Dharmadhatu refers primarily to the aspect of emptiness, and sugatagarbha refers primarily to the aspect of wisdom. The inability to recognize this basic nature of mind is called ignorance. It is the beginning of the eighth (*alaya*, or all-base) consciousness. This failure to recognize the mind's nature occurs because the empty aspect of the mind's nature is not recognized due to the appearance of its lucid aspect. This causes ignorance and the arising of the eighth consciousness along with the habits it holds, which produce confused appearances. As these bewildered appearances increase, from the eighth consciousness arise the afflicted seventh consciousness and then the six functioning consciousnesses (the five sensory consciousnesses and the mental consciousness). At that point, the structure of the bewildered appearances of samsara is fully established. This process of intensification is described in the verse: "When stupidity is clear, wisdom is unclear." As the stupidity of samsara becomes more and more vivid and distinct, the underlying wisdom becomes less and less clear and more and more obscured. This is the same idea expressed in the previous verse with the lines, "If a supreme gem is placed in a swamp, its radiance will not be clear." The radiance of the wisdom is obscured by the intensity of the stupidity.

When the mind is bewildered, the alaya consciousness begins to accumulate negative habits and tendencies. The alaya consciousness itself is not confused; it is mere cognitive lucidity. Nevertheless, it functions as the foundation for accumulating negative habits and for misperceiving the existence of the self. When we have this incorrect view that takes the self to exist, we also develop the incorrect view that the other exists as well. Through the increase of negative habits, based on thinking that a self and other exist, negative karmic latencies enter the alaya consciousness, and this leads to the arising of the other seven consciousnesses.

Even though they are nonconceptual consciousnesses, the five sense consciousnesses arise as the result of habits accrued in the alaya consciousness. The five sense consciousnesses are limited to perceiving a specific sensory input; for example, the eye consciousness just sees, the ear consciousness just hears, and so forth. The sensory consciousnesses do not appraise, recognize, judge, or in any way conceptualize what they see, hear, and so on. The sixth consciousness, the mental consciousness, is the consciousness that appraises, identifies, and judges what is perceived by the five sense consciousnesses. Therefore, it is the sixth consciousness that makes errors, such as believing different things to be essentially one and the same.

With the development of all eight consciousnesses, there is a state of full-blown ignorance, which is clear. The verse reads, "When stupidity is clear, wisdom is unclear." When wisdom is clear, the nature of the mind is realized. But when bewilderment, stupidity, and ignorance are clear, the true nature of mind is obscured. This leads to disturbing emotions, which in turn lead to the accumulation of negative karma, which then leads to suffering. Strictly speaking, not everything that results from actions causes suffering, because actions are of different types (positive, negative, and neutral), and so their results may be different. Nonetheless, directly or indirectly, the result of the disturbing emotions is suffering. For example, being very ill is obviously suffering and is called the suffering of suffering. But even an experience of happiness or well-being will change into a state of suffering because it is impermanent. In this sense, even states of temporary well-being are called the suffering of change. Furthermore, the pervasive environment of impermanence in which we live causes everything to turn eventually into suffering; this is called all-pervasive suffering. These three types of suffering are the result of the bewildered projections or appearances of samsara.

This verse presents an analogy to illustrate how the progressive intensification of stupidity causes suffering: "From a seed, a seedling arises; with this seedling as a cause, offshoots appear." Ignorance is the seed. When it is planted in the ground, it produces a seedling, from which emerges a stalk, and eventually branches grow from the stalk. In the same way, through increasing stupidity, we begin to suffer. This suffering keeps us in the midst of samsaric appearances, which always entail suffering in one way or another. Sometimes we experience the suffering of suffering, sometimes we experience the suffering of change, and sometimes we experience all-pervasive suffering. But we always experience suffering.

The verse also shows us, by implication, how to put an end to suffering. Everyone wants to stop suffering. Since the immediate cause of suffering is the disturbing emotions, it is clear that in order to get rid of the three kinds of suffering, we have to eliminate the disturbing emotions. When we look for the cause of disturbing emotions, we see that it is ignorance; obviously, we have to get rid of our ignorance if we want to lose these disturbing emotions. Remember that ignorance began with not seeing *dharmata*, the true nature of our mind. So the remedy for ignorance is evident: seeing our mind's true nature.

If we see the true nature of dharmata, then ignorance and bewilderment will vanish. Within the sutras, which emphasize vastness, we would refer to this nature as the dharmata, the nature of all things, often explained as the unity of space and wisdom. Within the secret mantra, or the Vajrayana, which emphasizes profundity and not so much the vast scope of the mind's nature, we would refer to this as the nature of our mind. We can also think of our mind as the nature of the sixth consciousness or the nature of the eighth consciousness. In either case, it is through looking at the nature of our mind that ignorance will be removed. We are bewildered and ignorant, because we have never looked into and realized this true nature. If we directly recognize it, we will eliminate ignorance, which is like the seed, and so the seedling will not grow, the stalk will not appear, and the branches will not develop.

Momma Zen

Karen Miller

Buddhism has many meditations on love, and often they begin by contem-
plating a mother's love for her child. It is the gold standard of love in this
world, of selflessness and compassion, and it is proof that the human heart
is innately kind and loving. If we could extend such love to all beings, not
just those closest to us, the world would truly be an enlightened place.

Even poor or suffering people raise their children with deep love.
Their hearts cannot be understood by others. This can be known
only when you become a father or a mother. They do not care
whether they themselves are poor or rich; their only concern is
that their children will grow up. They pay no attention to whether
they themselves are cold or hot, but cover their children to protect
them from the cold or shield them from the hot sun. This is extreme kindness. Only those who have aroused this mind can know
it, and only those who practice this mind can understand it.
—DOGEN ZENJI, *INSTRUCTION FOR THE TENZO*

It strikes me as best to begin my discussion of motherhood with
love. The word will never again mean so much.

Of course you love your spouse. You love your parents and
brothers and sisters. You love your friends. You love your home and
perhaps your hometown. You love your dog. You may love your

work. You might attest to loving your alma mater, mashed potatoes, or reading on a rainy day.

But *this* is love. The feeling you have for your child is so indescribably deep and consuming that it must qualify as one of the few transcendent experiences in your plain old ordinary life. It arrives spontaneously as though part of afterbirth. It is miraculous and supreme and irrevocable. It makes all things possible. There is a certain attitude, perhaps unavoidable, that most of us seem to adopt as we grow up. It is a kind of self-satisfied conclusion that our parents didn't love us. Oh, they might have loved us, but they didn't love us *enough*. They didn't love us the right way. They didn't love us just so.

Have your own child and you will penetrate into the utter absurdity of that idea. You will love your child as your parents loved you and their parents loved them. With a love that is humbling and uncontrived, immense and indestructible. Parents err, of course, and badly. They can be ignorant, foolish, mean, and far worse, in ways that you can come to forgive in them and try to prevent in yourself. But this wholesale shortage of parental love at the crux of everyone's story must be the product of shabby and self-serving recollections. Now that you are a mother, set that story aside, forgetting everything you thought you knew about love.

When my daughter was born, I saw my husband fall in love for the first time. He is a good and loyal man, and he loves me. But he has never lost his footing with me, not in the goofy, tumbledown way he surrendered on first sight to his baby girl.

Within days of bringing our tiny daughter home, my husband took dibs on the nighttime feedings. Born six weeks early, she had mastered bottle-feeding in the hospital but was weak and reluctant at the breast. There was a double bed crowded into our nursery, a relic of the room's recent use for guests, and there he slept, inches away from the mews, rasps, and mysterious "eaps" that emanated from her crib. He slept there eagerly and even well, waking every three hours to dispense her bottles. Although most nights I was waking too, like a shell-shocked soldier, to pump my raw and weeping breasts, the nights belonged to him.

So intense were his affections that I was jealous. Not jealous of him, jealous of *her*. He was hurrying home in the late afternoons to see *her*. Calling home hourly to check on *her*. Cradling *her* in the warm hollow of his chest for that last hour of sleep at dawn's early light. How could he possibly love an old, tired slob of a frump like me anymore? I looked at my love-struck husband looking at her and raised an eyebrow.

I was all wound up and wrongheaded, and I hadn't yet realized that there was plenty of love to go around. Leave it to our cat to state the obvious. She was a whiny and temperamental thing, and we expected her to make trouble when the baby came home—jumping in the crib, taking wide swipes and big bites out of the unsuspecting adversary. I had searched the baby stores and the Internet for some kind of delicate-looking defense that I could install over the crib to keep our sweet kitty from eating the rival child. I'd draped a mosquito net over the bed to foil the attack.

The cat knew better; the cat knew everything, and she recognized a good thing when she saw it. Within hours of our arrival from the hospital, the cat was sitting peaceably as close to the three of us as she could get. Forever after, there would never be the slightest menace in her approach. The net over the crib would only ensnare dust. Our family was a love fount, and kitty was more than happy just to be in on the overflow.

In these early and unending days, I was exhausted all of the time and depressed most of the time, but I came to a different and awed understanding of what life is. It's not what you think it is. First, what you call your life is not yours at all—not yours to plan, manipulate, or control, at least not very often. That's a staggering realization. I was humiliated to see that the maturity and serenity I thought I had achieved was simply the result of having things my way all the time. If life wasn't mine, what was it? In fleeting moments of deep satisfaction and insight, I saw the absolute truth of life: the unbroken line of love that had led to my existence and would lead on through my daughter. My mother's love, her mother's love, her mother's love, and back and back forever ago. Love that is no mere word, love that goes beyond feeling, love that is life itself. I was filled with a rush of respect for all mothers everywhere. *This* was how we all got here. What miracles, what sacrifice, what love! I never knew, nor could I have, before now. Can you imagine this love? Can you anticipate it, fabricate it, measure and evaluate it? No, you can't; you can only *be* love, and your child will release its magnitude within you.

Turns out you can take or leave the mashed potatoes. No matter how miserable I was at the moment, I knew that life itself was overwhelmingly and infinitely good. This is the balm for all the bad days ahead. This is the only fix. This is the source and strength that lifts you up as you bottom out time and again.

Just love.

Reflections on My Mother's Love

Ajahn Amaro

She was his shining example of kindness and generosity. As his mother approached death, the British monk Ajahn Amaro spoke to his students about why Buddhist practice, with all its emphasis on wisdom and emptiness, always comes back to the loving heart of the family.

This is probably the last Saturday night talk that I'll be giving for quite a while. I have received news from my sister in England that our mother is extremely ill, and the signs are that she won't live for more than a few months. So I plan to fly to England in a week to be with her.

The Buddha once said (*Anguttara Nikaya* 2:32) that if you were to carry your parents around with you for their whole lives—your father on one shoulder and your mother on the other—even to the point where they were losing their faculties and their excrement was running down your back, this would not repay your debt of gratitude to them. But you could repay the debt if your parents were not virtuous and you established them in virtue; if they were not wise and you established them in wisdom; if they were stingy and you established them in generosity; if they had no faith in the spiritual path and you led them to it.

One day, many years ago, I spoke of this teaching very matter-of-factly with my mother, assuming that she would be as impressed as I was with how highly the Buddha praised the role that parents play in one's life. She responded, as she almost invariably did anytime I tried to spout some spiritual statement, by saying, "What utter balls!" She is very good at keeping me level, as I can get somewhat airy-fairy at times. Her point was that it isn't a one-way process. She said, "Why do you talk about it in terms of being in debt? What could be more wonderful and satisfying than bringing children into the world and watching them grow? It isn't like a job that you need to be paid for." I was really impressed by that.

For obvious reasons, recently I've been reflecting a lot on my mother's influence on my life, and it occurred to me that until I met the *dhamma* (Pali; Sanskrit: *dharma*) when I was twenty-one, she was the main—if not the only—source of my ability to see what was noble and good in the world. I didn't grow up in a religious household (England is a very nonreligious country), but both my parents were very good people, especially my mother. She really embodies unselfishness, kindness, generosity, and a tremendous harmlessness toward all living beings—she is physically unable to hurt any creature. When I wonder where I got the inclination toward that which is good and wholesome and useful, I realize that it came almost entirely from her.

After my mother's father died, she told me that she'd received much of her guidance and direction from him. She deeply respected her inheritance of his gentleness, self-effacement, and benevolence toward all things, and she passed those qualities on. She was my main spiritual influence before I went to Thailand; anything that kept me operating somewhere in the neighborhood of balanced human behavior was thanks to her. So I've developed a great sense of gladness and gratitude toward her for imparting this to me.

Another realization that has become clearer to me over the years is that people who come from broken homes, or who have had very unstable family situations, assume that life is unsteady and unpredictable; they often have a deep sense of insecurity. I remember being struck by this during my first few years of meeting and living with such people—and there are a great many of them in this world. I never would have conceived of the experiences they'd had. Even though my parents had plenty of faults and our lives were not easy, they gave our family an astonishing sense of stability and reliability, especially our mother. (My father was often kept busy, first with the farm and then traveling with his work. And besides, I think it was Robert Bly who defined the Industrial Age father as "that which sits in the living room and rustles the newspaper.")

I've begun to reflect on the sense of security that arises from this intuition that life has a reliable basis. In stable families, parents impart this. If one doesn't have this, then one has to find it later on in other ways. For a child, the parents are a kind of substitute for the dhamma, that basis upon which everything rests and around which everything revolves.

I didn't always get on with my parents. But they never argued in front of us, and they were always there, establishing a continuity of presence and support. And thinking about that, I've seen that they reflected two qualities of dhamma that are crucial: *dhamma-niyamata*—the orderliness, or regularity, or patternedness of the dhamma—and *dhammatthitata*—the stability of the dhamma.

In a way, that's the job or role of parents—to be stable, the rock that things rest upon. They exhibit that quality of regularity, orderliness, or predictability that we can rely on and be guided by.

When I was about twelve, some of my mother's extraordinary qualities became apparent to me in a very powerful way. I was a growing lad who ate a cooked breakfast every morning before going off to school. In the late afternoon, I would come back and eat cream doughnuts for tea, and an hour later scarf down huge amounts of food at supper. I was turning into a burly youth. And every afternoon my mother waited in her car at the bus stop at the end of the lane, a mile away from our home. One day I got off the bus and she wasn't there. I thought, "That's strange." I started walking—I thought maybe she was just a bit late—and I walked and walked, but she didn't appear. I got all the way back to the house and she wasn't there either. When my sisters returned from school, we found out that our mother had collapsed and had been hospitalized. She was found to be suffering from malnutrition.

For months my mother had been living only on tea and toast, trying to make our food supply go a bit further by not eating. None of us had noticed, because we'd all been so busy gobbling our meals. She'd never made a fuss, never said anything. And the next thing we knew, she was in hospital. It hit me like a ton of bricks that she would actually starve herself while feeding all of us and not complain. And when we went to visit her in the hospital, she apologized as if she were wasting our time! After all, we could have been doing our homework or out somewhere enjoying ourselves.

Now my mother is eighty-two years old and her body seems to be reaching its limit. How does one hold that? How does one use the practice to relate to the situation, to bring balance to the heart, and to be of benefit to her and to others?

The wonderful Thai forest master Luang Por Duhn teaches us that the *citta*, the heart, *is* the Buddha. "Don't look for the Buddha anywhere else," he says, "the aware quality of the heart is the Buddha." This is an extraordinarily forthright, clear, and completely nondualistic teaching.

The problem that arises when we love or hate someone is that there is a polarity, a duality that the heart easily can be drawn into: there's "me" here and there's the "other" out there. And the more intense the emotion, the greater the feeling of duality.

Although we can be very focused on generating loving-kindness toward another being, there's also the matter of sustaining the liberating insight that recognizes selflessness, *anatta*, which sees that all phenomena are not-self and that the impression of a self-existent, separate entity is merely based upon ignorance and the activity of the senses. This conundrum can be a focus of practice.

In this light, it's interesting to reflect on the great masters and the relationships between their spiritual practices and their families. The famed Vipassana teacher Ajahn Chah was a highly accomplished being, and when he started at Wat Pah Pong monastery, one of his first disciples was his mother. She moved out of her village, was ordained as a nun, and went to live in the forest with him and his cluster of monks. When she died, Ajahn Chah made a great ceremony of her funeral; it was a huge affair, and he ordained eighty or ninety people during the event to make merit for her. Later, the main temple at Wat Pah Pong was built on the exact spot where his mother was cremated.

Sri Ramana Maharshi was also said to be a supremely detached being; he was famed for having such equanimity that rats sometimes nibbled on his legs when he sat in *samadhi*, and he allowed doctors to treat him because it made *them* feel better. Like Ajahn Chah, Sri Ramana's mother became his disciple and went to live at the bottom of Arunachala Mountain, while he was in a cave at the top. After she died, he too built his ashram on the place where she was cremated.

So here are these two highly accomplished, extraordinarily detached beings who both built their temples on their mothers' ashes. Of course this may have no significance whatsoever, but to me it indicates that they're *not* saying, "All *sankharas*—conditioned phenomena—are impermanent, my mother is just a formation in nature like any other, and it's no big deal." There's a mysterious twinning here of both the realization of ultimate truth and the recognition of the unique quality of that personal connection on the material plane. It's almost as if the mother is the primordial symbol of the source of reality, just as she is the source of life on the physical plane. After all, in the West we freely use the term *Mother Nature*, and *nature* is another word for *dhamma*. So perhaps it is natural and perfectly appropriate to accord this being with whom we have a unique relationship a special position among all the dimensions of life that we experience.

These days I have found myself practicing, first of all, to establish a clear insight of the nondual, or you might say, to establish the heart in pure knowing. And then I've been bringing up a question, or an investigational statement, such as Where is my mother? or

What is my mother? The purpose of this process is to let go of any habitual identification, to break down that notion of *me* here and the *other* over there, and to open the heart to the present moment.

Then, within that basic space of awareness, I consciously bring forth the intentions and emotions of loving-kindness, compassion, sympathetic joy, and equanimity.

There needs to be a balancing within that, however, because as soon as those intentions or qualities are aroused, one can slip back into the idea of me over here sending it to you over there, which is a dualism. But there's a way that dhamma practice can guide us toward both seeing things as completely empty (the ultimate truth of things) and also respecting the convention that there's a being here and a being there (the relative truth of things). On one level, that convention is pertinent. But it's only a partial truth, a half-truth, and it exists within the context of dhamma.

One of the ways that the Buddha spoke about stream-entry—the irreversible breakthrough to realization of the dhamma—was as a "change of lineage." The phrase relates to the idea that "I am a personality; this is me, this is mine, this is what I am." This belief is called *sakkayaditthi*, or "personality view." And as long as "I am the body," then, of course, Pat Horner and Tom Horner are my parents. But if the body is not-self, and perceptions are not-self, and feelings are not-self, and the personality is not-self, what does that say about Mr. and Mrs. Horner? What does that mean? If this body is not-self, then the lineage of the body can't be the whole story.

This is a subtle point of dhamma and it's easy to grasp it in the wrong way, as I most painfully did when I was a young novice in Thailand. I can't believe I actually did this, but I recall a letter I sent to my mother from Thailand in 1978 in which I wrote, "You know, in truth, you're not really my mother." Something in me doesn't want to remember having done that, but I have a sinking feeling that I did.

Anyway, we exchanged a number of rather tense letters in those days, when I was "full of the light" in Thailand, but this one certainly represented the nadir. In retrospect, it was pretty awful and very embarrassing. When my mother received this particular inspired declaration, she pointed out that she definitely was my mother since nobody else was. She wrote, "I care about you because you are my son, not because you are a Buddhist monk—*compris?*" Even at that time, I realized this was a totally appropriate response. I wasn't taking hold of the principle correctly. However, when that insight is present and we don't pick it up wrongly, we can genuinely see this change of lineage, without getting the relative and the ultimate planes confused.

There *is* that relationship with our parents in this flow of karmic formations, but the lineage of our true reality is fundamentally rooted in the dhamma. That's the source, the origin, the basis. Rather than thinking of one's physical parents as the origin, we can have the clear realization that that's just part of the situation. It's the Uncreated, the Unformed, the Unborn, the Unconditioned that's the genuine source, the genuine origin, the basis, the ground of reality.

We can fully respect the convention *and* we can base our practice on the insight that all sankharas arise and cease, that all dhammas are not-self. There's nothing to get heated about, nothing to get carried away by; it's just life doing its dance. The heart can remain serene, stable, clear, and bright. Which, of course, is what makes it possible for us to be of benefit to others, whether they be our parents, our children, our teachers, or our students.

Hardwired
for Altruism

Daniel Goleman

Daniel Goleman, author of the best-selling Emotional Intelligence, *stands at the forefront of the dialogue between Buddhism and science, as Western neuroscientists, psychologists, and social scientists test Buddhism's ancient insights into human nature—and frequently find them to be true. Here, Goleman considers the evidence that humans are innately disposed toward kindness and empathy, as Buddhism has long proclaimed.*

One afternoon at the Princeton Theological Seminary, forty students waited to give a short practice sermon on which they would be rated. Half the students had been assigned random biblical topics. The other half had been assigned the parable of the Good Samaritan, who stopped to help a stranger by the roadside, an injured man ignored by people supposedly more "pious."

The seminarians worked together in a room, and every fifteen minutes one of the seminarians left to go to another building to deliver their sermon. None knew they were taking part in an experiment on altruism.

Their route passed directly by a doorway in which a man was slumped, groaning in evident pain. Of the forty students, twenty-four passed right by, ignoring the plaintive moans. And those who were mulling over the lessons of the Good Samaritan's tale were no more likely to stop and help than were any of the others.

For the seminarians, time mattered. Among ten who thought they were late to give their sermon, only one stopped; among another ten who thought they had plenty of time, six offered help.

Of the many factors that are at play in altruism, a critical one seems to be simply taking the time to pay attention; our empathy is strongest to the degree we fully focus on someone and so loop emotionally. People differ, of course, in their ability, willingness, and interest in paying attention—a sullen teen can tune out her mother's nagging, then a minute later have undivided concentration while on a phone call to her girlfriend. The seminarians rushing to give their sermon were apparently unwilling or unable to give their attention to the moaning man, presumably because they were caught up in their thoughts and the press of hurrying, and so never attuned to him, let alone helped him.

People on busy city streets worldwide are less likely to notice, greet, or offer help to someone else because of what has been called the "urban trance." Sociologists have proposed that we tend to fall into this self-absorbed state on crowded streets, if only to guard against stimuli overload from the swirl around us. Inevitably, the strategy requires a trade-off: we shut out the compelling needs of those around us along with the mere distractions. As a poet put it, we confront "the noise of the street dazed and defeated."

In addition, social divides shutter our eyes. A homeless person sitting dejectedly on the streets of an American city asking for money may receive no attention from passersby, who a few steps away will gladly listen and respond to a well-dressed, outgoing woman asking for signatures on a political petition. (Of course, depending on our sympathies, the attention we give may be just the reverse: sympathy for the homeless person, but none for the political appeal.) In short, our priorities, socialization, and myriad other social-psychological factors can lead us to direct or inhibit our attention or the emotions we feel—and thus our empathy.

Simply paying attention allows us to build an emotional connection. Lacking attention, empathy hasn't a chance.

When Attention Must Be Paid

Contrast those events at the Princeton seminary with what happened one rush hour in New York City as I headed for the Times Square station after work one day. As usual, a steady torrent of humanity was sweeping down the concrete stairs, rushing to get on the next subway train.

But then I saw something troubling: sprawled across the steps midway down was a shabby, shirtless man, lying motionless, eyes closed.

No one seemed to notice. People simply stepped over his body in their rush to get home.

But, shocked by the sight, I stopped to see what was wrong. And the moment I stopped, something remarkable happened: other people stopped too.

Almost instantly there was a small circle of concern around the man. Just as spontaneously, messengers of mercy fanned out—one man went to a hot dog stand to get him some food; a woman scurried to get him a bottle of water; another summoned a subway patrol officer, who in turn radioed for help.

Within minutes the man was revived, eating happily, and waiting for an ambulance. We learned he spoke only Spanish, had no money, and had been wandering the streets of Manhattan, starving. He had fainted from hunger there on the subway steps.

What made the difference? Just noticing for one. By simply stopping to take in the man's plight, I seemed to snap passersby out of their urban trance and called him to their attention. As we tuned in to his predicament, we were moved to help.

No doubt all of us upright citizens on our way home from work were susceptible to silent assumptions about that man on the stairs, stereotypes built from walking by the hundreds of homeless who, sad to say, inhabit the streets of New York and so many other modern urban centers. Urbanites learn to manage the anxiety of seeing someone in such dire straits by reflectively shifting attention away.

I think my own shift-away reflex had been altered by an article I had recently written for the *New York Times* on how closing mental hospitals had converted the city's streets into psychiatric wards. To do research for the article, I spent several days in a van with workers for a social agency that administered to the homeless, bringing them food, offering them shelter, and coaxing the mentally ill among them—a shockingly high proportion—to come to clinics to receive their medications. For quite a while afterward I saw homeless people through fresh eyes.

In other studies using the Good Samaritan situation, researchers find that those who do stop to help typically report that on seeing the other's distress, they felt upset too—and an empathic sense of tenderness. Once one person noticed the other enough to feel empathy, the odds were very high that he would offer some help.

Just hearing about someone lending a helping hand can have a unique impact, inducing a warm sense of uplift. Psychologists use the term *elevation* for the glow stirred by witnessing someone else's kindness. Elevation is the state reported repeatedly when people tell how they feel on seeing a spontaneous act of courage, tolerance, or compassion. Most people find themselves moved, even thrilled.

The acts most commonly named as stirring elevation are helping the poor or sick, or aiding someone in a difficult predicament. But these good deeds need not be as demanding as taking in an entire family, nor as selfless as Mother Teresa working among the poor in Calcutta. Simple thoughtfulness can elicit a bit of elevation. In a study in Japan, for instance, people readily came up with accounts of *kandou*, times when the heart is so moved—for example, by seeing a tough-looking gang member give up his seat on a train to an elderly man.

Elevation, the research suggests, may be catching. When someone sees an act of kindness, it typically stirs in them the impulse to perform one too. These social benefits may be one reason mythic tales worldwide are rife with figures who save others through their courageous deeds. Psychologists speculate that hearing a story about such kindness—when it is told vividly—has the same emotional impact as seeing the act itself. That elevation can be contagious suggests that it travels the low road.

FINE-TUNING

On a five-day visit to Brazil with my son, we noticed that the people we met seemed to get friendlier day by day. The change was striking.

At first we largely sensed aloofness or reserve from the Brazilians we met. But by the third day we encountered noticeably greater warmth.

On the fourth day it followed us wherever we went. And by our trip's end we were hugging people good-bye at the airport.

Was it the people of Brazil who had changed? Certainly not. What had melted away was our own uptightness as gringos in an unfamiliar culture. Our defensive reserve had initially closed us off to the Brazilians' open, friendly manner—and it may well have signaled them to keep their distance.

At the beginning of our trip—like a radio set to a slightly off-channel signal—we were too preoccupied to take in the friendliness of the people we encountered. As we relaxed and tuned in to those around us, it was as though we had zeroed in on the right station, the warmth that was there all along. While we are uptight or preoccupied, we fail to register the sparkle in someone's eye, the hint of a smile, or the warm tones of voice—all prime channels for sending messages of friendliness.

A technical explanation for this dynamic spotlights the limits on attention itself. Working memory, or the amount of memory that we can hold in our attention at any one moment, resides in the prefrontal cortex, the citadel of the high road. This circuitry plays a major role in allocating our attention by managing the backstage business of an interaction. For instance, it searches our memory for what to say and do, even while it attends to incoming signals and shifts our responsibility accordingly.

As the challenges thicken, those multiple demands increasingly tax our capacity for paying attention. Signals of worry from the amygdala flood key regions of the prefrontal cortex, manifesting as preoccupations that steal attention away from whatever else we are dealing with. Distress overtaxes attention: merely being an uptight gringo will do it.

Nature puts a premium on smooth communications among members of a given species, sculpting the brain for a better fit— sometimes on the spot. In certain fish, for instance, during courtship a female's brain secretes hormones that temporarily reshape her auditory circuits to improve their attunement to the frequencies of the male's call.

Something similar can be seen in a two-month-old baby who detects his mother approaching: he will instinctively become still, quiet his breathing a bit, turn toward her and look at her face, focus on her eyes or mouth, and orient his ears toward any sounds coming from her, all the while making an expression researchers call "knit-brow with jaw-drop." Each of these moves enhances the perceptual ability of the baby to attune to what the mother says or does.

The more sharply attentive we are, the more keenly we will sense another person's inner state: we will do so more quickly and from subtler clues in more ambiguous circumstances. Conversely, the greater our distress, the less accurately we will be able to empathize.

In short, self-absorption in all its forms kills empathy, let alone compassion. When we focus on ourselves, our world contracts as our problems and preoccupations loom large. But when we focus on others, our world expands. Our own problems drift to the periphery of the mind and so seem smaller, and we increase our capacity for connection—or compassionate action.

INSTINCTIVE COMPASSION

- A laboratory rat, suspended in the air by a harness, screeches and struggles. Catching sight of the imperiled rat, one of its cagemates becomes upset too and manages to come to the rescue by pressing a bar that lowers the victim safely to the ground.

- Six rhesus monkeys have been trained to pull chains to get food. At one point a seventh monkey, in full view of the others, gets a painful shock whenever one of them pulls for food. On seeing the pain of that shocked monkey, four of the original rhesus monkeys start pulling a different chain, one that delivers less food to them but that inflicts no shock on the other monkey. The fifth monkey stops pulling any chain at all for five days, and the sixth for twelve days—that is, both starve themselves to prevent shocking the seventh monkey.

- Virtually from birth, when babies see or hear another baby crying in distress, they start crying as though they too are distressed. But they rarely cry when they hear a recording of their own cries. After about fourteen months of age, babies not only cry when they hear another, but they also try to relieve the other baby's suffering somehow. The older toddlers get, the less they cry and the more they try to help.

Lab rats, monkeys, and babies share an automatic impulse, one that rivets their attention on another's suffering, triggers similar distressed feelings in themselves, and leads them to try to help. Why should the same response be found in very different species? Simple: nature conserves, preserving whatever works to use again and again.

In the design of the brain, winning features are shared among various species. Human brains have vast tracts of well-proven neural architecture in common with other mammals, especially primates. The similarity across species in sympathetic distress, coupled with the impulse to help, strongly suggests a like set of underlying circuitry in the brain. In contrast to mammals, reptiles show not the least sign of empathy, even eating their own young.

Although people can also ignore someone in need, that cold-heartedness seems to suppress a more primal, automatic impulse to aid another in distress. Scientific observations point to a response system that is hardwired in the human brain—no doubt involving mirror neurons—that acts when we see someone else suffering, making us instantly feel with them. The more we feel with them, the more we want to help them.

This instinct for compassion arguably offers benefits in evolutionary fitness—properly defined in terms of "reproductive success," or how many of one's offspring live to parent their own offspring. Over a century ago Charles Darwin proposed that empathy, the prelude to compassionate action, has been a powerful aid to survival in nature's toolkit. Empathy lubricates sociability, and we humans are the social animal par excellence. New thinking holds that our sociability has been the primary survival strategy of primates species, including our own.

The utility of friendliness can be seen today in the lives of primates in the wild, who inhabit a tooth-and-claw world akin to that of human prehistory, when relatively few infants survived to childbearing age. Take the thousand or so monkeys that inhabit Cayo Santiago, a remote island in the Caribbean; all descend from a single band transplanted from their native India in the 1950s. These rhesus macaques live in small groups. When they reach adolescence, the females stay, and the males leave to find their place in another group.

That transition holds real dangers: as the young males try to enter an unfamiliar troupe, up to 20 percent of them die in fights. Scientists have taken spinal fluid samples of one hundred teen macaques. They find that the most outgoing monkeys have the lowest levels of stress hormones and stronger immune function, and—most important—that they are best able to approach, befriend, or challenge monkeys in the new troupe. These more sociable young monkeys are the ones most likely to survive.

Another primate data point comes from wild baboons living near Mount Kilimanjaro in Tanzania. For these baboons, infancy holds great perils: in a good year about 10 percent of infants die; in bad times up to 35 percent die. But when biologists observed the baboon mothers, they found that those who were the most companionable—who spent the most time grooming or otherwise socializing with other female baboons—had the infants most likely to survive.

The biologists cite two reasons that a mother's friendliness may help her infants survive. For one, they are members of a clubby group who can help one another defend their babies from harassment or find better food and shelter. For another, the more grooming the mothers give and get, the more relaxed and healthy they tend to be. Sociable baboons make better mothers.

Our natural pull toward others may trace back to the conditions of scarcity that shaped the human brain. We can readily surmise how membership in a group would make survival in dire times more likely—and how being a lone individual competing for scarce resources with a group could be a deadly disadvantage.

A trait with such powerful survival value can gradually fashion the very circuitry of the brain, since whatever proves most effective in spreading genes to future generations becomes increasingly pervasive in the genetic pool.

If sociability offered humans a winning strategy throughout prehistory, so have the brain systems through which social life operates. Small wonder our inclination toward empathy, the essential connector, has such potency.

An Angel on Earth

A head-on collision had left her car crumpled like a piece of paper. With two bones broken in her right leg, pinned in the wreckage, she lay there in pain and shock, helpless and confused.

Then a passerby—she never found out his name—came over to her and knelt by her side. He held her hand, reassured her while emergency workers tried to free her. Despite her pain and anxiety, he helped her stay calm.

"He was," as she put it later, "my angel on earth."

We'll never know exactly what feelings moved that "angel" to kneel at that woman's side to reassure her. But such compassion depends on that crucial first step, empathy.

Empathy entails some degree of emotional sharing—a prerequisite to truly understanding anyone else's inner world. Mirror neurons, as one neuroscientist put it, are "what give you the richness of empathy, the fundamental mechanism that makes seeing someone hurt really hurt you." Constantin Stanislavski, the Russian developer of the famed Method for stage training, saw that an actor "living" a part could call up his emotional memories from the past to evoke a powerful feeling in the present. But those memories, Stanislavski taught, need not be limited to our own experiences. An actor can as well draw on the emotions of others through a bit of empathy. As the legendary acting coach advised, "We must study other people and get as close to them emotionally as we can, until sympathy for them is transformed into feelings of our own."

Stanislavski's advice was prescient. As it turns out, brain imaging studies reveal that when we answer the question, "How are you feeling?" we activate much of the same neural circuitry that lights up when we ask, "How is *she* feeling?" The brain acts almost identically when we sense our own feelings and those of another.

When people are asked to imitate someone's facial expression of happiness, fear, or disgust, and thereby to generate that emotion in themselves, this intentional "feeling into" activates the same circuits involved when they simply observe the person (or when they spontaneously feel that emotion). As Stanislavski understood, these circuits come even more alive when empathy becomes intentional. As we notice an emotion in another person, then we literally feel together. The greater our effort or the more intense the feeling expressed, the stronger we feel them in ourselves.

Tellingly, the German word *Einfühlung*, which was first rendered into English in 1909 as the newly coined word *empathy*, more literally translates as "feeling into," suggesting an inner imitation of the other person's feelings. As Theodore Lipps, who imported the word *empathy* into English, put it, "When I observe a circus performer on a high wire, I feel I am inside him." It's as though we experience the other person's emotions in our own body. And we do: neuroscientists say that the more active a person's mirror neuron systems, the stronger her empathy.

In today's psychology, the word *empathy* is used in three distinct senses: *knowing* another person's feelings, *feeling* what the other person feels, and *responding compassionately* to another's distress. These three varieties of empathy seem to describe a 1-2-3 sequence: I notice you, I feel with you, and so I act to help you.

All three fit well with what neuroscience has learned about how the brain operates when we attune to another person, as Stephanie Preston and Frans de Waal observe in a major theory linking interpersonal perception and action. These two scientists are uniquely suited to make the argument: Preston has pioneered using the methods of social neuroscience to study empathy in humans, and de Waal, director of Living Links at the Yerkes Primate Center, has for decades drawn lessons for human behavior from systematic observations of primates.

Preston and de Waal argue that in a moment of empathy, both our emotions and our thoughts are primed along the same lines as those of the other person. Hearing a frightened cry from someone else, we spontaneously think of what might be causing their fear. From a cognitive perspective, we share a mental "representation," a set of images, associations, and thoughts about their predicament.

The movement from empathy to action traverses mirror neurons; empathy seems to have evolved from emotional contagion and so shares its neural mechanisms. Primal empathy relies on no specialized brain area but rather involves many, depending on what we are empathizing with. We slip into the other's shoes to share what they experience.

Preston has found that if someone brings to mind one of the happiest moments of her life, then imagines a similar moment from the life of one of her closest friends, the brain activates virtually the identical circuitry for these two mental acts. In other words, to understand what someone else experiences—to empathize—we utilize the same brain wiring that is active during our own experience.

All communication requires that what matters for the sender also matters for the receiver. By sharing thoughts as well as feelings, two brains deploy a shorthand that gets both people on the same page immediately, without having to waste time or words explaining more pointedly what matters are at hand.

Mirroring occurs whenever our perception of someone automatically activates an image or a felt sense in our own brain for what they are doing and expressing. What's on their mind occupies ours. We rely on these inner messages to sense what might be going on in the other person. After all, what does a smile or a wink, a stare or a frown, "mean," except as a clue to what's happening in the other person's mind?

AN ANCIENT DEBATE

Today most people remember the seventeenth-century philosopher Thomas Hobbes for his assertion that life in our natural state—absent any strong government—is "nasty, brutish, and short," a war of all against all. Despite this tough, cynical view, however, Hobbes himself had a soft side.

One day as he walked through the streets of London, he came upon an old, sickly man who was begging for alms. Hobbes, his heart touched, immediately gave the man a generous offering.

When asked by a friend if he would have done the same had there been no religious dictum or philosophical principle about helping the needy, Hobbes replied that he would. His explanation: he felt some pain himself when he saw the man's misery, and so just as giving alms to the man would relieve some of the man's suffering, it "doth also ease me."

This tale suggests that we have a bit of self-interest in relieving the misery of others. One school of modern economic theory, following Hobbes, argues that people give to charities in part because of the pleasure they get from imagining either the relief of those they benefit or their own relief from alleviating their sympathetic distress.

Latter-day versions of this theory have tried to reduce acts of altruism to disguised acts of self-interest. In one version, compassion veils a "selfish gene" that tries to maximize its odds of being passed on by gathering obligations or by favoring the close relatives who carry it. Such explanations may suffice in special cases.

But another viewpoint offers a more immediate—and universal—explanation: as the Chinese sage Mencius (or, Mengzi) wrote in the third century B.C.E., long before Hobbes, "All men have a mind which cannot bear to see the suffering of others."

Neuroscience now supports Mengzi's position, adding missing data to this centuries-old debate. When we see someone else in distress, similar circuits reverberate in our brain, a kind of hardwired empathic resonance that becomes the prelude to compassion. If an infant cries, her parents' brains reverberate in much the same way, which in turn automatically moves them to do something to soothe their baby's distress.

Our brain has been preset for kindness. We automatically go to the aid of a child who is screaming in terror; we automatically want to hug a smiling baby. Such emotional impulses are "prepotent": they elicit reactions in us that are unpremeditated and instantaneous. That this flow from empathy to action occurs with such rapid automaticity hints at circuitry dedicated to this very sequence. To feel distress stirs an urge to help.

When we hear an anguished scream, it activates the same parts of our brain that experience such anguish, as well as the premotor cortex, a sign we are preparing to act. Similarly, hearing someone tell an unhappy story in doleful tones activates the listener's motor cortex—which guides movements—as well as the amygdala and related circuits for sadness. This shared state then signals the motor area of the brain, where we prepare our response, for the relevant action. Preston and de Waal argue that our initial perception prepares us for action; to see readies us to do.

The neural networks for perception and action share a common code in the language of the brain. This shared code allows whatever we perceive to lead almost instantly to the appropriate reaction. Seeing an emotional expression, hearing a tone of voice, or having our attention directed to a given topic instantly fires the neurons that that message indicates.

This shared code was anticipated by Charles Darwin, who back in 1872 wrote a scholarly treatise on emotions that scientists still regard highly. Although Darwin wrote about empathy as a survival factor, a popular misreading of his evolutionary theories empathized "nature red in tooth and claw" (as Tennyson phrased the notion of a relentless culling of the weak), a notion favored by "social Darwinists," who twisted evolutionary thinking to rationalize greed.

Darwin saw every emotion as a predisposition to act in a unique way: fear, to freeze or flee; anger, to fight; joy, to embrace; and so on. Brain imaging studies now show that at the neural level he was right. To feel *any* emotion stirs the related urge to act.

The brain's circuitry that operates beneath our consciousness makes that feeling-action link interpersonal. For instance, when we see someone expressing fear—even if only in the way they move or hold their body—our own brain activates the circuitry for fear. Along with this instantaneous contagion, the brain areas that prepare for fearful actions also activate. And so with each emotion—anger, joy, sadness, and so on. Emotional contagion, then, does more than merely spread feelings—it automatically prepares the brain for appropriate action.

Nature's rule of thumb holds that a biological system should use the minimal amount of energy. Here the brain achieves that efficiency by firing the same neurons while both perceiving and performing an action. That economizing repeats across brains. In the special case of someone in distress, the perception-action link makes coming to their aid the brain's natural tendency. To feel *with* stirs us to act *for*.

To be sure, some data suggest in many situations that people tend to favor helping their loved ones over helping a stranger. Even so, emotional attunement with a stranger in distress moves us to help that person just as we would our loved ones. For instance, in one study the more saddened people were by the plight of a displaced orphan, the more likely they were to donate money or even offer the child a temporary place to live—regardless of how much social distance they felt.

The preference for helping those similar to ourselves washes away when we are face-to-face with someone in agony or dire straits. In a direct encounter with such a person the primal brain-to-brain link makes us experience their suffering as our own—and to immediately prepare to help. And that direct confrontation with suffering was once the rule in human affairs, in the vast period when encounters were always within feet or yards, rather than at the artificial removes of modern life.

Back to the quandary of why—if the human brain contains a system designed to attune us to someone else's distress and prepare us to act to help, why don't we always help? The possible answers are manifold, enumerated by countless experiments in social psychology. But the simplest answer may be that modern life militates against it: we largely relate to those in need at a distance. That separation means we experience "cognitive" empathy rather than the immediacy of direct emotional contagion. Or worse, we have mere sympathy, where we feel sorry for the person but do not taste their distress in the least. This more removed relationship weakens the innate impulse to help.

As Preston and de Waal note, "In today's era of e-mail communication, frequent moves, and bedroom communities, the scales are increasingly tipped against the automatic and accurate perception of others' emotional state, without which empathy is impossible." Modern-day social and virtual distances have created an anomaly in human living, though one we now take to be the norm. This separation mutes empathy, absent which altruism falters.

The argument has long been made that we humans are by nature compassionate and empathic despite the occasional streak of meanness, but torrents of bad news throughout history have contradicted that claim, and little sound science has backed it. But try this thought experiment. Imagine the number of opportunities people around the world today *might* have to commit an antisocial act, from rape to murder to simple rudeness and dishonesty. Make that number the bottom of a fraction. Now for the top value, put the number of such antisocial acts that will *actually* occur today.

That ratio of potential to enacted meanness holds at close to zero any day of the year. And if for the top value you put the number of benevolent acts performed in a given day, the ratio of kindness to cruelty will be always positive. (The news, however, comes to us as though the ratio was reversed.)

Harvard's Jerome Kagan proposes this mental exercise to make a simple point about human nature: the sum total of goodness vastly outweighs that of meanness. "Although humans inherit a biological bias that permits them to feel anger, jealousy, selfishness and envy, and to be rude, aggressive or violent," Kagan notes, "they inherit an even stronger biological bias for kindness, compassion, cooperation, love and nurture—especially towards those in need." This inbuilt ethical sense, he adds, "is a biological feature of our species."

With the discovery that our neural wiring tips toward putting empathy in the service of compassion, neuroscience hands philosophy a mechanism for explaining the ubiquity of the altruistic impulse. Instead of trying to explain away selfless acts, philosophers might contemplate the conundrum of the innumerable times that antisocial acts are absent.

Impermanence
Rocks! ☺﹚

Daniel Dancer

Impermanence is Buddhism's basic truth and samsara's basic secret. How intently we shield ourselves from the truth of impermanence (which is really just a euphemism for death), and how much more we try to shield our children from it. But what if we asked children not just to acknowledge impermanence but to celebrate it? Daniel Dancer gave it a try in his program for children called Art of the Sky.

Okay, boys and girls. Please say the word *im-per-man-nence.*" Without hesitating (they know the drill), fifty bright-eyed, first-grade faces repeat back in unison, "Im-per-ma-nence!"

"Okay, once more. Louder this time," I ask them.

"IM-PER-MA-NENCE!" they echo back with enthusiasm.

I wonder if such a concept can really be taught at this early age. I still struggle with it at age fifty-four. And yet, I didn't even think about it until I began reading Buddhist texts in my late twenties. What if we started coming to terms with our temporary existence and the fleeting nature of all things when we were five?

Physically experiencing the concept of impermanence in the body is one of the core teachings of Art for the Sky, a weeklong artist-in-residency program that I offer to elementary schools across the country. Each residency culminates with the entire school taking the form of a giant living painting by becoming human paint drops on their playing field: a two hundred-foot-wide salmon, bear, or bighorn sheep. The huge images only make sense when seen from above, at a distance, and this is a central point. Immanuel Kant said that "for peace to reign on Earth, humans must evolve into new beings who have learned to see the whole first." We can best make sense of our world by using our imaginations to rise above it, by employing our "sky sight" to see how everything is connected, to indeed *see the whole first.*

"IM-PER-MA-NENCE!" the children repeat back a third time. This is the first day of my residency, the first day they begin to learn about an art form that dates back four thousand years to the Nazca Desert in Peru. This desert is the driest place on Earth, and the ancients who lived there left hundreds of miles of lines, shapes, and figures on the earth that only make sense from the sky. I talk with the children about flying dreams; the power of collaboration; and the beauty of making art that is not a material product but simply a gift for the Sky, the Creator, the Great Mystery—a gift that leaves no trace.

On the morning of our event day, the flat, lifeless lined image of a bighorn sheep is painted on grass with nontoxic latex paint. And then suddenly, as children and teachers pour out onto the field, the entire student body is overflowing with joy and excitement. There is a moment, an almost still point, when everyone achieves just the right position and the bighorn comes alive. Looking at it from high above in a bucket truck, I can tweak the design and talk to everyone with a megaphone, and there truly is an "aha" moment when "IT" happens. And then, just as quickly, the form dissolves back into chaos, then into silence . . . coming from nowhere, returning to nowhere.

Form is emptiness, emptiness is form. I don't know when I first tripped over this slippery koan at the heart of Buddhism. Ever since, deciphering it has been like trying to spin around fast enough to catch a glimpse of my backside.

Sometimes when we do Art of the Sky in midafternoon, shadows can be a big problem, as if we spilled black paint all over the picture. Then I ask everyone to squat down low with their hands upon the earth. But sometimes the extra blackness adds depth to the image. When a cloud passes overhead and the shadows disappear, suddenly form slips into emptiness. Shadows coming and going have helped me understand the koan.

This art form is a metaphor for how change happens, how life begins. When all the participants align in the shape of a salmon, a bear, or a bighorn, suddenly the image comes to life. Each individual is vital to the whole. It's just the way an atom becomes an atom. A certain number of electrons have to arise out of chaos and align with each other, and when that critical mass occurs, an atom is formed. One electron less and there would be no "birth" of an atom. Physicists call this moment "phase transition." The Buddha might call it simply "becoming." Everyone kneeling on the earth in the shape of a bighorn has created a field of energy that all could sense. That energy is called *love.*

As our version of the endangered Sierra bighorn sheep dissolves suddenly into joyous children dashing to the four directions, I trust that a deep teaching has been felt in the soul of each participant.

After photographs are taken, with everyone still in position, kneeling down with hands upon the earth, I speak to them through a megaphone from the top of a high bucket truck or, if I am lucky, from a hot-air balloon. "On the count of three, everyone say, 'Impermanence rocks! Thank you, Great Mystery!'" Like good elementary school students everywhere, well practiced in recital, they do so in unison, hundreds of voices rising to the sky in thankfulness.

The next morning the entire school gathers for the final assembly. After giving thanks for their wonderful performance, I come back again to the subject of impermanence: "Impermanence is a natural phenomenon, at the very heart of life. Extinction of a species is something entirely different, however. To erase an entire lineage of fellow beings, who have been traveling with us for four billion years of evolution, is not acceptable. When you and all your schoolmates were part of the bighorn, in that moment you saw through the eyes of bighorns everywhere. I bet you wanted to live and evolve, didn't you?"

"Yes!" the students roar.

"You craved habitat and wildness, didn't you?"

"Yes!" they roar again.

"To protect bighorns and all species, we must take good care of the mountains, the rivers, the forests, and the sky. When we learn to see through the eyes of all beings, we understand how important this is. We understand the Wild is the Way, and we must dedicate ourselves to protect that way."

Next, I invite everyone to sing the chorus to "Wings to Fly," a song I wrote that contains many of these lessons. They have learned this song during the week. This final singing is a powerful part of each residency. Everyone in the entire school raises their voices loudly and with heart, before they see what they have made. When the song is over, the energy is supercharged as everyone anticipates the view from the sky of their giant, living creation. When the first image of the bighorn is projected, large, on the wall, showing the living, breathing work of art made with their very bodies, a joyous cacophony rises up and threatens to lift the roof off the auditorium. Children laugh. Teachers cry.

What seemed like chaos on the ground was beauty after all.

Beautiful Snowflakes ☺))

Norman Fischer

*Buddhism's signature doctrine of emptiness is simple enough to understand
intellectually: everything is transitory and without essence. But it's a long
journey to really seeing that nothing is real in the way we think it is. That
experience cuts the ground out from under us, but as poet and Zen teacher
Norman Fischer says, there is joy and freedom in realizing that we and our
world are as passing and beautiful as falling snowflakes.*

From the first time I encountered the word in English, I liked the
sound of it: *emptiness*. Some would find it chillingly abstract, even
scary. But I took to it immediately. I chanted the *Heart Sutra* ("form
is emptiness, emptiness form . . .") alone and with sangha every day
for years before I ever bothered to find out what the great teachers of
the past meant by emptiness. It didn't matter to me what they
meant. I knew what emptiness was.

Of course I had no clue. But intuitively I knew. I remember
once, at the beginning of my practice, wandering in the woods during a blizzard, drifting snow piled two feet high, chanting the *Heart
Sutra* over and over again. In the snow, with trees, bushes, and
ground covered in white, white, white, and the sky white with whiteness falling down, the sutra's meaning was perfectly clear. It wasn't
until much later that I plunged into the vast philosophical edifice of
Mahayana Buddhism, from the *Diamond Sutra* and Nagarjuna on,
that elucidates this saving and elusive teaching.

The logic of emptiness is wonderfully airtight. Like all simple truths, its clarity is immediately self-evident: we are. And there is no moment in which we are separate and apart: we are always connected—to the past; to the future; to others; to objects; to air, earth, and sky. Every thought, every emotion, every action, every moment of time has multiple causes and reverberations—tendrils of culture, history, hurt, and joy that stretch out mysteriously and endlessly.

As with us, so with everything: all things influence one another. This is how the world appears, shimmers, and shifts, moment by moment. But if things always associate with and bump up against each other, they must touch one another. If so, they must have parts, for without parts they couldn't touch (they'd melt into one another, disappearing). But the parts in turn are also things in their own right (a nose, part of a face, is a nose; an airplane wing, part of a plane, is an airplane wing), and so the parts must have parts (nostrils, wingtips), and those parts have parts, and so on: an infinite proliferation of parts, smaller and smaller, clouds of them. (This is true of thoughts and feelings as well as physical objects.) If you look closely enough and truly enough at anything, it disappears into a cloud, and the cloud disappears into a cloud. All is void. There is no final substantial something anywhere. The only thing real is connection: void touching void.

This simple but profound teaching is delightful. As a way of thinking and understanding, it is peerless and impossible to confute because it proposes nothing and denies nothing. Appearances remain valid as appearances, and there is no reality beyond appearances, other than the emptiness of the very appearances. So there is nothing to argue for or against! In being empty, everything is free of argument. Lighter than air.

But it is the taste of emptiness in the body, spirit, and emotions that has meant the most to me. Knowing that what happens is just what happens. My body; my thoughts; my emotions; my perceptions, desires, hopes, actions, words—this is the stuff that makes up my life, and it is never desperate because I feel its cloudlike nature. That cloud is all I am; it is my freedom to soar, my connection to all. I can float in it and watch it form and reform in the endless sky.

This doesn't mean I am disconnected from life, living in a Buddhist nirvana of disassociation. Quite the contrary, I know there is no way not to be connected, no person or place that is beyond my concern.

When I practice meditation, I rest in emptiness: my breath goes in and out, a breath I share with all who have lived and will live, the great rhythm that began this world of physical reality and will never cease, even when the Earth is gone. It's nice, in the predawn hours, to sit sharing that widely, knowing that this zero-point underlies all my walking and talking and eating and thinking—all activity—all the day through; in fact, it is it.

They say that wisdom (the faculty that cognizes emptiness) and compassion are like the wings of a great bird. Holding both in balance against the wafting winds allows you to float, enjoying the day. Really, though, the two wings are one wing. When you can appreciate the flavor of emptiness on the tongue, you know immediately (without mediation) that love is the only way and that everything is love and nothing but love. What a pleasant thing to hold in mind! All problems, all joys, all living, and all dying—it's love.

Traditionally, emptiness refers to the fact that phenomena have no "intrinsic existence." This means not that phenomena don't exist, but that they don't exist as we think they do, as freestanding, independent, solidly real entities. This is as true of us as it is of the world around us: everything is contingent, not solid, ceasing the moment it arises, moment after moment. Everything is like space, real in its own way and absolutely necessary, but not something you could put your finger on.

We, of course, don't know this. We are, according to the emptiness pundits of Buddhism, deeply ignorant of the one thing we should not be ignorant of: the real nature of ourselves and the world we live in. *Ignorance*, unfortunately, doesn't mean we don't know. It would be better if we didn't know. Ignorance means we know something very firmly, but it is the wrong thing: we know that things are solid and independent and intrinsically existent. But they actually are not. So ignorance is not not-knowing; ignorance is a form of knowing, but it is a misknowing. And spiritual practice is the process of coming to see our misknowledge and letting it go, to begin to experience, accept, and live the truth about how we and the world actually are. When we begin to understand and to live in this way, there is a great decrease in the fear and dread, so common in human experience, caused by the huge gap between our expectations and the way things actually are. With an appreciation of the empty nature of things, there are no more foiled expectations. There is a lot more joy, peace, and love.

The Buddhist literature on emptiness, the *Prajnaparamita,* is vast. It includes many sutras that run to many thousands of pages. On top of that, the commentarial literature on the sutras is also vast and intricate, as are the scholastic treatises on the subject. So many words to discuss the voidness of all phenomena—and the fact that words do not actually refer to things the way we think they do! Why so much talk about all this? For most of us, who are simply trying to live our lives with less suffering, all this complicated philosophical discourse is really beside the point. The Buddha said, in so many words, "I am not a philosopher; I am a doctor, and the purpose of my teaching is not to explain the nature of reality but simply to offer a path that will lead to suffering's end." Why then did the later Buddhists feel the necessity of producing such vast quantities of metaphysics?

Well, it turns out that it is naive to think that we can treat the human illness without having an accurate view of how things really are. Whether we are aware of it or not, we are all philosophers; we are all living our lives based on philosophical assumptions, however unexamined or even unconscious they may be, and this unconscious misknowledge is the root cause of our anguish. This misknowledge is not mere doctrinal incorrectness; it really matters to our lives.

In Buddhism, *suffering* means suffering of the mind, suffering that comes from the way we take things. Physical suffering is not preventable: if there is illness or injury, there will be pain, and even the Buddha suffered pain. But pain is not suffering. Mostly what we call suffering is suffering of the mind. Even most of our seemingly physical suffering is mind-caused. It is emotional suffering, suffering due to our complaining and our disappointment and feeling of being cheated and ruined because we are experiencing pain. This suffering is worse than the physical sensation of pain, though we mistakenly think it necessarily goes along with the sensation of pain. Suffering is afflictive emotion—anger, fear, regret, greed, violence, and so on. When we exercise these emotions, no matter how justified they may feel, we cause suffering in ourselves, and that suffering has a way of spreading out all around us. But what's the root of these afflictive emotions? How do they arise in the first place? They arise out of clinging—clinging to the self and to our opinions and to all that is external to us that we identify with. We take all of this as intrinsically existing and so are naturally—spontaneously and convincingly—upset when any of it is threatened. But the truth is that nothing can be threatened, because it doesn't exist in the way we think it does. Free of intrinsic existence, everything is free of all threat. When we really know this, through and through, down to the bottom of our souls, then the afflictive emotions don't arise. Instead there is peace and there is affection, even in tough situations. There is no sense of fearing or hating or desiring what is intrinsically nonexistent, empty.

That things are empty doesn't mean, as I have said, that they are unreal or that they don't exist. Here I think we can trust our common sense: we know that things are, we know that something is going on. We go to the movies, we read or hear stories of various kinds, and these matter to us. They are, in their own way, real, but we know the difference between stories or images and real life. The emptiness teachings are not telling us that things don't exist or that they are unreal. They are just telling us that things exist in a mode other than the one we think they exist in.

In Zen practice, we are fond of not-knowing. The not-knowing mind is the mind that knows that all phenomena, in being empty, are unknowable. Which means that all phenomena are marvelous, connected, magical. To see things in this way is to wake up from the dream of intrinsic reality, to walk out of the darkened movie theater into the light of day. In the dream, in the movie, various solid and menacing, separate, independent monsters are out to get us. But when we walk outside, we see that this was never really true. We have awakened to the connectedness and indescribable meaning that is and has always been our real life.

The emptiness sutras speak of these things in magnificent ways and promise fabulous rewards once we become enlightened to this truth. In Zen practice too, there's an emphasis on the experience of enlightenment, which is, more or less, the immediate, experiential recognition of emptiness—seeing emptiness with your own eyes. All the things that are said about this in Zen and other forms of Buddhism are extravagant and idealistic. This extravagant idealism is perhaps helpful: it gives us some faith and enthusiasm. After all, if we stick too much to the so-called real world, to being mired in identity and all our emotional and physical problems, that's no fun, is it? Although all this is taken for granted as life, in fact it is a kind of narrow-minded and naive metaphysical assertion we could do without. On the other hand, to take literally all this talk about enlightenment and emptiness, about becoming omniscient buddhas (omniscience is a key concept in the emptiness sutras), may be going too far, especially if it causes us to be frustrated with our progress in practice or to imagine that other people have become enlightened and that we should therefore abrogate our personal responsibility and listen to what they tell us about our lives.

Practically speaking, there's a progression in our appreciation of the emptiness teachings. In Zen practice, we begin with some modest, everyday experience. We sit. We practice *zazen*. Maybe even one period of sitting is enough. When you sit, something always happens. Maybe you don't know what, maybe you cannot identify it, or you barely notice it, but something does happen. You can feel that sitting is real, powerful. I travel here and there, and sometimes I go into a room in a hotel or some other institutional setting, maybe with doctors or businesspeople, not faithful sutra-reading Buddhists, and I say, "Breathe and sit up straight and be quiet," and in a few minutes something happens; something always happens. So there is some experience. What it amounts to is a faint glimmering that the world one has always assumed to be the world, the only world, the whole world, and nothing but the world, may not be as it seems. The mind, the self, may not be as it seems. So our appreciation of emptiness begins with something that is really very common. It's common not so much because sitting is a magical practice, but because it really is the nature of the mind to be empty of intrinsicality. So if you give it even a small chance, it will sense that, even if only a little bit.

The appreciation of emptiness begins there. Then you sit some more and experience it repeatedly. Possibly you sit long *sesshins* and retreats, experiencing it more deeply and more frequently. Then you hear teachings and reflect on them, and little by little you become more and more convinced that this is really how it is. You may begin to notice—maybe with some frustration—that you persist in giving rise to afflictive emotions anyway, that you persist in seeing being as intrinsic. But still, you are beginning to know better. You are beginning to see how unsuccessful, how painful, that old knee-jerk way of living is. And so in this way, you are beginning to train yourself in emptiness.

Then you might work directly with afflictive emotions, trying to let go of anger and greed and jealousy and so on, to begin to reduce their grip on you. Meanwhile you continue with your sitting and your study of the teachings and the verification of the teachings by your own experience. Someday you may or may not have a powerful experience of seeing directly, immediately, and powerfully that indeed things are empty, that they are like smoke or mist, like space, like the blue sky, like the movie, the dream: free and nondifferent from yourself. This would be lovely and it is certainly possible. But even if you don't have an experience like that, you continue to study and learn and experience; you apply the teachings of emptiness, of selflessness, of love and compassion, to your daily experience and to your relationships; and you see the results of this, that there is more peace, more affection, more happiness, and more clarity in your life.

You probably still experience confusion and afflictive emotion, but after a while it doesn't bother you so much. You are not tempted to be caught by it because you know that just leads to suffering, and you have gotten over your long-term love affair with suffering. So in this way, little by little, you develop an understanding of and a grounding in emptiness. You don't need to call it emptiness. In fact, it's better if you don't. *Emptiness* is just a word you can repeat to yourself in a blizzard. But you know how things are and you are happy to live in accord with them.

Eight Flashing Lances

Khenpo Tsultrim Gyamtso

Yes, Buddhism talks a lot about suffering, impermanence, and death, because we always need to hear the bad news (from the ego's point of view) first. But ultimately, Buddhism is about joy, freedom, even bliss. Otherwise, what would be the point? Khenpo Tsultrim Gyamtso is a joyous yogi who encourages his students to celebrate the dharma in spontaneous song and dance. Here, he gives a commentary on just such a song of realization, composed by a famed tantric yogi. It explains how realizing the true nature of mind through Mahamudra practice makes our lives joyous and free, like a lance flashing through the open sky.

The Eight Flashing Lances is a song of realization that was sung by Gyalwa Gotsangpa (1189–1258), who was renowned as an emanation of the lord of yogis, Milarepa. Born in southern Tibet, Gotsangpa went to central Tibet where he met his two teachers, Drogon Tsangpa Gyare and Sangye On. He wandered then from one mountain retreat to the next, practicing meditation and bringing his realization to perfection.

Gotsangpa made a commitment never to meditate in the same place twice. If he went somewhere and stayed for a few years, he never returned. He wandered continually to help himself abandon attachment to any particular place.

The Homages

Namo Ratna Guru

Gotsangpa begins the song with the Sanskrit homage *Namo Ratna Guru*, meaning "I prostrate" (*Namo*) to "the precious" (*Ratna*) "lama" (*Guru*). With body, speech, and mind filled with great devotion, Gotsangpa prostrates before the precious guru.

Next he offers a homage in Tibetan, which when translated into English reads:

> To that paragon, the dharmakaya, treasure isle
> And the treasure too, sambhogakaya's range of forms
> Who as nirmanakaya fills the needs of beings
> To the precious lord I bow respectfully

In this opening verse, Gotsangpa pays homage to his guru, who is a paragon, a supreme being, an unsurpassable guide. In particular, he pays homage to the guru's three *kayas*, his three dimensions of enlightenment. Gotsangpa compares the *dharmakaya* to a treasure isle, because the dharmakaya, the enlightened mind itself, is the source of all that one needs and desires. The *sambhogakaya*, the subtle light-form of a buddha that appears to pure disciples who are noble bodhisattvas, is like the gold, silver, diamonds, and all the other jewels one finds on this treasure island. The *nirmanakaya*, the buddha's form that appears to ordinary disciples as well as to noble bodhisattvas, is what fulfills the needs of all wandering sentient beings. "To the precious lord who embodies these three kayas," he says, "I bow with body, speech, and mind filled with great respect."

The dharmakaya is the ultimate dimension of enlightenment, the ultimate kaya. The sambhogakaya and the nirmanakaya are the relative dimensions, the form kayas. The dharmakaya, the true nature of reality, is inexpressible and inconceivable. The sambhogakaya and the nirmanakaya, therefore, are necessary because they appear in relative forms to be of benefit to all disciples who have not yet realized the dharmakaya. In this verse, Gyalwa Gotsangpa pays homage to his own root guru, Drogon Tsangpa Gyare, for embodying the three kayas.

THE FLASHING LANCE OF VIEW

Decisive understanding of your basic being
No bias toward samsara or nirvana
Conviction reached, you change your mind no more
These are three which render view unhindered
Like a lance that flashes free in the open sky

The view that is like a lance flashing free in the open sky has three characteristics. The first is that you have a decisive understanding of genuine reality. Genuine reality is the actual, ultimate way things are; it is your basic, ultimate being. You know this essence as it is, free from negating or affirming, free from contrivance. You achieve this by applying unobscured intelligence to listening to and reflecting on teachings about the view. Reflection means that you analyze until you have doubt-free certainty about what the true nature of reality is. Here we are not talking about the true nature of outer things. It is not enough merely to determine the true nature of what is outside. You must ascertain the true nature of mind.

What is the true nature of mind? According to the final turning of the wheel of dharma, the sutras that teach about buddhanature, this true nature of mind is explained to be luminous clarity, the essence of enlightenment itself—buddhanature. According to the Mahamudra tradition, the true nature of mind is clarity-emptiness Mahamudra, or bliss-emptiness Mahamudra. At the outset, it is important for you to ascertain mind's true nature.

The next characteristic of this view that is like a lance flashing free in the open sky is that you are not biased toward either samsara or nirvana. From the perspective of thoughts, samsara and nirvana are different—samsara is of the nature of confusion, and nirvana is liberation from that confusion. So from concept's point of view, samsara and nirvana appear to be opposites. But from the perspective of the true nature of reality, samsara is not something bad that needs to be abandoned, and nirvana is not something that needs to be attained. There is actually nothing to choose from between samsara and nirvana, because in their true nature, samsara and nirvana are undifferentiable.

As the protector Nagarjuna writes in *The Fundamental Wisdom of the Middle Way,*

> Samsara is not the slightest bit different from nirvana
> Nirvana is not the slightest bit different from samsara

It is important to be decisive in being unbiased toward samsara and nirvana. You can do this when you have gained certainty that samsara and nirvana are equality.

The third quality of this view is unchanging certainty about the first two points. You have perfectly determined what the true nature of reality is, and you are free from bias toward samsara or nirvana. You are doubt-free and have unchanging certainty about this.

When you have these three qualities, your view is profound. It is like a lance flashing in the open sky, because when you twirl a lance in open space you never hit any impediment. You do not hit any obstacles and nothing stops you. This is what your view is like—it is free from any hindrance.

The Flashing Lance of Meditation

> Cutting through the root, it holds its own ground
> Sixfold consciousness unspoiled by artifice
> Free of effort aimed at recollection
> These are three which make meditation fully free
> Like a lance that flashes free in the open sky

"Cutting through the root" means that in meditation that is like a flashing lance, you cut through mental confusion at its root. The way you do that is to realize that confusion is groundless. When you analyze the true nature of your own mind, you find not the tiniest basis for confusion. You do not find the tiniest source where confusion could possibly originate from. So you cut through confusion when you realize that you cannot actually find any confusion in the first place. You might have thought, "This or that is the source of my confusion," but when you analyze it, you cannot find the tiniest bit of confusion or any source of it.

"It holds its own ground" refers to mind's true nature, clarity-emptiness undifferentiable, holding its own ground. This means you are able to self-settle (Tibetan: *rang bab;* to settle within the true nature of mind in a nondual way) within clarity-emptiness and sustain that. Whatever mind's nature may be, however you find it to be, without negating or affirming it, you are able to settle naturally within it.

The next quality of this meditation is that the six consciousnesses—the five sense consciousnesses and the mental consciousness—are "unspoiled by artifice." You leave the six consciousnesses just as they are, without trying to alter or improve how they are functioning or what they are perceiving. There is no flaw in the essential nature of the six consciousnesses' experiences, so you can leave them just as they are. Leave your six consciousnesses to perceive just as they will and rest in the essential nature of that, free from trying to fix or change anything about it.

The third point is "free of effort aimed at recollection." Be free of mindfulness that is conceptual, that clings to the idea of needing to be mindful. Be free from mental contrivance and effort. Let your mindfulness be effortless and natural.

Thus, when you realize confusion is groundless and you can rest in clarity-emptiness, when your sixfold consciousness is unspoiled by artifice and your mindfulness is free of effort, then you have meditation that is unhindered, like a lance flashing free in the open sky.

THE FLASHING LANCE OF CONDUCT

> Experiences just naturally unhindered
> Free of fear, depression, and anxiety
> The triumph over all perceived/perceiver split
> These are three which render conduct fully free
> Like a lance that flashes free in the open sky

The first quality of this conduct is that the experiences you have are natural and effortless. You do not need to put effort into your conduct; it happens naturally and easily. At the same time, you are not afraid of anything. Nor do you get depressed or fall into despair. You never lose your courage and you do not get anxious over anything. You are triumphant over the duality of perceived object and perceiving subject.

To triumph over duality means to transcend it by ceasing to cling to dualistic appearances as being truly existent. This does not mean that dualistic appearances disappear; it just means you do not cling to what appears as real. Then dualistic appearances of perceived and perceiver are self-arisen and self-liberated, as in a dream when you know you are dreaming.

Thus the point of practice is not to try to eliminate the appearances of perceived objects and perceiving subjects, but rather to realize that these dualistic appearances are the energy and play of the true nature of mind, which is luminous clarity, Mahamudra, and therefore, they are self-arisen and self-liberated, like appearances in a dream when you know you are dreaming. That is how you should consider dualistic appearances to be: like appearances in a lucid dream. When you dream and you know you are dreaming, perceived and perceiver appear but you are free from clinging to them as being truly existent—they are self-arisen and self-liberated.

When your conduct has these three qualities, it is like a lance flashing free in the open sky—nothing hinders or impedes it. It is conduct that enhances your view and meditation and that is enhanced by your view and meditation.

THE FLASHING LANCE OF FRUITION

The kayas, five, pristinely self-occurring
Directly manifest in your experience
Ambition for achieving buddhahood consumed
These are three which make fruition fully free
Like a lance that flashes free in the open sky

The five kayas—the five dimensions of enlightenment—are the dharmakaya, sambhogakaya, and nirmanakaya; plus, fourth, the undifferentiability of these three kayas from the perspective of their true nature, called the *vajrakaya;* and, fifth, the three kayas' distinct appearances in relative reality, called the kaya of manifest enlightenment.

These kayas are "pristinely self-occurring," meaning that they are spontaneously present in your mind's true nature and have been since the beginning. This is the most subtle explanation of the kayas: dharmakaya is mind's emptiness; sambhogakaya is its natural luminous clarity; and nirmanakaya is mind's ability to manifest unimpeded as and cognize an infinite variety of images. Furthermore, it is not that mind's nature starts out as an ordinary composite thing and then transforms into the kayas. The kayas are mind's nature itself.

When you realize the fruition, these five kayas "directly manifest in your own experience." Then the fact that the true nature of mind is the five kayas is not just something you believe; it is your actual experience. When you have this realization of the natural presence of the five kayas as the true nature of your mind, you no longer have any ambition or longing to achieve an enlightenment that has not been present all along. You do not desire to become or turn into a buddha, because you realize directly the enlightenment that is the true nature of your own mind.

You should free yourself from the wish to achieve enlightenment as if it were something newly created, because if it were like that, then like all newly created things, it would be impermanent and decay. It would be unreliable. So train in recognizing this genuine buddha that is originally the true nature of your mind. When you do perfectly recognize that, when you have these three profound aspects to your fruition, it is like a lance flashing free in the open sky.

THE FLASHING LANCE OF SAMAYA

> Transgressions, downfalls pure from the beginning
> Experience: stainless clarity and emptiness
> When you have made your peace with self-importance
> These are three which make samaya fully free
> Like a lance that flashes free in the open sky

The three profound aspects of *samaya,* or tantric vow, are: to realize that transgressions of samaya vows and downfalls from them are originally and perfectly pure; to recognize that the true nature of all your experiences is flawless, unstained clarity-emptiness; and to abandon self-importance, so that you stop thinking, "I am more important than everyone else," and "I want things to come out well for me." When you have these three qualities, your samaya is like a lance flashing free in the open sky.

THE FLASHING LANCE OF COMPASSION

> Self-concern's ambitions are exhausted
> Uplifting waves of love without contention
> Tireless, relentless, not self-seeking
> These are three which make compassion fully free
> Like a lance that flashes free in the open sky

The first quality of this compassion is that it is free of self-concern. You are compassionate toward others without hope of getting something back for yourself.

Second, this compassion is filled with "uplifting waves of love without contention." The image here is of powerful waves of great love and compassion that are free of anger. The opposite of this would be if you felt love toward victims but anger toward aggressors. That is not authentic compassion. Authentic compassion is not angry at anyone; it sends out love equally toward victims and aggressors both.

Third, if you are going to benefit others with your compassionate mind, you must be tireless, free from despair or burnout, and unselfish. However, it is not required that tiredness, despair, and selfishness totally disappear. When they do appear, simply recognize that they are mind's true nature, Mahamudra's energy and play, and let them be self-arisen and self-liberated. In general, the Mahamudra instruction is that you do not need to make thoughts go away or prevent thoughts from arising. Whatever thoughts arise, look straight at their essence, self-settle, let go, and relax. Then thoughts will be self-arisen and self-liberated.

When your compassion has these three qualities it is like a lance flashing free in the open sky—nothing can hinder or stop it.

The Flashing Lance of Dependent Arising

> The murkiness of clinging clarified
> Causes and conditions, like reflections
> Knowing what to do and not, that subtle art
> These are three which make relations fully free
> Like a lance that flashes free in the open sky

This verse is about the dependent relationships between causes, conditions, and results. When you cling to these things as being truly existent, that clinging is like mud in water, preventing you from seeing what is actually happening. But when water is free of even the tiniest bit of mud, you can see through it perfectly clearly. Similarly, when you are free from clinging to true existence, you are able to see things clearly. In the clarity of your freedom from clinging, causes and conditions become vividly apparent, like reflections shining in the water. Like reflections, the causes and conditions of things appear vividly as appearance-emptiness, and you do not cling to them as being truly existent.

When these first two qualities are present, the third one arises—a subtle knowledge of what to do and what not to do in relating to these causes and conditions, which you see vividly as appearance-emptiness. In a subtle and precise way, you can abandon faults and adopt good qualities.

When these three essential points of dependent arising are complete, dependently arisen relationships between causes and results are fully free, like a lance flashing free in the open sky.

THE FLASHING LANCE OF ENLIGHTENED ACTIVITY

Prayers of aspiration long sent, wakening
Whatever's done contributing to benefit
Effortless spontaneous performance
These three make activity unhindered
Like a lance that flashes free in the open sky

In the Mahayana it is important to make many different prayers. We pray that more and more benefit will come to sentient beings and to the dharma, and we aspire that our ability to be of benefit to sentient beings and the dharma will increase and increase. The aspiration prayers for the benefit of others that we make over the course of many lifetimes accumulate a lot of altruistic positive energy, and when that energy wakes up, when it actually turns from potential into manifest ability, then you can really be of benefit.

Before the power of your aspiration prayers manifests, you cannot benefit beings in a vast way. But when it does, then you can do a lot. For example, when, due to your past aspiration prayers, you reach the first noble bodhisattva ground, called Excellent Joy, you are able to simultaneously send out a hundred emanations, which can benefit sentient beings in a great variety of ways. As you progress through the ten grounds (Sanskrit: *bhumis*), your ability to benefit others increases and increases, until, when you attain the level of buddhahood, you benefit others effortlessly and spontaneously.

All of the benefit you bring when you are a noble being is the result of the aspiration prayers you have made while on the path. Even when you are feeling physically or mentally weak due to sickness, mental agitation, or despair, you can always make aspiration prayers that your ability to benefit others will increase. This is one of the skillful methods of Mahayana practice, because even when you are not feeling capable of benefiting others in the present, your prayers will give you increasing ability to benefit others in the future.

The next aspect of enlightened activity is that whatever you do with your body, speech, and mind is excellent and benefits others. Everything you do is altruistic. Finally, your activity is effortless and spontaneous—it comes naturally. When these three qualities are complete, the result is profound, unhindered, enlightened activity, like a lance flashing free in the open sky.

A good example of effortless spontaneous activity for the benefit of others is Milarepa. Once, Milarepa was meditating in a forest and a frightened deer came running across his path. Milarepa sang the deer a song and the deer lost his fear. He sat down at Milarepa's feet like a student would sit at the feet of a teacher. Then came an angry hunting dog who was chasing the deer, and Milarepa sang her a song. She calmed down and sat down with the deer like they were mother and child. Finally there came the hunter, Gonpo Dorje, who was an angry person to begin with but became even angrier when he saw his dog sitting next to the deer. He accused Milarepa of putting a spell on his dog, and he raised his bow and arrow to shoot him. Milarepa raised his hand and said, "There is plenty of time for you to shoot your arrow, so first please allow for some time to listen to my song." Hearing Milarepa's song made Gonpo Dorje lose his anger and shortly thereafter he became Milarepa's student. That is what effortless spontaneous activity for the benefit of others is like.

CONCLUDING VERSE

> This tune upon this well-known site in Chungkar
> That tells of eight whole lances flashing freely

Borne on the blessing waves of able gurus
Appeared in mind and now has been put to song.

This is not a long song, so Gotsangpa calls it "a tune." He sang it in the well-known mountain retreat of Chungkar, due to the power of the blessing he received from his gurus. The power of his gurus' blessing allowed for this vajra song of realization to shine in Gotsangpa's mind, and he sang it.

QUESTIONS AND ANSWERS

Question: How should we apply Mahamudra practice to a strong habitual tendency of feeling tired?

Khenpo Tsultrim Gyamtso Rinpoche: When you feel tired, recognize that it is like being tired in a dream when you know you are dreaming. Recognize tiredness to be an expression of mind's energy and play. Let it be self-arisen and self-liberated as luminous clarity, Mahamudra.

The Mahayana teaches that when a practitioner reaches the first noble bodhisattva ground, Excellent Joy, then birth, aging, sickness, and death cause no suffering or hardship. From the Mahamudra perspective, it is understood that this can happen because the bodhisattva realizes that the appearances of suffering are self-arisen and self-liberated.

In a dream, all forms are appearance-emptiness undifferentiable, all sounds are sound-emptiness undifferentiable, and all states of mind are clarity-emptiness undifferentiable. Therefore, there is actually nothing to get tired from or that can cause any difficulty. When you do not know you are dreaming, however, things appear to be truly existent; you think they truly exist, and your experiences seem to confirm that. All of this produces tiredness and other forms of suffering. But when you recognize that you are dreaming, tiredness, despair, and all other forms of suffering are self-arisen and self-liberated.

It is helpful to consider this example of a dream. When we do not know we are dreaming, we cling to dream appearances as being truly existent and experience a variety of hardships as a result. When we recognize we are dreaming, nothing is difficult—appearances of difficulty are self-arisen and self-liberated. From the dream's perspective, their quality of being appearance-emptiness does not change, but your experience is quite different depending on whether or not you recognize you are dreaming. Thinking about that difference will help us understand these points.

Recognizing or not recognizing the dream state makes a difference in whether or not you assert that outer objects are truly existent. When you dream and do not know you are dreaming, you believe that the outer objects in the dream truly exist, that matter truly exists. When you dream and know you are dreaming, you do not believe that outer objects truly exist. This shows that outer objects' existence comes from conceptual clinging.

When you directly realize the true nature of mind, or Mahamudra, dualistic appearances of perceived and perceiver are like in a dream when you know you are dreaming—they are self-arisen and self-liberated. As Jamgon Kongtrul Lodro Thaye (1813–1899) teaches in his *Song of Mahamudra:*

> From mind itself, so difficult to describe,
> Samsara and nirvana's magical variety shines.
> Knowing it is self-liberated is view supreme.

From mind's true nature, which is inexpressible, shine all the appearances of samsara and nirvana. Like a magical display, samsara and nirvana appear but are not truly existent, and knowing they are self-liberated is the supreme view. One does not need to try to stop samsara and nirvana's magical variety of appearances, but only to know that these appearances are self-arisen and self-liberated. When you know appearances are self-arisen and self-liberated, you have the supreme view. This view of self-liberation sees that the difficult experiences in life are like difficult experiences in a dream—they arise due to clinging to appearances as being truly existent, and at the same time, they themselves do not truly exist.

As the *Song of Mahamudra* continues,

> Samsara's great waterwheel is turning,
> While it turns, its essence is unstained.

The confused state of samsara is like a giant waterwheel that is continuously turning, but from the perspective of its true nature, even while it turns, its essence is unstained. In essence, samsara does not inherently exist, so it is unstained. It is like walking through mud in a dream—however dirty you may appear, in essence, you are unstained.

In a dream, at the very moment you experience suffering, the experience does not truly exist. When you analyze wisely, you can know that this is how it is; you can gain certainty in it. In terms of actually experiencing it, that will come gradually as a result of cultivating your certainty in meditation. And when you reach the first noble bodhisattva ground, you realize it directly.

Similarly, at the very time in your lives that disturbing emotions and suffering arise, in their true nature they do not arise. As in a dream, at the very time disturbing emotions and suffering appear to arise, they do not truly arise at all. *The Song of Mahamudra* teaches:

> What arises in its true nature is unarisen,
> The unarisen is unceasing,
> And between these two that do not exist, there is no abiding.

The true nature of reality is free from arising, abiding, and ceasing. If you think about what dream experience is like, you will gain certainty in this. And like the appearances in a dream, this life's appearances do not exist while they appear, and while appearing, they are empty of true existence—they are appearance-emptiness undifferentiable. As Milarepa sang,

E ma, the phenomena of the three realms of samsara,
While not existing, they appear—how incredibly amazing!

Q: You have explained how this song teaches that ultimately samsara and nirvana are equality; they are undifferentiable. But Chögyam Trungpa Rinpoche also said that while acknowledging that equality, we still have a bias toward nirvana. It seems true that while recognizing the ultimate equality, in relative terms we should favor the uplifted over the degraded and well-being over suffering. So how do we hold the ultimate view of equality and the relative need to differentiate at the same time?

KTGR: From thoughts' perspective, one makes a choice; non-conceptual original wisdom does not make a choice. That's enough. [Laughter] Is that okay? [Laughter]

Q: Could you say more about how the subtle art of knowing what to do and what not to do arises from knowing causes and conditions?

KTGR: It is like when the reflection of your face shines in a clear pool of water. You can use the reflection to remove even the subtlest blemishes from your skin, to trim every follicle of facial hair, and to make yourself look beautiful. In this way, from the perspective of appearances, there are things to be adopted and to be rejected. From the perspective of the true nature of reality, there is no adopting or rejecting.

Q: From the perspective of appearances, how should we subtly adopt and reject?

KTGR: Adopt the actions that benefit others and abandon those that harm others. When the reflections of causes and conditions manifest, you can adopt those that are of subtle benefit to others and abandon those that subtly harm.

From the perspective of the causes and conditions in your mind, use a variety of meditation methods to cultivate love and compassion, which benefit others, and abandon anger and maliciousness. Relatively speaking, anger and maliciousness should be abandoned.

However, even though one adopts and rejects in relative, apparent reality, in the true nature of reality there is no adopting or rejecting. While conceptual consciousness adopts and rejects, there is no adopting or rejecting for nonconceptual original wisdom. Even though in relative reality one cultivates compassion for sentient beings and practices generosity and other virtuous actions toward them, in genuine reality the three spheres of generosity do not truly exist. These points are important to know. You must know how to bring relative reality and genuine reality together.

If you think about it from the perspective of what you meditate on, in relative reality, in dependence upon thoughts, you contemplate birth, aging, sickness, and death. At the same time, reflect well on how it is that from original wisdom's perspective, the true nature of reality transcends birth, aging, sickness, and death. Milarepa sang a song in which in successive sets of verses he described the respective suffering of aging, sickness, and death in great detail, and then at the end of each set of verses, he sang, "If you do not realize that aging does not truly exist, the suffering of aging is inconceivable," "If you do not realize that sickness does not truly exist, the suffering of sickness is inconceivable," and, "If you do not realize that death does not truly exist, the suffering of death is inconceivable." Thus, use thoughts to consider the suffering of aging, sickness, and death, and use wisdom to understand how genuine reality transcends the suffering of aging, sickness, and death.

When you put the two truths together in this way, you get Milarepa's two lines:

E ma, the phenomena of the three realms of samsara,
While not existing, they appear—how incredibly amazing!

The three realms of samsara are dreamlike—while not existing they appear, while appearing they are empty of inherent nature, and so they are miraculous.

Reentry

Jennifer Lauck

The truth, of course, is that Buddhist practice is hard work for most of us, and it doesn't bring about any instant transformations. In Buddhism, you always "come as you are," with all your baggage and problems, and your good stuff too. It's never about pretending to be something you're not. Jennifer Lauck, author of the best-selling memoirs Blackbird *and* Still Waters, *discovered that truth when she came home after a meditation retreat.*

Here's the scene. The house smells stale. The mail is stacked so high that it's not a stack anymore but more like a mound that covers six feet of countertop. The refrigerator is empty. There are no fewer than twenty-two e-mails in my inbox and ten messages on my answering machine, six more on my cell phone voice mail, and in about ten minutes, my three-year-old and eight-year-old will be racing through the front door.

"Mommy! Mommy!" they'll scream, wrapping themselves around me like pythons while drilling me with questions: "Did you miss us?" "Why didn't you call, even one time?" "Did you bring a present from your retreat?"

Their non-Buddhist father will be right behind them asking his own questions: "Are you all better now?" "Get plenty of rest?" "Have fun walking in circles?" This question inspired by a photo he once saw of retreatants circumambulating a stupa.

It's called reentry.

I heard the term after my first weeklong retreat at a Tibetan Buddhist center in Colorado. All that week, I studied, meditated, studied, meditated, and studied some more, all the while camping at 7,000 feet, being consumed by mosquitoes the size of Texas and little bugs so small they are actually called "no-see-ums."

My first reentry ritual was to inhale two double mint chocolate chip ice cream cones in the Denver International Airport, while standing.

Since, I've been on eight retreats and I've come to realize that reentry requires more than ice cream. Reentry is powerful. It's a transition from one reality to another, and sometimes it is so difficult, I have seen all the bliss I have achieved vaporize like mist under the rising sun.

After a *dakini* retreat, I found out that I lost a major lawsuit with a crooked contractor.

After a peaceful buddha retreat, I found out a lover had cheated on me.

After a silent *prajnaparamita* retreat, I found out my basement flooded and ruined my carpeting. I've come home to a car with a dead battery, a house that had been broken into, and kids who are sick.

My teachers are very pleased with all this reentry disaster. "Good, you're burning off karma, very good!"

My reactions have been less than enlightened though, and I have watched myself plummet from ecstasy to deep depression within a few hours of reentry.

I cannot change the reality of samsara or the way life seems to take on a specific kind of intensity when I return from these retreats, but I can devise a plan that enables me to preserve a bit of the wisdom I have achieved.

Here's the scene now: On the day I return from a retreat, I get a few groceries, open all the windows in my house, leave the mail on the counter, and draw myself a long, hot bath. I do not check e-mail. I do not check my telephone messages. I do not even check the messages on my cell phone. I arrange to have my children come home the following morning, since twelve more hours won't change their lives or the life of their father, and after my bath, I thank the buddhas and the lama and the deities for my safe return, and I go to bed.

There is one more thing. In the morning, I wake up and do my practice.

A teacher once told me that you can't love anyone until you love yourself, and that lesson has been the true inspiration of my reentry ritual. I am allowing for the fragile state of my mind and my spirit. I am being gentle with myself, in the way a mother is gentle with her new baby. I am welcoming myself back to samsara, slowly, with compassion and wisdom and love.

Birthing

Nancy Bardacke

Birth, old age, sickness, and death—these were the four discoveries made by the pampered young Prince Siddhartha that turned his mind toward the dharma. All are fraught with suffering; all are permeated by deep meaning. In this powerful memoir, Nancy Bardacke talks about the lessons she has learned as a midwife about the great cycles of in-breath and out-breath, contraction and relaxation, birth and death.

As my fingers gently slid into the warm, wet space of Susan's vagina, my eyes closed in concentration, riveting my attention on the sensations. An aspiring young midwife, I was doing the second vaginal exam I had ever done on a woman in labor. Yes, I could feel the bag of water and . . . and then it happened. Susan's breath quickened and a contraction began. As the wave grew stronger, I felt the hardness of the baby's head moving downward and the yielding tissue of Susan's cervix expanding around it until, at the crest, I could feel only a tight thin band. Slowly the wave subsided. As it did, the cervix released its tension and the uterus and Susan's entire being rested.

When I had examined her a few hours earlier, what I had felt deep inside was thick, soft, and spongy. The tip of my finger had barely been able to find the opening of the cervix. The difference between then and now was stunning. In those vivid moments of feeling the cervix, my fingers had touched the very process of change—the truth of impermanence.

"I can't do this much longer." Susan's voice was plaintive as her mind catapulted into the future. "Just stay right here with me," I whispered. "We'll do it together, one breath at a time." The next contraction began and Susan's eyes locked into mine. Breath by breath we rode the wave, anchored in the present moment.

Suddenly Susan's body began to push. She surrendered to the process in a rhythm of work and rest, work and rest. Before long the baby's scalp, with wet dark hair, appeared at her vagina. The obstetrician arrived and prepared for the delivery. Slowly the entire area between Susan's legs stretched and opened, and a head and tiny features of a baby's face emerged. My mind couldn't comprehend what my eyes were seeing. Another contraction, a little downward pressure by the doctor's hands, and a shoulder appeared. Then the chest, the other shoulder, arms, hands, impossibly tiny fingers, belly, back, pelvis, vagina, legs, feet, toes. As if startled, the baby flung out her arms and drew in her first breath. Dark eyes popped open. A loud cry. We were witnesses to the first breath. A new being was here. Now. Though I couldn't have described it in this way then, the birth process had become my teacher.

I wasn't to encounter the dharma for another eight years, but when I did, the teachings found easy resonance. When I heard of moment-by-moment change, I thought of labor, where I used my entire being—touching, seeing, hearing, smelling, my intelligence, and my heart—to encourage and welcome the process. When I heard how "this fathom-long body contains all the lessons we need to know," it rang true. When I heard about charnel grounds practice, I felt a curious kinship with the monks who sat day and night in the graveyard watching the decomposition of bodies. I had also sat day and night witnessing change in bodies, at the beginning of life's process rather than the end.

Twelve years and hundreds of births later I was working as a midwife in a county hospital. The population we served was poor. Many were immigrants. It was my first day back at work after a silent ten-day retreat. I was caring for nineteen-year-old Maria, newly arrived from Mexico with her husband, José. She was in labor with her first baby.

I felt grateful that the labor and delivery unit was quiet and that Maria was my only patient. I hoped to bring the presence and inner stillness from the retreat into the labor room. Maria's contractions had done their magic opening her womb, and she was bearing down, bringing the full power of her young body to the work of birthing her baby from the water-breathing to the air-breathing world. My hands told me the baby was small. I expected it would be born soon.

The baby descended through Maria's pelvis, and the muscles and skin around her vagina expanded in that astonishing capacity of the female body. A head and face emerged into my waiting hands. Even after all these years, I was still unable to comprehend the truth of this remarkable moment. Another push and a shoulder appeared. Maria cried out in pain and relief as the rest of the body—the torso, little arms, hands, fingers, pelvis, tiny penis, legs, feet, and toes—easily slid out.

Guiding the baby onto Maria's belly, my hands immediately told me to pay attention. Something was amiss. This baby felt soft, loose, almost flaccid. The first breath came, but weakly. He was pink . . . but barely. Deliberate drying with a warm blanket improved his color but brought only a feeble cry. The vibrancy of life in the body . . . where was it?

The nurse and I exchanged glances as I took the baby from Maria's arms to the resuscitation cart. Maria and José had only a brief look at their sweet little boy, whom they immediately called Juanito. The resuscitation team arrived quickly and began the work they were trained to do. Their faces looked worried. Juanito was breathing, but not well. His color was still pale.

"We have to take him to the nursery," they said to Maria and José, who didn't seem to understand the gravity of the situation.

In the nursery, Juanito's tiny features were obscured by a breathing tube in his nostrils. An IV tube snaked upward from his little arm. Wires were stuck to his chest with round blue stickers, and the muscles between his ribs were working hard to bring air into his lungs. I looked expectantly at the attending pediatrician. The pain in his eyes belied the almost matter-of-fact tone of his voice: "Congenital anomalies incompatible with life."

Now it was my turn to feel a contraction. It was in my chest, around my heart. "How long does he have to live?" I asked.

"Probably just a few hours, once we take out his IV and remove the O_2."

My ten days of intensive practice were not far away. I came to the breath. I noted sensations—a lump forming in the throat, a heaviness in the body. I watched the mind. It was once again confronted with something it couldn't comprehend.

A huge NO, almost like a howl, reverberated through my being. Breathe, I told myself. I do not want this to be happening. But there it was. And what was there to do but be with what was so and continue my work—which had just become midwifing Maria and José through Juanito's death. With as much care, attention, and presence as I had tried to bring to his birth.

It has been twenty years since that night with Maria, José, and Juanito, and I still remember moments. Like the moment when I nestled Juanito into Maria's arms, and she looked at him with such a sweet, sad, quiet smile. Or the moment Father Patrick arrived to baptize Juanito and I left the room so that the four of them could be alone. Or the moment at the nurse's station when a tear fell onto Maria's chart as I wrote the orders for medication to stop the milk that would soon be filling her breasts. Her body didn't know that there would be no baby to feed.

But mostly I remember the breathing. Sitting together in the quiet semidarkness of the hospital room, we listened to Juanito's breathing, as first Maria held him, then José, then I too, deeply touched to be asked. By the time I had put Juanito into Maria's arms, his breathing was already irregular. And shallow. A little sigh came on each out-breath. As the night wore on, the spaces between Juanito's breaths grew longer and longer. My attention would shift back and forth between feeling my breath and listening to his. Several times the thought arose that a particular breath was his last . . . and I would come again to my own. Then, suddenly, in what seemed like forever later, Juanito would take in another breath. Followed by another little out-breath sigh. And then we would wait. And wait. Finally, no more.

When I returned home, I was able to sleep only a few hours. I awoke knowing that my meditation cushion was the place I needed to be. Opening the door to my meditation room, I paused to read the framed calligraphy on the wall: "Birth will end in death. Youth will end in old age. Meetings will end in separation. Wealth will end in loss. All things in cyclic existence are transient. Impermanent."

Images of the previous night filled my mind as I settled onto my *zafu*. Breathing in . . . life in this world begins on an in-breath. Breathing out . . . this life ends on an out-breath. Breathing in . . . knowing the truth of change. Breathing out . . . knowing in this moment with utmost clarity that—just like Juanito and Maria and José and Father Patrick and all the babies who have ever come into my hands and all the parents I have ever cared for and everyone I know or have ever known or ever will know—there will be a time when I too will breathe in . . . and will breathe out . . . and will not breathe in again.

Through the Lens of Attention

Michael Krasner

A lot has been written in recent years about the cognitive problems facing health professionals who are trying to diagnose what is wrong with a patient. The kind of open, unbiased attention recommended by Buddhism can be a good antidote to the fast judgments, narrow thinking, and easy answers that cause mistaken diagnoses. Michael Krasner, an MD trained in Zen as well as Mindfulness-Based Stress Reduction, offers this meditative approach to attention that can be used not just by doctors, but by any of us when we have to weigh difficult decisions.

> The faculty of voluntarily bringing back a wandering attention, over and over again, is the very root of judgment, character, and will. No one is *compos sui* if he have it not. An education which should improve this faculty would be the education par excellence. But it is easier to define this ideal than to give practical instructions for bringing it about.
> —WILLIAM JAMES, *Principles of Psychology* (1890)

During my first two years of medical school, I had a professor of pathology named Dr. Katsumi Miyai who, with a thick and barely decipherable Japanese accent, insisted that my fellow students and I examine pathologic specimens with a "low-power microscope, high-power brain!" At nearly every opportunity, he would repeat this, sometimes as an admonition in the laboratory. It became a mantra. As he uttered the first words, we would all join in a chorus of "high-power brain!"

On one level, he was merely reminding us to avoid the obvious and common mistake of narrowing our visual focus prematurely and thereby missing critical patterns and features visible only from a more expansive point of view. Yet on another level, it became increasingly clear—especially as my education began to move from the laboratory and classroom to the bedside—that he was also reminding us how very easy it is to "miss the forest for the trees." We often lack awareness of a larger perspective and are unable to sense the fresh, new, and unique aspects of experience unfolding at each and any moment. The ability to use all the senses in meeting experience, approaching it as freshly as possible, while over and over bringing back the wandering of attention, is a skill that is imperative in the practice of medicine or in any endeavor where a meeting of beings takes place for the purpose of healing.

It seems almost paradoxical that the process of narrowing down a set of symptoms and signs to reveal a precise diagnosis, sometimes reflecting very specific aberrations in physiologic and psychologic processes, requires an open and attentive awareness that encourages a "beginner's mind" that is nonjudgmental and is not attached to outcome. Yet how can one possibly see clearly through the nearly infinite domain of diagnostic possibilities inherent in the complexities of human illness without being familiar, attentive, or even intimate with this kind of awareness? It follows naturally that for the education of health care providers to be effective (not to mention to be an education "par excellence"), it must focus on the cultivation and development of these innate human faculties of paying attention.

Open, attentive, and *nonjudgmental* are words that have been used to describe mindfulness. Yet what does it mean to be open and attentive? And is it possible to be truly nonjudgmental, or at least to acknowledge judgment when it arises? Thich Nhat Hanh has stated that one of the reasons to practice mindfulness is that we are actually practicing its opposite most of the time, and therefore becoming quite adept at it. The cultivation of a nonjudgmental awareness of the unfolding of experience from moment to moment balances out these human tendencies to be unaware and inattentive.

One Friday afternoon, at the end of a busy day and long week, I saw a patient of one of my partners who had called, he said, because his wife thought he was depressed. Upon hearing the patient's chief complaint, I became immediately aware of my desire, right at that moment, to have a stern word with my secretary for scheduling the appointment with this gentleman whom I had never seen before and who would be better taken care of, or so I thought, by seeing his regular physician. As I was planning a strategy to defer the evaluation of his problem until he could see my partner the following Monday, he said, "My wife calls me a loser."

Suddenly, my ears perked up. Just that very day I'd heard someone remark that the worst thing one can be called in the United States of America is not a four-letter word, but a five-letter word, *loser.* I asked him what his wife meant. "She says I never do anything right," he said. "Even the simplest things! What was I supposed to do with the hose? Put it in through the car window as I sat in the garage with the engine running?"

My mouth literally fell open, and the pen I was taking notes with hit the floor as I was momentarily dumbfounded. My shock at what I was hearing suddenly opened me up, and I found myself much more attentive and radically less judgmental of him, of my secretary, of the entire situation. Having opened to a larger context, my perception of the problem expanded, and I became far better able to work with him and his wife, arranging for an emergency evaluation and the beginning of effective treatment.

Seeing a situation with fresh eyes and a beginner's mind can be a challenging task in the practice of medicine, where pattern recognition and knowledge based on prior experience are so important.

After all, how would it be possible to diagnose such diverse things as rashes, migraine headaches, acute stroke, or appendicitis without the ability to integrate and interpret information acquired from patterns of symptoms and signs and biopsychosocial factors, an ability acquired through experience over years? In many ways we rely on the mind's remarkable ability to fill in a picture using incomplete data. But that ability can lead to some of the most common mistakes made in medicine when we rely too heavily on it.

This was brought home to me after my young daughter fell onto her outstretched hand while playing at home with her brother. My wife took her to the pediatrician, our daughter crying and holding her arm and hand close to her side.

After a medical student took a detailed history of the accident, the doctor entered, took one look at my daughter, and without listening to the history turned to the student and stated, "It is a classic case of a nursemaid's elbow, a frequent occurrence from being pulled by the arm." My wife interrupted, "But she wasn't being pulled by the arm. She fell onto her hand." The doctor replied, "Look how she's holding her arm close to her side. It's textbook!" and taking hold of the wrist, manipulated the arm in the usual way for a nursemaid's elbow. My daughter let out a very loud scream of pain. After two more unsuccessful and very painful attempts, she was sent next door for an x-ray of the elbow. This was negative for a fracture, and as she was sent home, the physician was overheard saying to the student, "Physicians' children. Always more complicated."

The next day my daughter was still in a lot of pain in her wrist, so I called the radiologist to see if the x-ray contained a view of the wrist. It did not. A subsequent x-ray demonstrated a fracture of the wrist. It was not so much that the wrong conclusion was initially made—in the diagnostic process many proposed hypotheses turn out to be incorrect and a methodical ruling-in and ruling-out process is standard—but that the attachment to a given idea was so strong that even in the face of new and conflicting data, that attachment did not loosen.

For the past four years I have been involved in teaching small groups of second-year medical students in a course called Master Clinician Rounds. This exercise involves the interview and examination of real patients, allowing the students to focus on unpacking the clinical decision-making process. This has been somewhat artificially, although neatly, broken down into a series of formal steps. The very first of these steps is the generation of an inclusive and unedited list of all the things that are known about the patient, relevant or not to the presenting complaint.

Just like the mind, the students often want to come quickly to certain conclusions, to produce a picture that makes sense, often based on very little or incomplete data, while ignoring other, perhaps important, pieces of information. It is valuable for the students to "unedit" themselves, to liberate themselves from the need to come up immediately with the right answer or the correct analysis at a time in the decision-making process when a more open approach is necessary. Making this list with a beginner's mind has the effect of loosening the hold of attachment to a particular outcome, such as presenting a case in a simple and tight fashion, in which everything makes sense and everything falls neatly into place. Many of the medical problems that come into the office are not so neat or simple. They are as complex as life itself. In medicine we often say that patients do not read the textbook for the purpose of having the right symptoms before coming into the office for evaluation of their problems.

Attachment to outcome also has a significant influence on end-of-life care. For not only is the loss encountered in dying a very challenging experience on so many levels, but there is often a desire for a certain kind of end-of-life experience, such as a painless one, a fully conscious one, or one in which healing occurs among family and friends, where problems are resolved and each can rest in peace. The "good death" experience is valued in our culture and reflected in our media. But life and death do not always unfold in quite that way. In dying, each person is unique, and each death, like each life, has never occurred before and will never occur again.

I had a recent end-of-life experience with a patient and family where, despite a disease that is uniformly fatal, and despite a not-so-abrupt but steady decline in his condition, the patient and family's attention seemed primarily focused on fixing many if not all of the physical, physiologic, and psychologic aberrations that regularly arose, such as weight loss, lack of energy, no motivation to exercise, minor variations in blood sugar levels, and insignificant fluctuations in blood pressure. At first glance, there seems to be nothing wrong with this focus of attention, especially if attention to these details would translate into an increased sense of well-being.

In this case, however, as he continued to deteriorate in these and other domains, the family members reacted as if he was failing them, and their resentment grew. It seemed it would be acceptable for him to die only if the problems were first successfully addressed. It was not until they could see the larger context of the dying process, until they could allow their awareness to hold not only the details but also the bigger picture, that things began to change. This new awareness included an awareness of the failure of the body in the process of dying, as well as the reality of all of them being very much alive together, right then. This orientation allowed them to make room enough not only for their resentment and great disappointment, but also for a loving-kindness that helped them to care for him with a fuller presence.

An open and attentive and nonjudgmental presence that is aware of attachment to outcome seems to be at the core of what it means to heal, whether one is a patient, a family member, or a health care provider. In one study of primary care physicians that used the writing of narratives about significant experiences to look at what doctors found most meaningful about their work, the authors were struck by how nearly all the physicians described humanistic and nontechnical interactions with patients as most fulfilling. "Rather than recounting tales of diagnostic and therapeutic triumphs, they uniformly told stories about crossing from the world of biomedicine into their patient's world," the authors wrote. "They described how relationships deepened through recognizing the common ground of each person's humanity. More than vehicles for medicine or surgery, these doctors discovered and were deeply gratified by the intrinsic healing capacity of simply being present."

For the past six years I have been teaching Mindfulness-Based Stress Reduction (MBSR) in patient settings, with first- and second-year medical students, and with practicing community and academic physicians. MBSR uses intensive training in mindfulness meditation, through instruction in a variety of formal practices, including sitting and walking meditation and mindful hatha yoga, as a skillful means of cultivating nonjudgmental, open, and attentive awareness. In this way, through observation of physical sensations, thoughts, and feelings, participants come to realize that there is something more fundamental to their being than simply their thoughts, feelings, or physical reactions. They practice responding with increased wisdom, rather than reacting mindlessly to life's difficult circumstances. They learn to cultivate a quality of awareness that allows for greater discernment in their appraisal of those circumstances.

At the end of MBSR courses with physicians and medical students, I ask the participants to review the classic and modern versions of the Hippocratic oath, and then to compose an oath of their own. The Hippocratic oath is one of the oldest binding documents in history and, like the bodhisattva vow, it reflects the deepest intentions of the one taking it. Because disease and illness and their attendant suffering are inevitable parts of the human condition, the vow taken to practice the science and art of medicine is as daunting as the vow to liberate all beings. The classical Greek version even speaks of freedom from "intentional injustice," which is very much akin to the "endless blind passions" referred to in the four bodhisattva vows.

As the participants read and discover personal meaning in the oaths, they find themselves contemplating what it means to be a physician. And as they make the oaths their own by taking authorship, they explore their intentions and their ideals, however unlikely to be fulfilled, in the same way that the ideals reflected in the bodhisattva vows are seemingly impossible to realize. If these vows are impossible to realize, then perhaps in taking this oath, one is committing to something more. To taking the hand of another human being who is ailing, seeing that person as truly unique, holding their being in awareness without judgment, remaining open to their needs, and not attaching oneself to any particular outcome are part of its essence. It is a commitment to the deepest level of presence between people, beyond words and action, grounded in the unfolding of every living moment.

Five Reasons to Get Cancer

John Tarrant

*Zen teacher John Tarrant was given a koan ("You have cancer"), and like
any good koan, it turned his world upside down and his mind inside out.
Here are five lessons he learned.*

Early last November an ancient Chinese koan came to me as if written on a billboard, and it has been with me ever since. Here it is:

> The teacher calls out, "Master!"
> And answers, "Yes!"
> "Are you awake?"
> "Yes!"
> "Don't be fooled by others!"
> "No! No!"

I was diagnosed with prostate cancer at the beginning of November, and here is what I've noticed.

*1. The kindness of mortals—if I don't expect them to be rushed or dis-
tracted or impatient or narrowly self-interested; in other words, if I am*

not rushed, etc., myself, almost every interaction emerges slowly and is deeply felt, the way athletes describe a big game, when time slows down and vision widens.

When the koan appeared, I took it as a response to the biopsy results. The diagnosis seemed all right at the time I got it, but I observed that the small consulting room became large, time slowed down, and everyone's eyes grew big. That room became a ship hanging in space, a ship I can still visit if I wish, and sometimes do. That moment was the last moment when I hadn't quite absorbed the news, when I didn't quite have cancer yet. Afterward, the thing that struck me was the feeling of nakedness with people, of falling into their eyes and swimming in the spaces there. In the end, this intimacy seemed to be more significant than the news about cancer—the response to a very interesting call.

At the same time, there were patterns that were the contrary of this nakedness. I noticed that I wanted people to be okay with where I would get surgery, which distracted me from the question, *I wonder where I'll get surgery?* There is a slightly craven piece in me that wants to be liked. I don't much like that part, but there it is. For me, this is a big good thing about cancer—cutting that imagined thread, not thinking that love is turning aside to manage other people and how they feel.

2. It's so obvious, once you know the trick. If you walk up to a cliff, a door will appear. The obstacle is itself the gate. This only happens if I'm willing to keep walking. Each wall is a large, rather smooth, dark expanse. I keep walking toward it without knowing what will happen, and then a doorway appears. This is like calling out, "Master!" and hearing, "Yes!"

When you get a diagnosis, you enter a different country, with different habits and laws. The customs officials don't care who you were, where you came from, what the spring flowers were like, or whether you walked by the sea with your child, counting the waves. They are not so much heartless as determinedly uninformed; their iron rule is that you will conform to the laws of the new country and that you must find out these laws for yourself.

Your initiation begins with insurance—what methods will be paid for, how much will be paid, to whom, and who is allowed to treat you? The density and heaviness of these tasks was puzzling until I realized that bureaucracy is just a feature of the underworld. It is just a set of customs and ceremonies that gathers around diagnosis. The Sumerian myth of Inanna describes the journey fairly closely: As you descend, you come to guardians at each gate, and though you negotiate, you surrender something—your crown, your jeweled belt, time, an idea you had, the belief that you would be able to function in a certain way for the rest of your life, the thought that you could avoid this journey. The prize for surrendering is to go farther down, to the next gate and the next surrender—in my case, closer to surgery.

The initiation phase took a couple of months: informing myself about the customs and treatments, wrestling the insurance guardians into opening the gates to the surgeon I wanted. Sometimes I knocked on doors with no one behind them, and at other times I had the image of stumbling in upon bird-headed beings making cuneiform incisions on clay tablets. This phase was devoted to the idea of the body as matter, money, plumbing, pain, something that involves time. The guardians were devoted to searching out and recording details that were minute and trivial in the land before diagnosis. I began to appreciate and even enjoy the monotonous repetition, the theater of it, the endless walking across an essentially featureless landscape. It occurred to me that perhaps this endlessness is the appeal of bureaucracy, a kind of false immortality that comes from immersion in trivia.

Hello, I have cancer and have been referred for a second opinion. I'd like my medical records.
      Who wants them?
      I do.

Which doctor?

Well, I was hoping to hand-carry them.

Where to?

To Stanford and Duke.

Why Stanford?

Well, they answered my telephone call; UCSF didn't.

What is the address for that?

I was hoping to hand-carry them.

We can't give you the records.

I think you can.

We can?

Yes.

Hang on a minute. . . . I'm back. OK, come in and fill out a form and then we'll put in a request. You'll get it in four to six weeks.

Um, my appointment with Stanford is tomorrow morning. I was hoping to come in this afternoon . . . etc.

Or a variation:

What kind of recovery rates do you get?

Forty to sixty percent of patients get good functioning after a year.

Um, how many of these surgeries do you do per year?

About twenty.

Is there somewhere that does more surgeries?

Not that I know of.

The quest became essentially about timing, a dance. People said yes or no or send more paperwork—just like the colleges my daughter was applying to at the same time. I came to feel warmly toward the people involved. It was a secret society, and gradually allies who knew the hidden passwords appeared.

The obstacle inside myself was also the gate. The thought that this or that bit of me wouldn't function after surgery or should function was refusing the call. It was like trying to see the gate before I was right against the cliff. When I just didn't know, I was much more lighthearted.

3. *The love of simple things—a wall, a chair. My ordinary thoughts can often have a certain amount of refusal in them—I don't like that chair, it doesn't look comfortable. That refusal disappeared. The chair, the wall, the eyes of the supermarket cashier are all monuments in a vast field.*

When I was first diagnosed, I noticed that I was attracted to archways and found tunnels with their promise of an endless journey, moving from twilight into deepest night, intensely appealing. Without thinking that there might be a connection, I bought a watch, bought time. I bought new luggage—for setting out. A winter coat and blankets—to keep me warm. Again without thinking about it, I found myself drinking pomegranate juice, the food of the underworld. Faced with any task, I thought, "Oh, I can do this because I have cancer." Clean up the dog shit, spend hours helping my daughter with a project. Time is what I have an infinite amount of, since I don't know when it will end. I can waste time, enjoy a raindrop soaking into the ground.

4. *My own reactions have sunk further into a kind of stillness or darkness, as if a wind is blowing out of the depths. I was driving along looking for a vacuum cleaner store. I noticed a guy tailgating me and then stopped noticing him. I slowed, found the store, turned, and parked. Then a man drove up toward me in a Subaru. He and his dog were both looking at me. I turned the ignition back on and wound down the window. He yelled at me for driving like an old lady and some other stranger beings. He had driven round the block to do this. I didn't go through the operation I sometimes do of explaining him to myself. I felt happy and simple, as if honey had been poured over me. "Thank you," I said, smiling radiantly. "Thank you." He paused. He rolled up his window and drove away.*

Meanwhile, the koan kept me company when I woke in the middle of the night, when I went to bed, when I taught retreats.

"Master!"
"Yes!"
"Are you awake?"
"Yes! Yes!"

The koan feels autonomous—that it has a development beyond my thoughts about it. It gives me a sense that the timing of events is probably perfect, that everyone has conspired to make the timing perfect. I can rest in uncertainty, held up by large forces moving in the dark. "Don't be fooled by others." The others are me.

I had a dream that went in this direction too. In the dream, I'm in the center of five or so very tall beings. They have wavy, thin bodies and are about sixty feet high: they are spirit beings called Mimis, which are seen on rock paintings in northern Australia. The Mimis are interested in me, and I keep seeing through the eyes of one of them. I see myself, the man below, dancing and moving about in connection with them. Because of this, his movements don't make sense in the day world. The Mimis might be able to heal. One stretches a long finger down toward me. They live in another realm that intersects with ours, and mostly their purposes are not to do with ours, but sometimes they intersect and are interested. That's what's happened here.

Aboriginal people of western Arnhem Land say that their ancient Mimi rock pictures were painted not by humans but by the Mimis themselves. The drawings, usually in red ocher, show elegant, graceful, extremely tall, and slender human figures in action—running, dancing, leaping, making love, hunting, fighting—the human things. Mimis live in the nooks and crannies of the rocky landscape, coming out at night. They are so thin and frail that they can come out from their hiding places only when there is no wind; otherwise they might be blown away. The Mimis are the Dreaming ancestors who taught people to paint, hunt, dance, and compose songs. It seemed good to have them interested in my case.

5. Cancer can be funny, like anything else. This is better than the alternative.

A friend, herself a surgeon, offered to come into the operating theater. "How is it watching someone you know get cut open?" I asked.

Her eyes grew wide in appreciation, the way they do when she looks at her two-year-old. "It's great. I'm fascinated."

She met my surgeon. "As you know, I'm in ob-gyn. I don't get to see inside guys."

"Oh good, you should come along. I'll tell the anesthesiologist."

Then we all laughed.

That there are excellent things about cancer seems a joke too. I understand odd things. For example, when I lose something precious, I can be happy for the person who found it.

All these forces led me to the G1 clinic in Duke University Medical Center. The medical center is defined by corridors that are color-coded—orange, brown, etc.—and are nonetheless incomprehensible at first. G1 is the urology place—the stream team, they call it. Anesthesia is the dream team, radiology the beam team. I decided not to ask about fertility. The physician's assistant has done the orientation so often that it's a kind of standup routine. He's a guardian spirit, helpful, skeptical, suggesting what to believe, what not to believe, how to get into a research protocol, offering his cell phone number.

How many surgeries does the team do in a year?

A couple hundred.

Surgery is, among other things, a manual skill like tennis, and it's generally acknowledged that you are better at it if you practice a lot.

Outcomes?

Over 90 percent have good functioning within a year, usually much sooner.

Transfusions?

We don't like to spill blood.

I'm scheduled for surgery, first on deck on the morning of February 22. Kind people have given me hypnotherapy, acupuncture, bodywork, tai chi instruction, and also refinanced my house. There is a rational part of my thinking that says, "This is good, I have a genetic history for this cancer. Get it out of me if you can." And then there is something more like a lizard consciousness that is deeply perturbed and says, "Knives, blood—bad!" Sometimes the lizard's eyes roll in his head. Sometimes he feels sad with an intimate, animal sadness. It's not a poor-little-me sadness—it's just that his eyes are wet with the kindness and sorrow in things. I must say that I like the lizard.

So far it all comes down to this. It's the joke of life, a funny joke, not a bitter one. I have stepped off an edge and am falling, happily, toward an outcome, like Alice down the rabbit hole. I can take marmalade jars off the shelves and look at the pictures as they go by, but no decisions are needed. The universe is managing things, and I imagine that I'll emerge in a place that's different from anything I might expect. I don't have to listen for the call. The call comes and the response just appears, "Yes." Unexpectedness is itself a kind of freedom.

"Master!"
"Yes!"
"You have cancer!"
"Yes, I do!"

Married to the Guru

Diana Mukpo and Carolyn Rose Gimian

"Diana, 16, Runs Away to Marry a Monk," screamed the English tabloid headline when young Diana Pybus married the Tibetan lama Chögyam Trungpa Rinpoche in 1969. Theirs went on to be an extraordinary if unconventional marriage, as Diana helped Trungpa Rinpoche to fulfill his destiny as one of the most important Buddhist teachers of the twentieth century. What follows is the story of their meeting and getting married, a time when Chögyam Trungpa was undergoing a decisive transformation, and even at the age of sixteen, Diana was his support.

The first time I saw Chögyam Trungpa Rinpoche was in December of 1968, during my Christmas break from Benenden School, an elite English boarding school for girls. I was fifteen at the time, and I was spending the holidays at home with my mother and my sister in London. The previous summer, my sister Tessa and I had traveled with Mother to Malta. At that point in my life, I couldn't communicate at all with my mother, and I felt claustrophobic around her. While we were in Malta, I withdrew more and more into myself, and I read many books about Theravada, Zen, and Tibetan Buddhism. When we got back to London, I started to go to lectures and other events at the Buddhist Society in Eccleston Square. Buddhism was not particularly popular at that time, and none of my friends were interested in it. However, my father had had an interest in Buddhism, and after his death, when I was thirteen, I began to question and explore my own spirituality, first reading about comparative religion and then focusing on Buddhist writings. In the autumn of 1968, I read *Born in Tibet,* Trungpa Rinpoche's book about his upbringing in Tibet and his escape from the Chinese. I thought it was an exciting and somewhat exotic story. However, the book was nowhere near as thrilling as meeting the author proved to be!

Over the Christmas holidays, I went to St. George's Hall to attend a rally for the liberation of Tibet, sponsored by the Buddhist Society. The program went on for several hours, with one speaker after another. I found it quite boring. One of the last speakers on the schedule was the author of *Born in Tibet,* Chögyam Trungpa Rinpoche, who appeared onstage in the maroon and saffron robes of a Tibetan monk. I looked up at him from the audience, and much to my amazement, I felt an immediate and intense connection. Before he could say anything, however, he collapsed and was carried offstage. We were told that Rinpoche had taken ill, but I imagine that alcohol may have been involved.

Although he was only onstage for a few minutes, I knew that I had a very deep and old connection with him, and it stirred up a great deal of emotion for me. The only way I can describe this experience is that it was like coming home. Nothing in my life had hit me in such a powerful way. I said to myself, "This is what I've been missing all my life. Here he is again." This wasn't just some exciting, powerful experience. I *knew* him, and as soon as I saw him, I realized how much I'd been missing him. From that moment on, I wanted desperately to meet him.

Since the age of thirteen, shortly after my father's death, I had had several very vivid dreams about previous lives in Tibet. I didn't tell anyone about them because I didn't know what to say about them, and I thought that people might misunderstand. I didn't really understand these dreams myself, although somehow I knew that the location was Tibet and they were about previous lives. When I saw Rinpoche, I knew that he was connected to the world that I had encountered in my dreams.

After seeing Rinpoche in London, I continued to read anything about Tibet or Tibetan Buddhism that I could get my hands on. Not long after the rally, I was able to attend a program that he was teaching at the Buddhist Society, which is one of the oldest Buddhist organizations in England. It was founded by Christmas Humphries, a very colorful and well-known judge. When Rinpoche first arrived in England, the Buddhist Society often invited him to teach there, and they published some of his early lectures in their journal, *The Middle Way*. However, at some point, the Buddhist Society and Rinpoche had a falling-out. I heard that, after they discovered he was drinking alcohol during a program, they never invited him back.

The particular program that I attended was a series of lectures on Padmasambhava, or Guru Rinpoche, the Indian teacher who was instrumental in bringing Buddhism to Tibet in the eighth century. Rinpoche told us stories of Padmasambhava's life and the lessons that one could take from it. Frankly, I don't remember the talks that well; I mainly remember staring at the teacher. I thought that he looked beautiful in his monk's robes, and although he had rather thick reading glasses, I found him quite good-looking.

The participants were told that we could have a private interview with the teacher if we requested one. Although I felt a bit shy and intimidated, of course I asked to see him. The lectures were conducted in a large room upstairs in the Buddhist Society, across from which was a small interview room. During the interview, Rinpoche was incredibly sweet. He gave me instruction in meditation, which I don't remember very well. I was just so hungry for *him*. To me, he seemed to be a very special being: so kind, so pure, so sharp. During the interview, I had the sense that he was touching my mind with his. There was absolutely no barrier in our communication. He seemed to fall in love with the mind of whomever he worked with. I felt that he had no personal agenda except to be kind and helpful.

In the interview room, Rinpoche sat on a cushion on the floor, and I sat across from him. There was a bowl of grapes in front of him, and at a certain point, he offered me some. Even though we had just met, I think there was already some sexual feeling between us, but I didn't really pick up on it. I was only fifteen and quite naive at that point. After the interview, I felt enchanted by the experience and by how close I felt to him. I resolved to spend more time with him.

In 1967 Rinpoche had cofounded a rural meditation center in Scotland, named Samye Ling. He spent most of his time there, and one could go to the center to practice meditation and hear lectures on Buddhism. Early in 1969, I heard about a program at Samye Ling that I wanted to attend during a long weekend that I had off from school. Being only fifteen, I had to have my mother's permission. When I asked her, she told me that the only way she would allow me to go was if she came too. The prospect of her accompanying me was unpleasant. Our relationship was not good, to say the least, and my mother also was extremely prejudiced against anybody who wasn't white and a member of the English upper class. She would have had a problem with Rinpoche if he were Italian, let alone an Asian who was an adherent of some strange religion—as far as she was concerned. However, I felt that I had no choice, so I told her that it would be fine if she came along. I think she was mildly intrigued by something as exotic as a Tibetan lama.

Mother, my sister Tessa, and I took the long drive up from London to Scotland. Although I wasn't looking forward to spending the weekend with my mother, I was excited to be going to Samye Ling, especially with Tessa, with whom I was quite close. The drive took us more than six hours. A few miles north of Eskdalemuir, a tiny Scottish village composed of a few houses here and there, we found ourselves at Samye Ling. The main building was a large, white stone house, several hundred years old, set starkly in the middle of its lawn. There were several small buildings spread around the property for people doing retreats. The well-tended grounds were surrounded by barren terrain, windswept hills with a mixture of green and brown long grass now flattened by the wind. Little clouds in the sky seemed to mirror the scattered sheep on the hillsides.

When we entered the house, we were directed down the main corridor. On our left was a room with large windows that looked out into the garden. Sherab Palden Beru used this room as his painting studio. He was one of the Tibetan monks in residence there and was a talented painter of traditional Tibetan religious paintings, which are called *thangkas*. The room was filled with his drawings and paintings in various stages of completion. They depicted Tibetan mandalas and deities, some of them quite fierce. I was somewhat familiar with these images, but it must have been quite strange to my mother's eyes.

Farther down the hall on the left was the main shrine room, a large room set aside for meditation and the conduct of various Tibetan practices and ceremonies. It was painted in deep reds, yellows, oranges, and gold, and a number of shrines were set up around the room. In addition to the more elaborate central shrine, there were smaller shrines in various parts of the room. There were butter lamps burning, and we noticed a number of bronze and gold statues. Thangka paintings hung on the backdrops to the shrines and on the walls of the room, and there was a heavy smell of Tibetan incense. There were low benches and cushions for people to sit on, as well as a sort of throne covered in brocade. We were told that this was where Rinpoche sat, as the presiding lama. Early morning services, or *pujas,* were held every day in the shrine room. Rinpoche used to come down to morning puja. There were stories about him falling asleep on the throne, and people used to drive around the driveway honking the horn to wake him up.

On the right was a room with nothing in it but a rug, a small table, and a few cushions on the floor. This was where Rinpoche conducted personal interviews. I can't imagine what my mother thought, as the whole place had the feeling of a Tibetan monastery.

We were given a room on the second floor with windows overlooking the grounds. Soon after we arrived, Rinpoche invited Mother to come for an interview. Most of the people who came to Samye Ling were not from my mother's social class and were much younger than she was, so I'm sure that Rinpoche was intrigued to meet her. My sister and I snuck down while she was talking with him and stood outside the room wondering what was going on in there. We had a good laugh, because my mother's high-heeled snakeskin shoes were neatly placed beside the closed door. We thought it was a hilarious image: my mother taking off her shoes and going barefoot to meet with somebody. We found it amusing and incongruous to see these two worlds coming together in that way.

When my mother came out of her meeting, she said, "He asked me to stay." She was absolutely enamored of Rinpoche. This was surprising, to say the least, but it was fantastic news for my sister and me. We all settled into the routine at Samye Ling. We took our meals at one of the long wooden tables in the dining room set aside for Western students. The food was quite simple; I remember we had soup and bread for supper. There were a number of other Westerners there for the weekend, as well as a number of resident students. There were several practice sessions every day. We got up around 6:30 and practice started at 7:00. My sister and I were asked to help with simple chores, such as doing dishes.

I also had an interview with Rinpoche while we were there. I remember telling him about my anxieties and my problems with my mother. He seemed very understanding. I asked him questions about his new book, *Meditation in Action*, which had just been published in England by Stuart and Watkins. However, the main thing for me was just being in his presence. I was pretty blissed out.

Most of the Western students at Samye Ling were English or Scottish. I don't remember meeting any Americans at that time. In addition to Rinpoche and the painter Sherab Palden Beru, we were introduced to another Tibetan: Akong Rinpoche, Trungpa Rinpoche's longtime companion and the cofounder of the center. Akong had escaped from Tibet with Trungpa Rinpoche and had lived with him at Oxford University, where Rinpoche had studied for several years after he arrived in England. Akong at this time was not teaching very much, although he was a rinpoche as well. He was in charge of the administration of Samye Ling, while Trungpa Rinpoche was the spiritual head of the center. Apparently, they had known each other for several lifetimes (the Trungpa *tulkus*, or incarnations, and the Akong tulkus had been very close in previous lives), and the two had been very close in this lifetime as well, like brothers. However, by the time I visited Samye Ling, they were having major disagreements,

222 Diana Mukpo and Carolyn Rose Gimian

though I didn't know this at the time. During our stay there was no evidence of discord. As far as I could see, it was a peaceful scene.

Both the morning and the evening services were chanted in Tibetan. The main emphasis at that time was on a traditional Tibetan approach to meditation practice, quite different from what Rinpoche eventually developed. Things were already in transition, however. Rinpoche had introduced a new liturgy that was practiced in English almost every day, and the atmosphere was changing rapidly.

One afternoon, after we'd been there for several days, I walked into the bedroom to find Mother sitting on the bed, absolutely frozen. She seemed to be in shock. She didn't move or say anything for several minutes. Then she said, "My God, I've been hypnotized. I've been hypnotized by this Asian. Pack your bags immediately. It's black magic. We have to get out of here."

Looking back, I realize that it was amazing that she stayed at Samye Ling as long as she did. In a way, it *was* magic. She had completely set aside her normal concepts of propriety during this period of time. I don't actually understand why this was possible. Whatever the spell was, it was now broken.

At the time, I didn't appreciate how remarkable her behavior had been. Rather, I was focused on wanting to stay longer and distraught that she insisted we leave. Both my sister and I tried to convince her that everything was all right, that it wasn't black magic, and that we could stay. I pleaded with her, but she said that we had to go *immediately*. I went to say good-bye to Rinpoche, whom I felt I'd barely seen while we were there. I told him that, because of my mother freaking out, we had to leave. He reassured me and told me not to worry, that it would be all right, and that we could get together in the future.

My sister had friends nearby in Scotland, and since she was older, Mother allowed her to stay with them for the rest of the weekend. I had to drive home alone with Mother. I loaded our cases into the car, a Jaguar sedan, and the two of us drove back to London. I didn't speak; I didn't open my mouth on the whole trip, except to give monosyllabic replies to direct questions. Several hours into the journey, Mother stopped and bought me an ice cream cone, thinking it might change my mood. I waited until we were on the road again, then I opened the window and threw the cone out. I remember her pleading with me, "We'll move to South Africa. You'll like it there. I'll buy you a horse farm. You can have as many horses as you want. Just please, please forget your interest in Buddhism and this strange man." Of course, I did nothing of the kind.

Soon after this, I went back to school. It was the spring of 1969, and I didn't see Rinpoche again for almost six months. During the spring term, I was shocked to hear that he had had a terrible car accident and was paralyzed on his left side. Shortly after that, I heard that he was slowly recuperating and was planning to marry a young Englishwoman by the name of Maggie Russell. That was another shock. Then, a little bit after that, I heard that Maggie had decided not to marry him. Strangely enough, that was the most disturbing news. I couldn't believe it. I remember thinking, "How could somebody say no to him? How could he want to marry somebody and they would turn him down like that? She has to be out of her mind." I thought to myself that if I ever had the opportunity to marry him, I wouldn't hesitate. I would have no second thoughts.

When Rinpoche later wrote about his car accident, he talked about overcoming hesitation, doubt, and self-deception. In the epilogue to *Born in Tibet*, "Planting the Dharma in the West," he wrote about the message that came through to him from this accident:

> When plunging completely and genuinely into the teachings, one is not allowed to bring along one's deceptions. I realized that I could no longer attempt to preserve any privacy for myself, any special identity or legitimacy. I should not hide behind the robes of a monk, creating an impression of inscrutability which, for me, turned out to be only an obstacle. With a sense of further involving myself with the sangha, I determined to give up my monastic vows. More than ever, I felt myself given over to serving the cause of Buddhism.

At the time, I knew nothing about the implications of the accident. For my part, I simply thought about Rinpoche constantly and couldn't wait to see him again. A young girl of fifteen, I was infatuated with him and caught up in my own life, my own dramas. I didn't stop to think about the deeper meaning of what he was going through.

Throughout the dismal autumn term, I thought about going up to Samye Ling to see Rinpoche again. It was out of the question to discuss this with Mother, so I decided to find my own way there, the first chance I got. At the end of October, I decided to leave school for the weekend without permission. I asked my friends at school to cover for me, and I hitchhiked up to Scotland.

When I arrived at Samye Ling, I discovered that Rinpoche wasn't staying there. He was living about a mile down the road to recuperate from his accident, at a residence called Garwald House, an old Scottish home owned by Christopher and Pamela Woodman, two students who were quite devoted to him.

Rinpoche also left Samye Ling because he and Akong had had a major falling-out. After his accident, Rinpoche had started to reach out to his Western students. He really wanted to explore the world beyond monastic constraints, and he didn't want to be typecast as a Tibetan monk. He wanted to go beyond all of the cultural boundaries. Akong became frightened of what Rinpoche was doing, and as Rinpoche told me later, Akong's fear became controlling. There was a huge discrepancy in the way that they wanted to treat Westerners and to be treated by them as well. Akong didn't mind Rinpoche's behavior—which included some sexual activity and the consumption of alcohol—as long as it was kept very private. But after the accident, Rinpoche was no longer willing to hide behind the pretense of religiosity. The only way that Akong seemed able to deal with Rinpoche's behavior was to say that Trungpa Rinpoche had gone crazy. Akong often would not allow Rinpoche to teach at Samye Ling, and it became a very limited existence for him there.

But at the time, I knew nothing about all this. Rinpoche's students who lived in and around Samye Ling may have known what was going on, but publicly everyone, except Rinpoche, was trying to keep things very hush-hush.

The first evening I was at Samye Ling, Rinpoche came by to have dinner with the Tibetans. After dinner, as he was getting ready to return to Garwald House, I saw him outside by the car. He was no longer wearing monk's robes. Instead he had on a layman's *chuba*, or robe, and he was walking slowly in a labored way with the aid of a walker. He was quite crippled from the accident. I managed to get close to him, and as he walked past me, he stopped to greet me.

Although I only saw Rinpoche that evening for a few minutes, in that short period of time I realized that he was a completely different person than he had been before his accident. Of course, he looked quite different physically because he was paralyzed on one side and had obviously been through a lot. However, it wasn't just his physical being that had changed. He manifested differently now, which I found fascinating. Before the accident, he had been so youthful, pure, and light. Now he was much more heavy and solid, and there was a well-processed feeling about him. He seemed much older, and he had an unfathomable quality that I hadn't experienced before. He was transformed.

His earlier manifestation had been one that Westerners, especially the proper English Buddhists, were more comfortable with. He was obviously powerful and accomplished, but not in a way that was threatening. He radiated loving-kindness. Now, although his kindness was still apparent, there was a wrathful quality. It was a little bit scary to approach him, and when he looked at you, it was penetrating and disconcerting. But for me, he was magnetic.

I desperately wanted to have an audience with him, but the people I spoke to at Samye Ling told me it would be impossible. Nevertheless, the next day I decided to visit him at Garwald House. I walked a little over a mile to the turnoff to the house, and then began to walk down the long driveway that wound through the Woodmans' property.

Near Garwald House, I met one of Rinpoche's American students, who was helping to care for him after the accident. When she asked me what I was doing there, I told her I had come to see Rinpoche. She said that he simply wasn't having any visitors. She was adamant, but so was I. I told her that if he didn't want to see me, I wanted to hear that from him directly.

I walked on down the driveway, and when I got to the house, someone went upstairs to tell Rinpoche that he had an unexpected visitor. A few minutes later, she came down and said that I would be allowed to go up to his bedroom for a few minutes. I was told to keep it short. I was led up the main stairs to a large room, whose only furnishings were a double bed and a small nightstand. When I entered the room, Rinpoche was in bed, and he was wearing maroon cotton pajamas. He spent a great deal of time in bed during this period, as he was still recovering from the accident itself and from the pneumonia and pleurisy that he had developed as side effects of the original trauma. However, as I soon found out, his injury didn't stop him from being sexually active.

I sat down on the side of the bed and we started to chat. I was so happy to see him. I couldn't believe that I'd finally found my way to him. He was very friendly, and I felt closer to him than I had ever felt before. Somewhat unexpectedly, but also much to our mutual delight, one thing led to the next between us. I reached out my hand to him, and he took it and we kissed each other. He sat up in bed, put his arm around me, and invited me to get into bed with him. I accepted with no hesitation. It was, in fact, exactly the invitation I was hoping for at that moment.

I had barely turned sixteen, and I knew very little about sex or about men, having grown up in a sheltered environment, having had my father pass away when I was just thirteen, and having attended boarding schools from the age of nine, where there were no boys. I had a boyfriend in Cambridge, but we hadn't done anything much more than kiss. As I was climbing into bed, Rinpoche started to take off his pajamas. I remember saying to him, "Where are your knickers?" And he replied, "Well, men don't wear knickers." I also was shocked to discover that men had pubic hair.

Once I entered his bedroom, his manner was so intimate that

it seemed natural for us to take the relationship to this new level. I had never been with a man before, but I didn't have any qualms about making love with him. When I visited him again a few weeks later, I asked him a number of questions about a religious teacher having sexual relationships and why he had given up his robes. But we didn't talk about any of that the first time we were together. I was so happy being there with him that I didn't question anything. Later on, I realized that it was rather outrageous for us to be sleeping together, but I also thought it was terrific.

After we made love, we stayed in bed and talked. In fact, we spent the entire weekend in bed together. Being with him made complete sense to me, in a way that nothing in my life had before. I had never connected with English culture, and I had always felt like an outsider. Basically, I thought the whole English thing was crackers from day one. I had felt emotionally repressed my entire life. Suddenly here was this person whom I could connect with, who could go anywhere with you in your mind. I felt that I had been rescued—and liberated, because it wasn't just that I could go anywhere with him; he would go anywhere with me too. During that weekend with Rinpoche, I discovered this tremendously vast playground. There was so much space, and I felt the freedom to be myself. That was one of the things that I always most appreciated about him: that fathomless quality.

I remember that at some point he turned to me and said, "Maybe one day, someday, we could get married." I pretty much melted at that point, and I said, "Yes, yes, I'd love to marry you." While we were together, he wrote me a beautiful poem. It began, "This marriage is the marriage of sun and moon."

People have many naive ideas about tantric sex and what it must be like to sleep with the guru. It was certainly amazing to be with him, but not because of exotic sexual positions or super orgasms. What was extraordinary about it wasn't the physicality at all. Rather, it was the atmosphere of pervasive gentleness and compassion. There was, I would almost say, a sense of being zapped by the huge space of his mind. I can only describe the experience as a combination of profundity and sweetness. By the end of the weekend, I was in a fog, but it was a soft, velvet fog, unlike the cold spaces I usually inhabited. It was difficult to leave, but I pulled myself away and caught a ride south with someone leaving Samye Ling. I managed to slip back into school undetected. I think they never knew that I'd been gone.

A few weeks later, I decided to go up to see Rinpoche again. Unless your parents made special arrangements, on weekends you were expected to stay at school. My mother, of course, had no idea what I was up to and hadn't given her permission for me to go anywhere, but I decided to leave school for the weekend anyway. This time, I didn't cover my tracks so well. I just split.

My mother wouldn't give me any spending money because she thought that I would use it to buy drugs. So there I was in the south of England, and I had to find a way to get up to Scotland without any cash. I called Rinpoche, and he said that if I could get to the Carlisle train station, which was the station nearest to Samye Ling, he would pay for my taxi the rest of the way.

I hitchhiked part of the way up to Scotland. A truck driver picked me up and drove me all the way up to Yorkshire. There I boarded the train to Carlisle. In England in those days, you had to give your ticket to the conductor at your destination. Since I had no ticket, I waited until the train slowed down coming into Carlisle station, and I opened the door and jumped off the train. I remember hitting the ground with a big *thonk* and rolling down an embankment. Then I had to climb over several fences, which led me into a chicken farm. There were hundreds of chickens running around in the yard. When I got out of the farm, I walked around to the front of the train station, relatively unscathed, and took the hour-long taxi drive up to Garwald House. Rinpoche, as he'd promised, paid for the taxi.

We had a fabulous weekend together. It only deepened my connection with him, and we were able to talk about a lot of things. I had some questions about our relationship and whether it was appropriate for a Tibetan lama to be sexually active. When Rinpoche and I were in bed together that second weekend, I said to him, "You know, I thought sex was bad, especially for people like you." I told him that I'd heard that the Dalai Lama had spoken about the value of sexual abstinence. Rinpoche told me that was true for some people, but that it wasn't true for everyone. He pointed out to me that he was no longer a monk.

In any case, Rinpoche and I spent the entire weekend in bed together, just as we had the first time we were together. I can remember lying awake one of the nights that I was there feeling how special it was to be with him. I was very much in love. The time went by quickly, and I was sad to have to leave. When I had to go, Rinpoche found someone to drive me partway, and then I hitchhiked the rest of the way back to school. This time, when I got back, the school officials as well as the police were waiting for me, and they demanded to know where I'd been. I refused to tell them. There were two or three policemen trying to intimidate me. I dug in my heels and didn't say anything. I knew that if I told them where I'd been or that I had been with Rinpoche or anything like that, it would destroy my chances of ever seeing him again. Finally, they told me, "All right, but if you ever leave school again without permission, you'll be expelled and put into juvenile detention."

Right after Christmas, Rinpoche called me in London, pleading with me to come up to Scotland for the New Year. I didn't know how to persuade my mother to let me go, but then I hatched a plan. I called some friends who were also students of Rinpoche's, Stash and Amalie, who lived near Eskdalemuir, and told them that I needed a cover so that I could see Rinpoche. Stash knew how to do the English upper-crust thing really well, so he called my mother and said that he and his wife were having a lovely New Year's Eve party at their home in Scotland. He told my mother, "I'd really like Diana to come for it. But please be very careful about train tickets, because of all the drunken people on the train this time of year. I think you'll have to spend the money on a first-class ticket, and we'll pick her up at the station in Carlisle." My mother was quite charmed, so this time I ended up having my way paid first class to Carlisle.

I had an instinct that I would never be coming back. When I was packing, my mother walked into the bedroom and said, "You're taking so many things. You're packing as if you're leaving home." I laughed and said, "Oh well, I just don't know what I'm going to need to wear."

When I got off the train, I got a taxi directly to Garwald House and met Rinpoche there. I never even saw Stash and Amalie that night. I arrived on December 30. The next night, New Year's Eve, was wild. Rinpoche and I drove around with some friends to visit various people. The first place we stopped, the people had put hashish in their Christmas cake. After they'd eaten it, they'd had a terrible fight and had broken every piece of china in the house. We went on from there to visit Stash and Amalie, who lived in a cottage in a remote area. We continued making the rounds at Eskdalemuir, stopping at a number of friends' houses.

Halfway through the evening, we joined up with the Woodmans, who owned the house where Rinpoche was living. After that, I remember encountering a lot of negativity toward Rinpoche, and some of that was directed at the two of us. I don't know exactly what had happened, whether Rinpoche had gone one step too far for them at that point, or if there was jealousy because of me, or what. However, the situation felt hostile and rather weird.

For Rinpoche at that time, there was so much personal crisis and personal growth taking place simultaneously. He was quite young, if you think about it, just twenty-eight, and he was dealing with incredible forces of change in his life. He'd lost his own culture in a horribly brutal way and had been exiled to a strange land. Then he'd had the big message of his car accident and the subsequent paralysis, which was a major turning point for him spiritually. He used to say to me that there was a point in your spiritual development where you could either go crazy or become enlightened. He was right there, on that point.

I think that he felt abandoned to a large extent, misunderstood both by the Tibetans and by his students. Most of the English students, even those who had been quite close to him, couldn't go along with him at this point. He just didn't fit the mold of a spiritual teacher that the English people wanted. They found him brilliant, but they were also intimidated by him. They could venerate an Asian guru if he remained a holy little man, but a powerful figure like Rinpoche was threatening.

So when I came into his life, there weren't very many people there for him. At the same time, although this era was terribly bleak, he was giving birth to something much more powerful than what had happened in the past. It was a very pregnant time. In October of 1969, Rinpoche had sent a letter to the lawyer for Samye Ling, who was also one of his students, in which he talked frankly about the whole situation. Early in the letter he talks about his decision to disrobe:

I have decided to give up the robe, which I feel stood as a subtle obstacle to the formulation of my teaching in the West. The monk's robe confused many here as a glorious image of spirituality. However, my teaching concerns actual experience. I don't feel that I need to hide behind something, though some people are critical of me for coming out and showing myself as a human being.

He continues,

To be quite frank with you, I feel that I must make it quite clear that the disapproval which has been directed toward me from some so-called Buddhists, including some of my compatriots, has been a fear of plunging in in this way. My very existence becomes an enormous threat to them because I am utterly without fear in this world of violent change.

That New Year's Eve, after we went round and visited Rinpoche's students in Eskdalemuir, we went back to Garwald House. Rinpoche got on the phone, and at first I thought he was calling people to wish them a happy New Year. I finally realized that he was calling his old girlfriends and inviting them up to the house. Four or five young women arrived within the hour, and they were each put up in a different bedroom for the night, while I slept with Rinpoche in his room. When I asked him what on earth he was doing, he said, "I'm trying to decide which of you I'm going to marry." Somehow I knew that it would be me, so I didn't feel threatened, as strange as that might sound. But what a bizarre spectacle!

In the morning when I woke up, I wanted to go down to the kitchen to get something to eat, but I couldn't find my nightgown or a robe to put on, so I grabbed Rinpoche's Tibetan robe, his chuba, wrapped it around myself, and went downstairs. Pamela Woodman was there, and when she saw me, she started screaming at me, "Who do you think you are? Who do you think you are that you can wear his chuba?" There was tremendous black negativity in the air.

Later that day, after saying good-bye to all the assembled ladies, Rinpoche and I decided to escape the whole scene at Garwald House and go to Edinburgh. I thought that we might be getting married there. Rinpoche just said, "Let's get out of here," and I agreed. I phoned my sister, and she and her boyfriend, Roderick, arrived at Garwald House to drive us. We packed a few things, got in their car, and headed north. We stopped in Glasgow for the night. We didn't have much money, so we stayed in a tiny, disgusting little place where every hour or two the heater would go off and you had to spend a half-crown to get it to come back on. Rinpoche and I would fall asleep, only to be woken up when it was freezing in the room. Then we'd have to find another half-crown and put it in the heater. We spent the whole night like that. The next night we moved into a nicer hotel in Edinburgh.

The period from Rinpoche's accident until we married and left for America a year later was one of the darkest times in his life. Rinpoche was often in the depths of depression. He was sick with pleurisy and pneumonia, he was crippled, his Tibetan compatriots were trying to control him, and many of his students had left him. He felt that his only reason for existence was to present the Buddhist teachings. Akong refused to support him in teaching the way that he wanted to, and he had very few students in England who could hear what he had to say. For Rinpoche, if he had no opportunity to present the *buddhadharma,* the Buddhist teachings, life was not worth living. He told me at several points that if he couldn't teach, he had no reason to go on. That night in the hotel, Rinpoche had a big jar of Seconals, which are sleeping pills. I don't know where he had obtained them. At one point that night, he turned to me and said, "Let's take all these pills. Let's just do it." I grabbed the bottle out of his hand and threw the pills out of the hotel window, saying, "We're not going to do that. There's a future for us." Then we went to bed.

I'm not sure if Rinpoche really meant it, if he actually would have taken an overdose. One might think he was testing me somehow, but I'm not so sure. If I had said, "Okay, yes, let's kill ourselves," I think he might have gone ahead. He loved those Japanese movies where the star-crossed lovers commit double suicide, a bit like *Romeo and Juliet.* I'm sure it's difficult to understand how a spiritual teacher could even contemplate taking his own life. But Rinpoche was just so real. He wasn't like anybody's concept of a spiritual teacher. Of course, I found the suggestion that we take all those pills quite shocking, although I felt tremendous sympathy for what Rinpoche was going through. In a way, it seemed like a very human response to his situation. Thank heavens I kept my faith in our ability to transcend this awful situation. I don't mean to suggest that I saved his life exactly. It was more that I was part of the circumstances or the atmosphere that gave him a future. I don't know if you can understand this, but there were many times in my husband's life when circumstances intervened and helped him. I felt as though I were part of that support system—which almost felt like a cosmic coincidence of some kind.

The next morning, January 3, 1970, we decided that we were going to get married. What an outrageous time to make this decision! Most people, looking back on their courtship and marriage, would see a happy picture, I think. Our bond, obviously, was not forged out of any such cheerful circumstances. What we had, however, was a true connection, and I never doubted my love for Rinpoche or his genuine love for me.

On January 1, a law had gone into effect in Scotland that made it legal to get married at sixteen years of age without your parents' consent. The morning of the third, Rinpoche called Akong and

Sherab Palden at Samye Ling and told them that we were getting married. They came up to Edinburgh right away, but it was like they'd come for a funeral. That's the only way I can describe it. Our marriage was a huge mistake as far as Rinpoche's Tibetan colleagues were concerned, further proof that he was not going to remain securely within the fold. Akong was sullen and wouldn't look me in the eye. I think the icing on the cake for him, so to speak, was that Rinpoche was going to marry a white girl. At that point, Akong might have given in and softened to the situation, but instead he seemed to become more rigid. In doing so, he sealed shut a door of intimacy that had been open between Rinpoche and him, not just in this life, but for many lifetimes. In the letter I quoted from earlier, Rinpoche also addressed his relationship with Akong:

> There is much that I think you ought to know about the situation at Samye Ling. . . . Most of the difficulty boils down to a basic disagreement between Akong and myself. I have not acted more forcefully as of yet because I feel that he is involved in a deep personal crisis through which I want him to discover his own way himself. At heart the problem is that same lack of courage and lack of faith which I have tried to impress on you as the ultimate danger. . . .
>
> The point is that Akong wishes to control me and use me in a very limited way. He feels that my "becoming Western" is a "disgrace to Tibet"—(pride lies very near the surface here). But my role is a far deeper one than a mere cultural mission, a representative of the East in the West. I am not Tibetan but *Human* and my mission is to teach others as effectively as I can in the world in which I find myself. Therefore, I refuse to be bound by any "national" considerations whatsoever. And if Akong wishes to work effectively now, he too must have the courage to break through his Tibetanness, to stop hiding behind our national background. . . .

I think that Akong was hoping that at the last minute Trungpa Rinpoche would change his mind about marrying me, but that didn't happen. Akong and Sherab went with Rinpoche and me to a very formal old Scottish building to apply for our marriage license. Rinpoche and I must have been quite a sight as we approached the registrar: a rather short, crippled Tibetan man, age twenty-nine, wearing a special caliper on his leg and a cumbersome walker to support him, and a tall, sixteen-year-old English girl with long, blonde hair. The registrar had a Bible, and he said to Rinpoche, "Put your hand on this Bible and swear before God." And Rinpoche said, "I'm sorry, I can't do that. I'm a Buddhist." That was all right for him, but then the registrar gave me the same instruction, and I said, "I'm also sorry I can't do this. I'm a Buddhist." This absolutely appalled him. Here I was, a young English girl who had obviously run away from home and a good family, and on top of that I had renounced Christianity. I thought for a moment that he might not give us the marriage licenses, but he did.

After we got the license, we had to go to the justice of the peace to perform the actual wedding. Before the ceremony, Akong and Sherab bowed out and went back to Samye Ling. Rinpoche had taken me shopping earlier in the day and had bought me a beige camel-hair suit, so at least I didn't get married in one of my hippie caftans. I think he was trying to clean up my act a little. He wore a dark gray flannel suit and tie. Before we got married, we got our picture taken in one of those booths where you put in a coin and take four pictures really quickly.

My sister, her boyfriend, and a couple of other friends went with us to a little hall where we were married by a justice of the peace. We took our vows sitting on folding chairs. We said all the traditional things: we promised to honor, obey, and love one another. I got two gifts: a muslin shirt and a bunch of daffodils. Later, Rinpoche said that we should get married again and have a proper wedding, but we never did.

When we came out of the hall after the ceremony, there was a scene with the press. Because of the new law, a number of reporters were hanging around to see who was getting married, and as we left the hall, they took photographs and tried to interview us. After we escaped the reporters, we went out to eat with our friends and then went back to the hotel and got in bed.

Shortly thereafter, our hotel room door burst open and more reporters came into the bedroom. They said to me, "We want to get some information. You've married your *gobo*. We need information. Tell us all about it." They didn't know what a guru was, so they kept calling Rinpoche my *gobo*, a meaningless word. We were both horrified. That was one of the few times in those early days that I saw Rinpoche become really angry. He yelled at them, "Get out of here before I smash your cameras." And they left.

There were other dramas that evening. The press went to my mother's house in London and said that they wanted to ask her some questions about the daughter who'd just married a Tibetan guru— or *gobo*. My mother went into shock and said, "Oh, my God. Oh, my God. Tessa got married. I can't believe it." Then they told her, "No, no, it's not Tessa. It's Diana." My mother fainted.

Rinpoche and I received a telephone call later that night from a friend of my mother's, saying that my mother was having the marriage annulled because I was underage. Rinpoche kept telling me not to worry, that it was okay, and that she wouldn't be able to do that because the marriage was legal and we had the marriage license to prove it. But it was still frightening.

The next morning we got the newspapers and discovered that our marriage had made the front page of the *People* and the *Express*, as well as the back page of the *Sunday Mirror*, none of which are among the better English papers. The *Sunday Mirror* featured a picture of Rinpoche and me, with the caption "Diana, 16, Runs Away to Marry a Monk." Seeing our picture in the tabloids must have been terribly humiliating for my mother.

However, for me, the most outrageous event occurred after all the reporters had gone away and the phone calls had ended. Late that morning, while we were lying in bed, Rinpoche decided he would call some friends to announce our marriage. His first call was to a friend in Wales, and I remember him saying, "Mary, a very exciting thing has happened to me. I'm married." And then he said, "Yes, yes, she's sixteen years old." Then I could hear her talking on the other end of the line, but I couldn't hear what she was saying. Rinpoche looked slightly quizzical, there was a pause, and then he said, "Hold on a minute." He put his hand over the mouthpiece of the telephone, and he turned to me and said, "Excuse me, sweetheart, but what's your name?"

He had actually forgotten my name! Rinpoche lived his life without the conventional reference points that most of us cling to as the anchors of our sanity. I don't know if you can possibly imagine what I felt at this moment. It wasn't that I felt he didn't care about me or that fundamentally he didn't know who I was. In fact, he knew me better than anyone else did. But on the morning after our wedding, he couldn't remember my name. Not at all. Not Diana, not Pybus, not any of it. So I told him my name, and he happily went back to his phone conversation as though nothing had happened.

I, meanwhile, was freaking out. There was no regret on my part, but I realized that I had gotten myself into the wildest situation possible. I lay in bed thinking, "I don't know what's going to happen in my life. You know, I really at this point do not know at all what lies in my future. But I do know one thing: my life will never be boring. It definitely is going to be amazing and unusual." On the whole, I was both excited and terrified at the prospect of spending my life with such a person.

That was how our marriage began. I don't really blame my parents for the unusual path I've taken. They had something to do with it, but it is also the result of who I am. I chose this marriage and this life. Until I met Rinpoche, I never could connect with the world as a whole. I always felt different. I never felt like I was one of "them" at all. Meeting Rinpoche and being in his world were the first real things that happened for me in my life.

Once I entered his world, I didn't have any objective reference points, nothing to fall back on and say, "Well, this is normal, this is civilized. This isn't." For me, there was absolutely no other reference point. Just him. Just us. Just our marriage. I spent a lot of years married to Rinpoche, operating in that space with him.

Later, when I started my intensive dressage training, I knew that I had to acknowledge the conventional world and some sort of conventional wisdom and behavior if I was going to find a place for myself in the riding world. I tried to keep those two worlds, my marriage and my career, separate so that I would be accepted in the riding world. Rinpoche's world was not a problem for me. It was just a bit of a balancing act.

My Life in Robes

Leonard Cohen

For seven years in the 1990s, the famed poet, man of the world, and lover of women Leonard Cohen lived a Spartan Zen life under the enigmatic Zen master Sasaki Roshi. But for all its rigors and discipline, the Zen life is an adult life, as these poems make clear, full of juice and desire and danger. Cohen has left Zen for now, but clearly Zen has not left him.

Roshi at 89

    Roshi's very tired
        he's lying on his bed
    He's been living with the living
        and dying with the dead
    But now he wants another drink
        (will wonders never cease?)
    He's making war on war
        and he's making war on peace
    He's sitting in the throne-room
        on his great Original Face
    and he's making war on Nothing
        that has Something in its place
    His stomach's very happy
        The prunes are working well
    There's no one going to Heaven
        and there's no one left in Hell

Roshi

I never really understood
what he said
but every now and then
I find myself
barking with the dog
or bending with the irises
or helping out
in other little ways

Disturbed This Morning

Ah. That.
That's what I was so disturbed
about this morning:
my desire has come back,
and I want you again.
I was doing so fine,
I was above it all.
The boys and girls were beautiful
and I was an old man, loving everyone.
And now I want you again,
I want your absolute attention,
your underwear rolled down in a hurry
still hanging on one foot,
and nothing on my mind
but to be inside
the only place
that has
no inside,
and no outside.

EARLY QUESTIONS

Why do cloisters of radiant nuns study your production, while I drink the tea called Smooth Move, alone in my cabin during the howling winter?

Why do you mount the High Seat and deliver an incomprehensible discourse on the Source of All Things, which includes questionable observations on the contract between men and women, while I sit on the floor twisted in the Lotus Position (which is not meant for North Americans), laying out the grid lines of shining modern cities where, far from your authority, democracy and romance can flourish?

Why do you fall asleep when, in order to familiarize you with our culture, I screen important sex videos, and then when they're finished, why do you suddenly wake up and say: "Study human love interesting, but not so interesting?"

Why can't the Great Vehicle, which rolls so merrily through the quaint streets of Kyoto, make it up the switchbacks of Mount Baldy? And if it can't, is it any good to us?

Why do irises bend to you, while dangerous pinecones fall from a considerable height on our unprotected bald heads?

Why do you command us to talk, and then talk instead?

It is because a bell has summoned me to your room, it is because I am speechless in the honor of your company, it is because I am reeling in the fragrance of some unutterable hospitality, it is because I have forgotten all my questions, that I throw myself to the floor, and vanish into yours.

My Life in Robes

After a while
You can't tell
If it's missing
A woman
Or needing
A cigarette
And later on
If it's night
Or day
Then suddenly
You know
The time
You get dressed
You go home
You light up
You get married

Suffering Too Insignificant for the Majority to See

Alice Walker

The Pulitzer Prize–winning novelist, poet, and activist Alice Walker says she isn't formally a Buddhist, but she's been deeply affected by Buddhist teachings, particularly those of the American nun Pema Chödrön. This essay is based on a talk she gave to one of the first Buddhist retreats specifically for African Americans. Like Gary Snyder's essay earlier in this book, it shows how political criticism, poetic sensibility, and Buddhist practice can combine to produce a powerful platform for personal and social progress.

This was not an area of large plantations, since the land is hilly with some bottoms of rich soil. Whites usually had small or medium-sized farms with slaves, but one pervasive thread of "southern life" ran through Leake County history. White masters raped black slave women who bore their children. The treatment of these children varied, and sometimes they were accepted or acknowledged as relatives of the white families.

And other perversity was always looming. Percy Sanders, a descendent of an early black family in the area, recalled hearing as a child about George Slaughter, a white farmer's son by a black woman, who came to a horrible death because he "didn't keep his place." Ambushed by white men, including his own father, he was shot while riding his horse because the saddle horse was "too fine." The story goes that when he was found, "the horse was drinking his blood."

—From *Mississippi Harmony: Memoirs of a Freedom Fighter,* by WINSON HUDSON AND CONSTANCE CURRY

When I went to live in Mississippi in the sixties and to work in the Civil Rights movement, whose aim was to emancipate and empower African Americans who were still, thousands of them, treated as badly as and sometimes worse than slaves, I met Winson Hudson. She was trying to write the story of her life. I helped her, until I left Mississippi to live in New England. We sat under a tree and I wrote what she dictated. Today her story has become a book.

I begin with this harrowing quote simply to ground us all in the reality of being African Americans, African Indians, African Amerindians. We are that mixture of peoples, brought together very often and for centuries in the most intense racial confusion, hatred, and violence. This horrible story, which has haunted me since I read it, is typical of the kind of psychic assault we endure, while it is exactly the kind of assault today's white majority takes no notice of, just as it took no notice one and two and three hundred years ago. This story, so chilling—The horse was drinking his blood? His own father was one of the assassins? His crime was that his horse was too "fine"?—unfortunately is one in a storehouse of such stories those of us present might hear or expect to hear on any given day of our lives. What do we do with the shock? What do we do with the anger? The rage? What do we do with the pain?

When I read this story recently, I was sitting in a federal courthouse, preparing to do jury duty. I felt ill immediately. But not as ill as I would feel an hour later upon entering the courtroom, when I was confronted with the fact that three young men of color, one Asian, two Latino, were to be tried for the murder of a policeman, whom they allegedly killed when he interrupted their burglary of a steak house. One glance at the accused trio revealed the faces of malnourished youths, barely out of their teens. The choice before the jury would be life imprisonment without parole or the death penalty. The judge, white and middle-class, well fed and well educated, seemed prepared to impose either choice.

Here were the contemporary brothers of George Slaughter.

My first version of this talk began with a poem by Basho:

> Sitting quietly
> Doing nothing
> Spring comes
> And the grass
> Grows
> By itself.

I was thinking of how I found my way from the backwoods of Georgia as a young woman into the company of the finest poets. It was a route of unbelievable, serious magic. When I was a child, my family had no money to buy books, though all of us loved to read. Because I was injured as a child and blinded in one eye, the state gave me a stipend that meant I could buy all the books I wanted. When I went north to college, my first stop after settling in my room was the bookstore, where I entered a state of ecstasy seeing before me all the books of poetry I was hungering to read. It was there in the Sarah Lawrence College bookstore that I encountered Basho and Buson and Issa, Japanese Buddhist haiku poets who had lived centuries before. And also a book called *Zen Telegrams* by Paul Reps. We connected on the profound level of Nature. That is to say, in these poets I discovered a kindred sensibility that respected Nature itself as profound, magical, creative, and intelligent. There was no hint, as there is in other poetry, that simply because humans are able to write about Nature, they are somehow, therefore, superior to it.

So this is the way I was going to start the talk. But then I thought, it is more honest to start with the harder, more collective stuff. The stuff that makes addicts and slaves of Africans a hundred and fifty years after the Emancipation Proclamation. For I knew while sitting in that courtroom, having read the story of George Slaughter and acknowledging the young men before me as today's version of him, that the pain I was feeling is the same pain that sends our people reeling into streets and alleys looking for a "fix" to fix all that is wrong with this gruesome picture. It is the pain that undermines our every attempt to relieve ourselves of external and internalized white domination. The pain that murders our every wish to be free. It is a pain that seems unrelenting. A pain that seems to have no stopping and no end. A pain that is ultimately, insidiously, turning a generous, life-loving people into a people who no longer feel empathy for the world. We need only listen to some of our African American comedians to see that our traditional compassion for life has turned into the most egregious cynicism.

We are being consumed by our suffering.

We are a people who have always loved life and loved the earth. We have *noticed* Earth. How responsive and alive it is. *We have appreciated it.* We have been a nation of creators and farmers who adored the Earth even when we were not permitted to own any part of it larger than our graves. And then only until a highway needed to be built or a condominium constructed on top of them.

I remember distinctly the joy I witnessed on the faces of my parents and grandparents as they savored the sweet odor of spring soil or the fresh liveliness of wind.

This compassionate, generous, life-affirming nature of ours, that can be heard in so much of our music, is our buddhanature. It is how we innately are. It is too precious to lose, even to disappointment and grief.

Looking about at the wreck and ruin of America, which all our forced, unpaid labor over five centuries was unable to avert, we cannot help wanting our people, who have suffered so grievously and held the faith so long, to at last experience lives of freedom, lives of joy. And so those of us chosen by life to blaze different trails than the ones forced on our ancestors have explored the known universe in search of that which brings the most peace, self-acceptance, and liberation. We have found much to inspire us in Nature. In the sheer persistence and wonder of Creation Itself. In Indigenous wisdom. In the popular struggles for liberation around the world, notably in Cuba, where the people demonstrate a generosity of spirit and an understanding and love of humankind that, given their isolation and oppression by our country, is almost incomprehensible. We have been strengthened by the inevitable rise of the Feminine, brought forward so brilliantly by women's insistence in our own time. And of course by our own African American struggle for dignity and freedom, which has inspired the world. In addition, many of us have discovered in the teachings of the Buddha wise, true, beautiful guidance on the treacherous path life and history set us upon.

Having said this, let me emphasize that I did not come to the study and practice of Buddhism to become a Buddhist. In fact, I am not a Buddhist. And the Buddha would not have minded this in the least. He would have been happy to hear it. He was not, himself, a Buddhist. He was the thing Itself: an enlightened being. Just as Jesus Christ was not a Christian, but a Christ, an enlightened being.

The challenge for me is not to be a follower of Something but to embody it; I am willing to try for that. This is how I understand the meaning of both the Christ and the Buddha. When the Buddha, dying, entreated his followers to "be a lamp unto your self," I understood he was willing to free his followers even from his own teachings. He had done all he could do, taught them everything he had learned. Now their own enlightenment was up to them. He was also warning them not to claim him as the sole route to their salvation, thereby robbing themselves of responsibility for their own choices, behavior, and lives.

I came to meditation after a particularly painful divorce. Painful because I never ceased to care for the man I divorced. I married him because he was one of the best people I'd ever encountered. However, life had other plans for us both. I left my home, as the Buddha left his two thousand and five hundred years ago, to see if I could discover how I at least could be happy. If I could be happy in a land where torture of my kind was commonplace, then perhaps there was a general happiness to be found.

The person who taught me Transcendental Meditation was teaching out of the Hindu tradition and never mentioned the Buddha; the Four Noble Truths (about the fact of human suffering, its causes, and the necessity to engage, endure, and transform it); or the Eightfold Path, which provides a guide to moral, conscious living. What she did teach me was the deeper value of sitting quietly. Doing nothing. *Breathing.* This took me back to childhood days when I did this without thinking. Days when I was aware I was not separate from the cosmos. Days when I was happy. This was actually a place where poets, time out of mind, have frequently lived. No wonder I felt at home there.

And so I laughed. The laughter bubbled up, irrepressible. I saw the path to happiness and to liberation at a glance. It was inside myself.

Now I understand that all great teachers love us. This is essentially what makes them great. I also understand that it is this love that never dies, and that, having once experienced it, we have the confidence always exhibited by well-loved humans to continue extending this same love. The Buddha, presumably raised as a Hindu, was no doubt disheartened by its racism, i.e., the caste system that today blights the lives of one hundred and sixty million Indians. Indians who were once called "untouchables" and now call themselves *Dalits,* "those broken to pieces." They are not allowed to own land. They cannot enter the same doors, attend the schools, or drink from the same wells as the so-called higher castes. Their shadow must never fall on those above them. They are brutalized and the women raped at will. Niggers of India, they are.

Traditionally it is taught that the Buddha discovered someone old, someone sick, and someone dying, after having lived a very sheltered life, and that because of this suffering, inherent to all humankind, he struck out into the world to find a remedy. There's no mention, usually, of the horrible caste system, everywhere in place in his area, which I personally find impossible to imagine the Buddha ignoring.

I like to think of the young prince, Siddhartha, observing this hypocrisy of his native religion, perhaps touching or loving an "untouchable," and deciding there had to be a better way. A higher truth. I like to think of him leaving his cushy home and delightful family, his loving wife and adorable son, and striking out into the wilderness. Searching for a way humans could rid themselves of the hideous affliction of spirit that forced division and degradation of part of the human family imposes.

Which is to say, I felt the Buddha's spirit long before I began to study his words. I felt him not as a god or as the son of a god but as a human being who looked around, as any of us might do, and said to himself: Something here is very wrong. People are such beautiful and wondrous creations, why are they being tortured? What have they done that this should be so? How can there be an end to their suffering?

The Buddha sat down.

Most of the representations of the Buddha show him sitting down. Sometimes he is lying down. Sometimes he is walking, though this is rare. Sometimes he is shown leaping to his feet and flinging up his arms in joy. Anyone who meditates recognizes these states. First, the sitting. The concentration on the breath. Sometimes the lying down, feeling our connection to the Mother, the great support of Earth. There is the walking, which integrates our bodies with our mind state. Then there is the feeling of exuberance when we realize we have freed ourselves. *Again.*

How does this happen?

I imagine there are people who turn to the Buddha because they've lost a lot of money. My experience, however, is that almost everyone I've met who has turned to the Buddha did so because they have suffered the end of a love affair. They have lost someone they loved. Perhaps they have lost a country as well, or parents or siblings or some function of their bodies. But very often, people turn to the

Buddha because they have been carried so deeply into their suffering by the loss of a loved one that without major help they fear they will never recover. (I actually love this about Buddhists: that though their reputation is all about suffering and meditating and being a bit low-key sexually and spiritually languid, they are in fact a band of hopeful lovers who risk their hearts in places a Methodist would rarely dare to tread.) This is what happened to me. I had lost my own beloved. The pain of this experience seemed bottomless and endless. Enter my teacher for that moment of my life, the Buddhist nun Pema Chödrön and her teachings on a set of tapes called "Awakening Compassion." Under her guidance, far in the country away from everyone, on my own retreat of one, I learned an ancient Tibetan Buddhist meditation practice called *tonglen,* along with the teachings that accompanied it, called *lojong.* This involved, during meditation, learning to breathe in the pain I was feeling, not to attempt to avoid or flee it. It involved making my heart bigger and bigger just to be able to hold it all. It involved breathing out relief and happiness for myself and for everyone on Earth who was feeling as miserable as I was. I stayed at this practice for a year.

It worked. So that today I sometimes wonder what my suffering over the loss of a loved one was really about. I have almost concluded that it was the love of the Buddha reaching through two thousand and five hundred years, wanting me to understand that I had some control over how much suffering I endure. Wanting me to try a remedy he had found and to see for myself whether it works.

My novel *The Color Purple* was actually my Buddha novel without Buddhism. In the face of unbearable suffering following the assassinations and betrayals of the Civil Rights movement, I too sat down upon the Earth and asked its permission to posit a different way from that in which I was raised. Just as the Buddha did, when Mara, the king of delusion, asked what gave him the right to think he could direct humankind away from the suffering they had always endured. *When Mara queried him, the Buddha touched the Earth.*

This is the single most important act, to my mind, of the Buddha. Because it acknowledges where he came from. It is a humble recognition of his true heritage, his true lineage. Though Buddhist monks would spend millennia pretending all wisdom evolves from the masculine and would consequently treat Buddhist nuns abominably, the Buddha clearly placed himself in the lap of the Earth Mother and affirmed Her wisdom and Her support.

It has been enormously helpful to me to learn that the Buddha's wife and son eventually joined him in the wilderness and that she became both a follower and a teacher. There was love between them. How I wish we had a record of her thoughts. The male effort to separate Wisdom from the realm of the Feminine is not only brutal and unattractive but it will always fail, though this may take, as with Buddhism, thousands of years. This is simply because the Feminine is Wisdom; it is also the Soul. Since each and every person is born with an internal as well as an eternal Feminine, just as everyone is born with an internal and eternal Masculine, this is not a problem except for those who insist on forcing humans into gender roles, which makes it easier for them to be controlled.

Sometimes, as African Americans, African Indians, African Amerindians, people of color, it appears we are being removed from the planet. Fascism and Nazism, visibly on the rise in the world, have always been our experience of white supremacy in America, and this has barely let up. Plagues such as AIDS seem incredibly convenient for the forces that have enslaved and abused us over the centuries and that today are as blatant in their attempts to seize our native homelands and their resources as Columbus was five hundred years ago. Following the suffering and exhilaration of the sixties, a pharmacopia of drugs suddenly appeared just as we were becoming used to enjoying our own minds. "Citizen Television," which keeps relentless watch over each and every home, claims the uniqueness and individuality of the majority of our children from birth. After the assassinations of Martin Luther King, Jr., Malcolm X, Che Guevara, and so many other defenders of humanity, known and unknown, around the globe, we find ourselves with an unelected president who came to office by disenfranchising black voters, just as was done, routinely, before Martin Luther King, Jr., and the rest of us were born. This is a major suffering for black people and must not be overlooked. I myself, on realizing what had happened, felt a soul sickness I had not experienced in decades. Those who wanted power beyond anything else—oil and the money to be made from oil (which is the Earth Mother's blood)—were contemptuous of the sacrifices generations of our ancestors made. The suffering of our people, especially of our children, with their bright, hopeful eyes, is of no significance to them. George Slaughter—the surname would have been his master/father's and deadly accurate—was not killed, we intuit, because his "saddle horse was too fine"; he was killed because *he* was too fine.

This is the bind we are in.

There is a private riddle I ask myself: Why did Europeans enslave us in Africa and take us to the United States?

The answer: Because we would not go voluntarily.

. The African Americans who are aiding and abetting the rape and pillage of Earth, helping literally to direct the bombs that fall on the innocent and the exquisite, are still another cause of our suffering. We look into their eyes and experience a great fright. They appear so familiar, and yet, somehow, we feel they are not. I do not call their names because essentially they are, as we are, energies. They are familiar because they have been around just as long as we have. It is also necessary to acknowledge that some of those energies we find so frightening exist within ourselves.

This poem, which I think of as one of my "bitter" poems, expresses something of their position, when they can bear to acknowledge it, throughout the long centuries:

They Helped Their Own

> They helped their own
> They did not
> Help us

We helped
Them
Help
Themselves

Beggars
That
We are.

Underneath what is sometimes glibly labeled racism or sexism or casteism, there lurk covetousness, envy, and greed. All these human states can, through practice, be worked with and transformed. This is the good news for our oppressors, as it is for humans generally, since we all have these qualities to a degree. The equally good news for us is that we can turn our attention away from our oppressors—unless they are directly endangering us to our faces— and work on the issue of our suffering without attaching them to it.

The teaching that supports that idea is this: Suppose someone shot you with an arrow, right in the heart. Would you spend your time screaming at the archer, or even trying to locate him? Or would you try to pull the arrow out of your heart? White racism, that is to say, envy, covetousness, and greed (incredible sloth and laziness in the case of enslaving others to work for you), is the arrow that has pierced our collective heart. For centuries we have tried to get the white archer even to notice where his arrow has landed; to connect himself, even for a moment, to what he has done. Maybe even to consider apologizing, which he hates to do. To make reparations, which he considers absurd.

This teaching says: enough. Screaming at the archer is a sure way to remain attached to your suffering rather than easing or eliminating it. A better way is to learn, through meditation, through study and practice, a way to free yourself from the pain of being shot, no matter who the archer might be.

There is also the incredibly useful assurance that everything is change. Everything is impermanent. The country, the laws, the Fascists and Nazis, the archer and the arrow. Our lives and their lives.

Life. Looking about at the wreckage, it is clear to all that in enslaving us, torturing us, trying to get "ahead" on the basis of our misery, our oppressors in the past had no idea at all what they were doing. They still don't. As we practice, let this thought deeply root. From this perspective, our compassion for their ignorance seems the only just tribute to our survival.

Who or *What* knows what is really going on around here, anyway? Only the Tao or Life or Creation or That Which Is Beyond Human Expression.

Sitting quietly.

This place of peace, of serenity and gratitude, does exist. It is available to all. In a way, this place of quiet and peacefulness could be said to be our shadow. Our deserved shadow. Our African Amerindian shadow. In European thought the shadow is rarely understood as positive, because it is dark, because it is frequently behind us, because we cannot see it; but for us, ultrasensitive to the blinding glare of racism and suffering daily the searing effects of incomprehensible behavior, *our shadow of peace,* which we so rarely see, can be thought of as welcoming shade, the shade of an internal tree. A tree that grows beside an internal river that bathes us in peace. Meditation is the path that leads to this internal glade. To share that certainty is the greatest privilege and joy.

I am grateful for the opportunity to join you in this first-ever African American Buddhist retreat in North America. Though not a Buddhist, I have found a support in the teachings of the Buddha that is beyond measure, as I have found comfort and support also in those teachings I have received from Ancient Africans and Indigenous people of my native continent and from the Earth itself. The teacher who has been most helpful to me, in addition to Pema Chödrön, is Jack Kornfield, an extraordinary guide and human being, whose books and tapes, among them *A Path with Heart, After the Ecstasy the Laundry,* and *The Roots of Buddhist Psychology,* I would recommend to anyone who seeks a better understanding of the enspirited life. Sharon Salzberg's book *Loving-Kindness, The*

Revolutionary Art of Happiness has been an incomparable gift. In a book called *Knee Deep in Grace*, I discovered the teachings of the Indian female yogi, householder, and mother Dipa Ma. Her instructions and observations seem endlessly potent.

I am deeply grateful to all the teachers who came before these four that I have mentioned. Teachers from Vietnam (Thich Nhat Hahn has been a beloved teacher), Thailand, Burma, India, China, and especially Tibet. I thank the Dalai Lama for allowing himself to be a symbol of good in a world that seems, at times, hopelessly tilted toward evil. I thank Martin Luther King, Jr., for the warm, brotherly touch of his hand when I was young and seeking a way to live, with dignity, in my native land in the South, and for the sound of his voice, which was so full of our experience. I thank him for loving us. If he had been able to live and teach, as the Buddha did, until the age of eighty, how different our world would be. It is such a gift to have his books and recordings of his words and to be able to understand his death as a teaching on both the preciousness of human existence and impermanence.

And, as always, I thank the ancestors, those who have gone on and those who are always arriving. It is because our global spiritual ancestors have loved us very dearly that we today sit together practicing ways to embody peace and create a better world. I feel personally ever-bathed in that love.

Let us sit for ten minutes.

Let us bring our attention to the life of our young brother, our murdered ancestor, George Slaughter. We know he was a beautiful young man and that it was this beauty and his freedom expressing it that caused his father, *himself unfree,* to seek his death. *We can see George sitting on his stunning saddle horse.* We do not know if his half-sister, white, confused by her liking for her darker brother, gave it to him. We do not know if his mother, dark and irresistible, as so many black women are, gave it to him. We do not know if he bought it himself. All we know is that *he is sitting there, happy. And the horse, too, is happy.*

George Slaughter, an English name. We might think of Bob Marley, half-English, with his English name; perhaps George had a similar spirit. A kindred look and attitude.

May you be free
May you be happy
May you be at peace
May you be at rest
May you know we remember you

Let us bring our attention to George's mother. She who came, weeping, and picked up the shattered pieces of her child, as black mothers have done for so long.

May you be free
May you be happy
May you be at peace
May you be at rest
May you know we remember you

Let us bring our attention to George's father. He who trails the murder of his lovely boy throughout what remains of time.

May you be free
May you be happy
May you be at peace
May you be at rest
May you know we remember you

Let us bring our attention to those who rode with the father, whose silence and whose violence caused so much suffering that continues in the world today.

May you be free
May you be happy
May you be at peace
May you be at rest
May you know we remember you

And now let us bring our attention to George's horse. With its big dark eyes. Who drank George's blood in grief after the horror of his companion's bitter death. We know by now that the other animals on the planet watch us and know us and sometimes love us. How they express that love is often mysterious.

May you be free
May you be happy
May you be at peace
May you be at rest
May you know we remember you

I cherish the study and practice of Buddhism because it is good medicine for healing us so that we may engage in the work of healing our ancestors. Both George and his father are our ancestors. *What heals ancestors is understanding them.* And understanding as well that it is not in heaven or in hell that the ancestors are healed. *They can only be healed inside us.* Buddhist practice, sent by ancestors we didn't even know we had, has arrived, as all things do, just in time.

This is not a time to live without a practice. It is a time when all of us will need the most faithful, self-generated enthusiasm (*enthusiasm:* to be filled with god) in order to survive in human fashion. Whether we reach this inner state of recognized divinity through prayer, meditation, dancing, swimming, walking, feeding the hungry, or enriching the impoverished is immaterial. We will be doubly bereft without some form of practice that connects us, in a caring way, to what begins to feel like a dissolving world.

In addition to contemplating the Hopi message "Know your garden and where is your water," we must also ask: What is my practice? What is steering this boat that is my fragile human life?

Take some time to contemplate what sort of practice appeals to you. If you are Christian, the words and actions of Jesus are excellent guides; especially the words and actions discovered during the past century in the Gnostic Gospels and the Nag Hammadi Scrolls. If you are an animist, there is all of Existence to be inspired by. Everything has life, everything has spirit! Perhaps singing in the choir of your church or trance dancing with friends is a connector to the All for you. Whatever it is, now is the time to look for it, to locate it definitely, and to put it to use.

Turning Your Whole Way of Thinking Upside Down ❂

Pema Chödrön

Pema Chödrön is often described as a beloved American Buddhist nun, and indeed, she is a kind and gentle person. But she is also honest, tough, and uncompromising. I think she is among the most radical and demanding of Buddhist teachers, who says our only hope—and the world's—is to do exactly the opposite of what we usually do.

On a very basic level all beings think that they should be happy. When life becomes difficult or painful, we feel that something has gone wrong. This wouldn't be a big problem except for the fact that when we feel something's gone wrong, we're willing to do anything to feel okay again. Even start a fight.

According to the Buddhist teachings, difficulty is inevitable in human life. For one thing, we cannot escape the reality of death. But there are also the realities of aging, of illness, of not getting what we want, and of getting what we don't want. These kinds of difficulties are facts of life. Even if you were the Buddha himself, if you were a fully enlightened person, you would experience death, illness, aging, and sorrow at losing what you love. All of these things would happen to you. If you got burned or cut, it would hurt.

But the Buddhist teachings also say that this is not really what causes us misery in our lives. What causes misery is always trying to get away from the facts of life, always trying to avoid pain and seek happiness—this sense of ours that there could be lasting security and happiness available to us if we could only do the right thing.

In this very lifetime we can do ourselves and this planet a great favor and turn this very old way of thinking upside down. As Shantideva, author of *Guide to the Bodhisattva's Way of Life*, points out, suffering has a great deal to teach us. If we use the opportunity when it arises, suffering will motivate us to look for answers. Many people, including myself, came to the spiritual path because of deep unhappiness. Suffering can also teach us empathy for others who are in the same boat. Furthermore, suffering can humble us. Even the most arrogant among us can be softened by the loss of someone dear.

Yet it is so basic in us to feel that things should go well for us, and that if we start to feel depressed, lonely, or inadequate, there's been some kind of mistake or we've lost it. In reality, when you feel depressed, lonely, betrayed, or any unwanted feelings, this is an important moment on the spiritual path. This is where real transformation can take place.

As long as we're caught up in always looking for certainty and happiness, rather than honoring the taste and smell and quality of exactly what is happening, as long as we're always running away from discomfort, we're going to be caught in a cycle of unhappiness and disappointment, and we will feel weaker and weaker. This way of seeing helps us to develop inner strength.

And what's especially encouraging is the view that inner strength is available to us at just the moment when we think we've hit the bottom, when things are at their worst. Instead of asking ourselves, "How can I find security and happiness?" we could ask ourselves, "Can I touch the center of my pain? Can I sit with suffering, both yours and mine, without trying to make it go away? Can I stay present to the ache of loss or disgrace—disappointment in all its many forms—and let it open me?" This is the trick.

There are various ways to view what happens when we feel threatened. In times of distress—of rage, of frustration, of failure— we can look at how we get hooked and how shenpa escalates. The usual translation of *shenpa* is "attachment," but this doesn't adequately express the full meaning. I think of *shenpa* as "getting hooked." Another definition, used by Dzigar Kongtrul Rinpoche, is the "charge"—the charge behind our thoughts and words and actions, the charge behind "like" and "don't like."

It can also be helpful to shift our focus and look at how we put up barriers. In these moments we can observe how we withdraw and become self-absorbed. We become dry, sour, afraid; we crumble or harden out of fear that more pain is coming. In some old familiar way, we automatically erect a protective shield and our self-centeredness intensifies.

But this is the very same moment when we could do something different. Right on the spot, through practice, we can get very familiar with the barriers that we put up around our hearts and around our whole being. We can become intimate with just how we hide out, doze off, freeze up. And that intimacy, coming to know these barriers so well, is what begins to dismantle them. Amazingly, when we give them our full attention, they start to fall apart.

Ultimately all the practices I have mentioned are simply ways we can go about dissolving these barriers. Whether it's learning to be present through sitting meditation, acknowledging shenpa, or practicing patience, these are methods for dissolving the protective walls that we automatically put up.

When we're putting up the barriers and the sense of "me" as separate from "you" gets stronger, right there in the midst of difficulty and pain, the whole thing could turn around simply by not erecting barriers; simply by staying open to the difficulty, to the feelings that you're going through; simply by not talking to ourselves about what's happening. That is a revolutionary step. Becoming intimate with pain is the key to changing at the core of our being—staying open to everything we experience, letting the sharpness of difficult times pierce us to the heart, letting these times open us, humble us, and make us wiser and more brave.

Let difficulty transform you. And it will. In my experience, we just need help in learning how not to run away.

If we're ready to try staying present with our pain, one of the greatest supports we could ever find is to cultivate the warmth and simplicity of *bodhichitta*. The word *bodhichitta* has many translations, but probably the most common one is "awakened heart." The word refers to a longing to wake up from ignorance and delusion in order to help others do the same. Putting our personal awakening in a larger—even planetary—framework makes a significant difference. It gives us a vaster perspective on why we would do this often difficult work.

There are two kinds of bodhichitta: relative and absolute. Relative bodhichitta includes compassion and *maitri*. Chögyam Trungpa Rinpoche translated *maitri* as "unconditional friendliness with oneself." This unconditional friendliness means having an unbiased relationship with all the parts of your being. So, in the context of working with pain, this means making an intimate, compassionate heart-relationship with all those parts of ourselves we generally don't want to touch.

Some people find the teachings I offer helpful because I encourage them to be kind to themselves—but this does not mean pampering our neurosis. The kindness that I learned from my teachers, and that I wish so much to convey to other people, is kindness toward all qualities of our being. The qualities that are the toughest to be kind to are the painful parts, where we feel ashamed, as if we don't belong, as if we've just blown it, when things are falling apart for us. Maitri means sticking with ourselves when we don't have anything, when we feel like a loser. And it becomes the basis for extending the same unconditional friendliness to others.

If there are whole parts of yourself that you are always running from, that you even feel justified in running from, then you're going to run from anything that brings you into contact with your feelings of insecurity.

And have you noticed how often these parts of ourselves get touched? The closer you get to a situation or a person, the more these feelings arise. Often when you're in a relationship it starts off great, but when it gets intimate and begins to bring out your neurosis, you just want to get out of there.

So I'm here to tell you that the path to peace is right there, when you want to get away. You can cruise through life not letting anything touch you, but if you really want to live fully, if you want to enter into life, enter into genuine relationships with other people, with animals, with the world situation, you're definitely going to have the experience of feeling provoked, of getting hooked, of shenpa. You're not just going to feel bliss. The message is that when those feelings emerge, this is not a failure. This is the chance to cultivate maitri, unconditional friendliness toward your perfect and imperfect self.

Relative bodhichitta also includes awakening compassion. One of the meanings of *compassion* is "suffering with," being willing to suffer with other people. This means that to the degree you can work with the wholeness of your being—your prejudices, your feelings of failure, your self-pity, your depression, your rage, your addictions— the more you will connect with other people out of that wholeness. And it will be a relationship between equals. You'll be able to feel the pain of other people as your own pain. And you'll be able to feel your own pain and know that it's shared by millions.

Absolute bodhichitta, also known as *shunyata*, is the open dimension of our being, the completely wide-open heart and mind. Without labels of "you" and "me," "enemy" and "friend," absolute bodhichitta is always here. Cultivating absolute bodhichitta means having a relationship with the world that is nonconceptual, that is unprejudiced, having a direct, unedited relationship with reality.

That's the value of sitting meditation practice. You train in coming back to the unadorned present moment again and again. Whatever thoughts arise in your mind, you regard them with equanimity and you learn to let them dissolve. There is no rejection of the thoughts and emotions that come up; rather, we begin to realize that thoughts and emotions are not as solid as we always take them to be.

It takes bravery to train in unconditional friendliness; it takes bravery to train in "suffering with"; it takes bravery to stay with pain when it arises and not run or erect barriers. It takes bravery to not bite the hook and get swept away. But as we do, the absolute bodhichitta realization, the experience of how open and unfettered our minds really are, begins to dawn on us. As a result of becoming more comfortable with the ups and the downs of our ordinary human life, this realization grows stronger.

We start with taking a close look at our predictable tendency to get hooked, to separate ourselves, to withdraw into ourselves and put up walls. As we become intimate with these tendencies, they gradually become more transparent and we see that there's actually space, there is unlimited, accommodating space. This does not mean that then you live in lasting happiness and comfort. That spaciousness includes pain.

We may still get betrayed, may still be hated. We may still feel confused and sad. What we won't do is bite the hook. Pleasant happens. Unpleasant happens. Neutral happens. What we gradually learn is to not move away from being fully present. We need to train at this very basic level because of the widespread suffering in the world. If we aren't training inch by inch, one moment at a time, in overcoming our fear of pain, then we'll be very limited in how much we can help. We'll be limited in helping ourselves and limited in helping anybody else. So, let's start with ourselves, just as we are, here and now.

Pitbull

Jarvis Jay Masters

*Can punching someone in the face sometimes be the "Buddhist" thing
to do? Under the right circumstances, yes, because Buddhism—like life—
doesn't offer us easy formulas about what's skillful or compassionate. Jarvis
Jay Masters is a prisoner on death row in California and the author of an
excellent book called* Finding Freedom: Writings from Death Row, *which
Pema Chödrön often quotes. In this harrowing story of prison life, he shows
us that in life-and-death situations, the best thing to do isn't always spelled
out in the ethics books.*

There are times when I look forward to being out in the open air, to
have a chance to take a slow, thoughtful walk around the prison
yard, and then to play a game of basketball or handball, or just to
chat with other prisoners before returning back to our cells. At other
times, I want to remain locked in my cell, cushioned on the floor by
my folded blankets beneath me, sitting in the stillness of meditation.
Those are the times when it feels as though my very existence depends on sitting and meditating.

It was the beginning of the day. The morning light of the sun
shone through the bars of my cell from the window opposite, and I
calmly sat on the floor, not wanting to move. A guard appeared at
my cell door, blocking the ray of light on my face, to ask if I was

going out or staying in. It wasn't until I said I wanted to go that I knew it was what I wanted to do. I sprang up from my cross-legged position and hustled to gather my clothing together. I could now almost taste the fresh spring air awaiting me. I desperately wanted out. The faster, the better.

When the back door of the Adjustment Center building finally opened to let me out, someone I'd never seen before stood on the yard by the electric entrance gate. "Who is he?" I thought. I had been hoping to walk quietly around the yard before the other fifty-plus prisoners got outside to join me for exercise.

I make it a point to familiarize myself with everyone on the yard, and this stranger's presence made me nervous. As the yard gate locked behind me, his hooded eyes stared me up and down, and his mean prison-mug look attempted to catch my eye. I tried to pay him no serious mind. Once upon a time, many years before, I had been a new prisoner myself, with a furious mask like his. Yet I felt uncomfortable. I walked past him, holding on to my Buddhist vows of nonviolence like an elderly woman clutching her purse.

"Man, where is you from?" he asked in a voice that matched the hooded black cap he had pulled down to his eyelids. "Where is you from, man?"

"Huh?" I said, trying to take very deep breaths without detection. "What do you mean, where am I from? Where are *you* from?"

His voice rose. "What set you from, dude? Where you stay at out there?"

I realized he wanted to know what street gang I belonged to. "Hey, shit! I've been in San Quentin for the past seventeen years or so. That's *your* world out there. Mine's been in here—you know?"

"Is that right?" he said, his eyes widening. "You been down that long?"

"I've been down a long while," I said. "Too damn long."

"Uh huh," he mumbled. "So what else is out here?" he then asked, wanting to know who and from what towns would be coming out to the yard.

"Hey, man," I said. "Just guys who wants to do their own thing, their own time, with anybody who wants to get along with them, you know? Why do you ask?"

"'Cause, man," he said with rage in his voice. "I've been gettin' 'em up, stabbin' and fightin' all these punk mothafuckas talkin' that beaucoup-ass shit all up in this here joint, you know? 'Cause I don't get along with none of 'em. It's to the death with them and me. 'Cause I don't give—"

"Man, like who?" I interrupted. "Who you talkin' about?"

"Dudes from all over," he said. "I hate 'em all. All the ones from Los Angeles, Bakersfield, Fresno, and the whole damn Bay Area, you know? Man, all these punkass bitches who thinks I'm some punk. In every unit I been in, dudes been thinkin' I'm a punk, callin' me a bunch of cowards, and I'm no punk or coward! You hear me? Huh? Huh? Hey, dude, I'm a pit-mothafuckin'-bull! Straight that, okay? You hear me? And I don't give a mad fuck, either. Them polices knows what time it is, 'cause I be spittin' in their damn faces each and every chance I get! 'Cause I am the O.G., the Original Pitbull."

"Oh, is that right, is that right?" I kept repeating, as this new prisoner, Pitbull, went on raging. Now I wished I had not come out to the yard. I had been enjoying all the comforts of meditation. If only I had stayed locked in my cell, sitting right there on my ass! But no! Hell, no! I just had to come out here to shake hands with a maniac, a real-life maniac! And why? To say: Hello there. *My name is Jarvis. I am a Buddhist!* No, this can't be real. This just can't be fuckin' real.

"So, hey, dude," said Pitbull. "You see where I'm comin' from, huh? I'm no punk, I'm no coward. I stay ready. You feel me, you hear me, dude?"

"Yeah, yeah, I hear you, Pitbull," I said. "But man, you have to slow down. It ain't that kind of party out here. The folks that will be coming out to this yard don't want no problem with you. They don't even know you, let alone want problems. You can see that I don't want no problems, right?"

"I hear what you're saying," he said. "But still, I've been tricked before. The police don't like me 'cause I been spittin' in all their faces—and they always tryin' to send other inmates to do their dirty work."

"Well, man," I said, "if that's the case, I advise you to wait until someone moves on you, attacks you first, because out here, if you attack first, the gun towers are goin' to shoot to kill you."

"Yeah, I know," he said. "So I'm just going to stand right here, right like I am now. And let it be known where I'm comin' from."

"No, not right there in front of the yard gate," I said to him. "No, you want to wait in the back of the yard, with your back against the fence—way over there." I pointed. "Man, way over there to where you can see everybody and can't anyone get you from behind, you know?"

"You right," he said. "You right about that! I'm goin' right over there and just wait for someone to run up on me. And boy, when they do, I'm a show them fools a thing or two. Man! I'm goin' to show them fools! *Bam! Bam!*" He was suddenly swinging his fists, shadowboxing his way to the far corner of the yard.

As I watched Pitbull fighting his own demons, I didn't know what to think. At least he was over in the far corner and not standing at the entrance gate, where others coming out to the yard would not have been able to avoid a physical confrontation. For this I felt relieved, but I feared I had only postponed the inevitable. I wondered if this guy would get off the yard without being stabbed. I wondered if he would even get off the yard alive.

I paced up and down along the fence, greeting all my friends being let onto the yard with only a look of warning, as I saw them observe Pitbull in the corner. The situation intensified, as everybody on the yard grouped up in lion packs. The camera of my eyes zoomed in with a split focus. One lens showed my friends gathering in groups, some of them encircling and positioning to block off escape routes. The strongest of them—Malcolm, Jambo, and Insane—were poised not more than a few feet from where I was. The other lens showed Pitbull over in the corner shadowboxing with the devil. This was real prison.

"Say, Jambo." I walked over to where Jambo, Malcolm, and

Insane were standing. "Man, what are you guys getting ready to do? Because you know I spoke with that dude before everybody was out today, and I think he is more bark than anything else and—"

"Check this out, Jarvis," Jambo interrupted me. I was glad he did. I didn't know what else I planned to say. "This dude cannot stay out here. No way! And man, you know I love you like a brotha. But all that Buddhist shit you gettin' ready to run on us is not workin' this time, not today."

"He's right, Jarvis," Malcolm joined in. "'Cause, man, look at that dude. Just look at him. He's over there fistfighting the damn air, man! He's over there talkin' to himself like he's killin' somebody."

"And just look at us," added Insane. "We're standin' here on this side of the yard while that nut case, that jackass fool, is over there trying to pump fear into us so we don't run over there and put a cold piece of penitentiary steel in his ass. We'll just have to see about all this, 'cause, man, I'm about ready to bum-rush over there and rip a hole in his guts. I'm goin' to push this shank I have right into his heart and leave it for the pigs to pull out! 'Cause they had no damn business puttin' him out here with us."

"Man, hold on. Hold the fuck on, Insane!" I said in total anger, as I saw the blade peeking out of the sleeve of his coat. "Man! That nut don't need to be killed. He only needs to be let off this yard. That's all. We all know that if he wasn't on this yard, all this other stuff about killing wouldn't even be on our minds. Hey, I'd be takin' your ass through the hoop on this basketball court, while Jambo and Malcolm, you guys would be working out over there on the pull-up bars. And everybody would just be glad to be out those damn cells."

"But that's not the case," said Jambo.

"Yeah, I know," I said. "But the problem is gettin' that nut off the yard and not standing over here waiting for the perfect time to kill someone. Man, you guys going to have to do a Judge Ito, you know. Like he says, take three long, deep breaths. And this is not my Buddhist shit, either! It's called *thinking*. But, man, you know, if none of you guys brought your thinking caps out today," I said, becoming frustrated, "and if you just want to go over there and kill just to kill, go right ahead! 'Cause it's none of my business. I'll let the chips fall, you know? But even so," I was almost talking out loud to myself now, "this guy still should not be stabbed."

"Well, I tell you what then," said Jambo. "The three of us are going to go over there. But not as planned, not just to kill that fool. No! We're going over there to ask this dude to leave the yard. And man, I swear, if he so much as swings at a fly, man, Jarvis, we're going to break him off another asshole!"

"Yeah, I hear what you're saying, Jambo," I said. "But still, man, it doesn't sound like you guys are going to give him a real chance to leave the yard. Hey, let me go over there with—"

"No! Hell, no!" said Insane. "'Cause you just goin' to be in the way in case this nut tries somethin'. Seriously, Jarvis, you be talkin' too damn much."

"OK! OK!" I said. "But you guys have to give this dude—his name is Pitbull—a chance to leave the yard."

"Man, Jarvis! Trip off this, check this out," Malcolm said angrily. "Man, if we weren't goin' to give this Pitbull a chance . . . shit, man, we'd jus' tell you we goin' to blast holes in his ass. It's that simple. Man, it's that simple!"

"OK, you're right. I hear what you're sayin'," I said, empty of words. All my Buddhist convincing had suddenly run its course. My friends' minds had been pulled back only a little. Was it enough? I feared not. I watched them walk straight to Pitbull's corner.

As the whole yard fell deep into silence, I glanced up at the gunman standing in the doorway of the tower shack. He, too, saw the jaws of this lion pack slowly opening as Jambo, Insane, and Malcolm headed directly toward the corner of the yard. The gunman quickly lit a cigarette, took two deep inhales, and flicked the butt to the ground from the tower. Then, calmly, as my three friends approached Pitbull, he went inside the tower shack and closed the door. I knew what that meant: "Do what you want to do. I'm not watching."

There was nothing in the way now. I remembered Pitbull's voice bragging about spitting in all the guards' faces and how the guards "send inmates to do their dirty work." I realized how Pitbull's paranoia played into this whole thing.

In seconds, my three friends were in front of Pitbull, face-to-face. He was no longer shadowboxing. I didn't know what I was witnessing. I held my breath, praying that this "nut" had the sense to leave the yard. It was too late for me to go over there—by now I would've had to run, and that probably would have incited the guys to attack. I started mumbling to myself: "Man, you jackass, leave the yard . . . come on, man, you can do it . . . just leave, man, just leave, I beg you, just leave the yard." I felt the pounding of my heart.

Then slowly a miracle happened. I watched Jambo point to the yard gate, in a fan motion, telling Pitbull to keep walking. Pitbull slowly walked toward the gate. As he did, he raised his hands over his shoulders and shouted loudly, getting the attention of the tower gunman, that he was "the greatest, the champion of the world," and wanted off the yard. This brought a sigh of relief to my heart.

Through the tower window, I could see the gunman get on the phone to call the Adjustment Center for someone to come and escort Pitbull back into the housing unit. I had known and seen quite a lot of mental cases over the years in San Quentin, but this was the worst case I had ever seen on an exercise yard. In most cases, the prison authorities place severe mental cases on "walk-alone" yards. I began to suspect that everything Pitbull had said was true.

The whole yard watched Pitbull leave. We all saw how the two guards who escorted him away were roughing him up and mocking him and calling him names under their breath. I didn't know if they wanted to see him simply beaten up, or worse, stabbed and killed. This question lingers in my mind to this very day.

After the tension subsided and everyone went about their business—playing cards, basketball, and handball—I went over to the pull-up bar area to talk to Jambo and the others. I wanted to thank Jambo for taking a chance in asking this person to leave the yard instead of resorting to violence as the only way. But I didn't use this particular language—it would have sounded too flat and awkward in speaking to my longtime friend, who had been born into violence just as I had. I just thanked him for using his head instead of the sword. Jambo appreciated this. We spent the rest of our yard time talking about Jambo's Vietnam experiences and working out together on the pull-up bars.

Several days later, I again traded in my meditation cushion for the exercise yard.

When the Adjustment Center door opened, letting me outside into the sky-blue air, I felt suddenly choked by it, nearly hyperventilating at the sight of Pitbull again. He was enraged, pacing up and down on the yard. My legs weakened. I wanted to stop and say to the smirking guard escorting me, "You ass! What in the hell is *he* doing back out here again?" But I did not. I kept walking toward the yard gate. With each step, I took a deep breath, trying to control my steaming anger. I had never hated San Quentin more.

I walked straight up to Pitbull and said, "Why, man, why? Why did you come out here again? Don't you know how lucky you were the last time you was out here?"

"Man, dude," he said, shouting in my face. "Them police been callin' me a bunch of cowards and shit. They said I was scared of you all, said, 'If you a man, you go back out there and prove it!'"

"And *that's* why you're back out here?" I asked angrily. "Because they told you some bum shit like this?"

"Yeah, man," Pitbull said. "They came to my cell this morning callin' me all kinds of bitches and cowards. And, man, I'm no mothafuckin' coward. And I'm not scared of any-mothafuckin'-body out here."

"So what are you goin' to do, huh? You goin' to wait 'til everybody come back out here to prove to the guards you ain't a coward?"

"You fuckin' right!" Pitbull answered. "That one guard said, 'A real man with real nuts is goin' to do what he have to do.'"

"Damn that!" I said, my adrenaline boiling. "I can't let you do this, Pitbull. I can't let you stay out here, just so you can prove your manhood to everybody."

"Dude! I don't give a husky fuck about what you not goin' to do," he blurted, inching up to my face with rage in his eyes. "Dude, I do what the fuck I wanna do, and who said *everybody*? Dude, we don't even need everybody."

"Hmmm," I mumbled, clenching my fist tightly. "You right! We don't need everybody." *Bam!* My fist landed squarely on his chin. I coldcocked Pitbull flat on the prison asphalt. With my adrenaline still pumping, I could only stare down at him. He was knocked out.

The tower gunman saw me standing over Pitbull and began blowing his alarm whistle. The scream of the whistle made me realize what I had just done. I tensed up waiting for a shot. I looked up, expecting to see a gun on me. The officer just looked at me, gave me a slight smile, and walked into his shack. I had just done something that over the years I had worked hard to convince others not to do. I stared down at Pitbull. "Man, I just punched the lights out of someone. Oh, man, what is Chagdud, my teacher, going to think or say now? And what about my court appeals?" My mind overfilled with shame and guilt at myself and anger at San Quentin.

I felt as if I were bending something inside my heart trying to explain all this to myself. But on a deeper level, something felt good about what I'd just done.

I was responsible for why this person was lying flat on the prison asphalt. I could not take back what I had just done, nor did I want to. I could have held back. But why? What for? To prove to everyone outside myself that I am a true Buddhist? To strictly keep to my vows of nonviolence, even at the cost of watching this human being get stabbed or killed? To be a witness to this guy lying dead on the prison exercise yard? "No way," I resolved. "Not today. Buddhist or not, Buddhist or not! And I am *not* returning my vows, either. I am not. *I* am not." I said the last part out loud.

I noticed Pitbull finally coming to, barely lifting himself to a clumsy position on the asphalt. We stared at each other.

"Ah, man. Dude!" he mumbled, holding his chin in pain. "Shit! Man, what did you hit me with?"

"A straight left, I think."

"Oh, so you's a southpaw, huh?" he said, with a broken half-smile. "OK. That's the way, that's how you got me. OK! But, man, now don't you see that I am a man? I am a man, not a coward. You tell them fools that, huh, will you? That I am a man, a real fuckin' man!"

Seeing Pitbull sitting there, wanting me to see him as a man, I didn't know what I was anymore. Was *I* a man? Was I a Buddhist? We were both escorted off the yard.

Later, to further prove his manhood, Pitbull insisted that both he and I get disciplinary write-ups for this fight. I was given a mixed blessing. I was confined to my cell for ten days, with no choice but to sit inside these awakening days of meditation.

Are You Joining a Cult?

Donna Lovong

This story and the one that follows are about how Buddhist practice helped two young people deal with family difficulties. Donna Lovong's story is proof that Buddhism is not monolithic and that Buddhist families can be as painful and troubled as any.

Are you joining a cult?" my mother asked, her eyebrows furrowing. My mom looked anxious as I told her that I would be going to a Buddhist meditation retreat the next weekend. I laughed. "No, Mom, this isn't a cult. Don't you remember what the monks did back when you lived in Laos? I'm doing meditation." She wasn't reassured. Even though our family frequently went to the local Buddhist temple, meditation by laypeople was as foreign to her as offering sticky rice to monks was to me. Mom continued, "Be careful. Don't let them brainwash you." She proceeded to tell me about people at her workplace who followed some kind of group. "I know these Asian women at work who stopped eating meat altogether . . . I think they are being brainwashed."

At first, I couldn't believe that my mother, herself an avowed Buddhist, would think that my meditation practice was weird. I have since come to appreciate the big cultural gap between my mom's

Asian past and my American upbringing, and between her ethnic Buddhism and my Western Buddhism. Looking for ways to bridge our differences, I've probed deeper into my family, my community, and myself.

My parents grew up in Southeast Asia during the 1950s, '60s, and early '70s. In those decades, the region was in constant war and conflict. When the Communist regime expanded into my parents' country in 1975, my mother—pregnant with me at the time—and my father fled and became refugees. We took shelter at a Buddhist temple temporarily, and there I was born. We emigrated to the United States, bringing with us generations of suspicion, mistrust, and anger. I suspect that my parents' experience of being uprooted and of witnessing their own country being "brainwashed" by the Communists is why my mom felt apprehensive when I joined a meditation group.

My mother grew up in a traditional ethnic Chinese family, which had Confucian and Taoist sensibilities mixed in with spirit and nature worship. She told me that no one in her family was Buddhist. She started going to the local Lao Buddhist temple as a teen simply because her friends went there and because the temple taught English classes. She told me that she was drawn to the peaceful grounds of the temple, the sounds of the temple bells, and the chanting of the monks in their colorful robes. My father's side of the family is not Buddhist either. He comes from an ethnic minority group who perform rituals to appease the spirit world. Thus my mother and father were the first ones in their families to partake in Buddhism. Similarly, I am embarking on a path never practiced by anyone in my family—a path of Zen meditation and mindfulness practice.

But the Buddhism I grew up with is very different. The Thai and Lao Buddhist temples in the Theravada tradition are centered on community events like Lao and Thai New Year celebrations. Monks performed blessings for a new house or for a sick person. At home, we celebrated Chinese New Year and gave offerings to the spirits of our ancestors at the ancestor altar. My parents and I were never taught meditation. We thought that only monastics meditated and that we laypeople were supposed to earn merit by donating money to the temple, making offerings to the Buddha, and cooking for the monks.

Despite being a Buddhist family, our home was actually filled with anger, violence, and hurtful speech. I remember trying to protect my siblings from my father's uncontrollable rage. The bathroom became our shelter, a place to retreat and find safety. There are many dents and scars in our home, evidence of unskillful actions. Like my father, and his mother before him, I also tried to discipline and control my younger siblings by instilling fear in them. I would be in my room reading alone quietly when I would hear my siblings making a ruckus outside. Instantly, I would lose my patience. I would yell, "Be quiet! Why are you being so loud? You are driving me crazy." I would come out and threaten to beat them if they did not shut up. One time, I lost control and threw a glass at my sister. Another time, I melted my brother's glasses in the microwave.

In high school, I sought ways to control my anger and keep myself sane at home. I asked a teacher how to find quiet time amid the busyness of life. He told me that he dedicated at least ten to fifteen minutes every day to doing nothing. He would sit or lie down in silence and relax, or gaze outside his window and see what was going on outdoors, in the skies and in the yard. He also suggested eating raisins slowly, one at a time, chewing each fifteen to twenty times, while breathing in and out, concentrating on tasting the raisin. I was not aware then that this was my first instruction on mindfulness and meditation—eating meditation, that is.

When I left home for college, I rebelled against my family and its traditions. I didn't want anything to do with the anger and instability of my parents' home, just as I didn't want anything to do with the Buddhist cultural practices of my parents. I felt that my family and my community were just using the Buddhist temple as a filling station. I felt that they partook in the many rituals just to accumulate merit and temporarily relieve their anxieties about life. But afterward, they went right back to their harmful habits of hurting their families, their community, and themselves. People prayed in front of the Buddha for a new car or to win the lottery, as if the Buddha were Santa Claus.

During my college years, I began reading books by Thich Nhat Hanh and Buddhist magazines. I learned about mindfulness, engaged Buddhism, and other Buddhist traditions. I thought to myself, "Wow, there is so much I am not aware of!" I started attending meditation sessions and retreats offered by a local Zen group, composed of mostly non-Asians. I felt a connection to this group of people who, like me, were all trying to cross over to the other shore of freedom and truth, where lies our true home. I began rediscovering the Buddha, dharma, and sangha in a new light, not through my ethnic Buddhist temple, but through Western culture and American Buddhist teachers. I found a Buddhism that spoke to me as a young, Asian American woman, opening my heart and mind. This path began to heal my wounds, and through mindfulness, I cultivated some sense of patience and compassion.

After eight years away from home, I recently returned to live with my parents. It's a little less chaotic now than when I was growing up, but there are still plenty of times I feel myself really challenged—in a way that living on my own didn't challenge me—to practice compassion, mindfulness, and patience. Still, things feel different. One night, a huge fight broke out between my sister and father. It started because my sister thought that my father was refusing to give her some documents that she needed for school. There was screaming, angry faces and words, hearts racing faster, and misery. An object went flying toward my sister. In that moment, I realized that as much as I tried to stop what was happening, I could not control the situation. I could not control the fear that arose within me. I certainly could not control another human being, whether it was my father, sister, or mother. Although I was scared, I also felt an indescribable sense of calm and stability in letting go of this desire for control.

After my father left the room, I walked past my other sister's room and saw that she was sitting on her bed, her body shaking from listening to the whole incident. When our eyes met, we both started to cry. I knew that this cycle of anger and violence needed to stop, because we were passing this on to younger generations. Somehow I sensed that our own family's cycle had an extended effect on the well-being of the Earth itself. I felt our unskillful actions reverberating through the past, present, and future—the consequences going far beyond what we can comprehend.

That night, I urged everyone in the household to practice noble silence (silence of body, speech, and mind) for the rest of the night. I said that unkind words were hurting us all. More than ever, I voiced that we need this quiet time now to calm down and heal and that we must try and refrain from hurting each other further. Amazingly, everyone gave it a try. The next morning, my father gave my sister the documents that she thought he was keeping from her.

Things are getting better at home. The teachings of the Buddha have provided me with the tools to look deeply and understand why my family and I say and do what we do. The study and practice of Buddhism has also helped me to look deeply and understand where my parents are coming from. I am now aware that my anger and hot temper were passed down from my parents and my parents' parents, many generations ago. I feel I am also absorbing the karma of my own country's violence and anger, and that of the world.

A few weeks ago, I came home late one night from a long day at work and was starting to prepare dinner for myself. My mom, who was washing dishes, suddenly asked, "When are you going to finish your thesis so that you can get another job that pays more? Hurry up and finish. My friend's son just finished his bachelor's and got a job starting at $60,000. . . ."

In the past, I would have instantly lost my patience and reacted defensively. "Stop getting on my case. I'll finish when I finish. And I've told you before that in my field of work, I won't make that high of a salary." She would respond, "Then why did you pick that field to study? Why didn't you pick doctor or lawyer?" We would argue some more and then I wouldn't even feel like eating my dinner, so I would storm upstairs to my room. These days, though, I'm less bothered by what my mom says. This time around, I responded, "I understand that you want the best for me and our family, but don't worry, I'll finish soon and get another job." I played along and avoided getting excessively involved. Then I said, "OK, I am going to eat dinner now. Let's talk about this another time." I ate peacefully as my seeds of anger didn't arise. These days, I can be patient for much longer periods.

Each day, I learn that all these barriers, problems, negative habits, anger, and jealousies are all part of my path—they are me. They are gifts too, gifts that provide me with opportunities to practice wholesome ways. For the first time, I feel I am being intimate with my fears by not running away anymore.

My father still asks me occasionally why I meditate. My parents do not understand my meditation practice fully, but they no longer call it a "cult." They seem to have come to some degree of acceptance of my practice. I still participate in the local Lao temple activities, but now I am not blindly following what others are doing.

Just recently, my mother came home from work one evening and asked if I could give her information on meditation places in town. She wanted to give it to her coworker who had inquired about it. Her coworker told her that she had a very good daughter because I practiced meditation. Having someone tell her this altered the way she thought about me and the practice of meditation—I am less odd now. A week later, my mother asked me how she could meditate herself, to calm her mind and be free of worries. The seeds of dharma are beginning to grow.

What's Crazy, Really?

Layla Mason

The Buddhist path is not a smooth and predictable road to enlightenment. The lives of Buddhist teachers are often marked by trials, disappointments, and dark nights of the soul. When Layla Mason discovered that the life of a great Korean woman teacher had been marked by a descent into apparent madness, she was able to see her own family's difficulties in a new and more accepting light.

I've got a cold, so I won't be coming to morning meditation tomorrow," my brother said over the phone. We were both students at the same college. "I'm going to sleep in and shake it off; so just carry on without me." The next morning, trudging through sludgy snow from my dorm toward the chapel meditation room, I passed my brother's freshman dorm, thought about his being sick, and decided to check in on him. Everyone was still sleeping, but his door was halfway open. I came into a room that was impeccably clean. In fact, all that was in it was the pale pine college furniture and a Douglas Adams book in the desk. Even the trash was empty.

My brother came in the door, I guess from the bathroom. His eyes were googling all over the place, and he could barely walk. I thought he might be drunk. "What's the matter?" He grunted something unintelligible and began weaving all over the room. "Come here and breathe out," I demanded, not sure of what vapor he'd emit. No alcohol. What was going on? I began to panic; he was clearly out of his mind. I called Dad and then the campus police. An officer and I carried him out to a patrol car and to the college clinic. In the psychiatrist's room, my brother began climbing on the furniture like a drugged ape and drooling on himself. The clinic called an ambulance and we took him to the hospital, strapped down on a stretcher.

The blood tests showed no irregular substances in his blood. After an overnight stay at the hospital, where I slept miserably in the lounge, the psychiatrist said he probably had a dissociative incident brought on by the stress of final exams. He was fine to return to college. When I got back to his dorm room, I found a note in the Adams book, *Life, the Universe, and Everything.* "Please return this book to my friend I borrowed it from. I've decided to end my life, and now I'm gone. I'm sorry if I've caused any pain."

This was my brother's first suicide attempt, through vodka and a new brand of sleeping pill, which inaugurated five years of hospitalizations, group homes, therapy, and medications—and it changed forever what it meant for me to be his closest friend. The most distressing part of my brother's sudden change from high school valedictorian and likeable, athletic young man was that I didn't know why it had happened. The doctors said it was most likely a biological predisposition to schizophrenia that often emerges at around eighteen, especially upon leaving the structured environment of a home. My dad was pretty happy with that answer, as it left everyone blameless but the genes. But there was another possible explanation.

The doctors asked me to give an extensive history of our childhood. I began telling them what had never been discussed before outside the family: that my father had been a violent and unpredictable parent for the last ten years that we'd been living with him. The beatings for small things like forgetting to lock the back door, the spit on our faces, the hundreds of push-ups of repentance for being disrespectful, the million little mind games, his paranoia of the outside world. The doctors began to change their diagnosis: "We think your brother may have post-traumatic stress disorder," they told me. My brother, after a decade of living in terror that this man would make good on his threats to "throw him out the window" and "break every bone in his body," had turned all of my father's rage inside toward himself.

The doctors sitting around the long table in the fluorescent-lit room were looking at me quietly, no longer writing on their yellow legal pads, as I finished telling them the truth. It felt good to tell the truth. As I did, it dawned on my nineteen-year-old brain that these stories were horrifying. And then I realized what they were thinking: how could I, who not only witnessed but experienced these things, have not gone crazy myself? I had straight As at college, was seemingly well adjusted, dating—and visiting my Thorazine-drugged, drooling brother every few weeks in the pink-painted locked ward.

Over the years, while my brother got worse, I did everything I could to prove to myself that I was not like him, that I would never become like him. I graduated with high honors, while he was slicing himself with the top of a soda can in the state hospital. I went to graduate school, while he attempted to set himself on fire at the group home. I got published, while he tried to shoot his eyes out with a BB gun. While my brother was dealing with our past by destroying himself, I dealt with it by becoming an overachiever.

But I was not ashamed that I had a brother like this. In fact, I wore the My Crazy Brother Story on my already-decorated coat like a badge of honor: not only was I a successful person, but I had become so despite circumstances that drove another person insane. What's more, I could tell people that I had devoted hundreds of hours to his care, arranging doctors, playing the mental health system, even letting him live with me for a summer. I told our story over and over and felt good when people said, "How did you do it? You are so strong for someone so young."

Then, this last summer, something happened that put a small

fissure in this thick wall I'd built between myself and my brother, between sanity and insanity. I encountered a Zen master. Dae-haeng Sunim is now in her late seventies. She's known as a powerful teacher, psychic, and leader of the enormous, wealthy, international Zen organization that she founded. In a rare opportunity, I was able to have an interview with her when I was visiting Seoul. To prepare well for the meeting, I began reading her biography.

Sunim's life began as terribly as ours: a violent and hypercontrolling father, a yielding and unprotective mother, living in poor and dirty conditions. Her father's abuse forced her to run away to the woods to sleep at night. Between the lines, I wondered if her father was a predator at night especially. When she reached young adulthood, she finally ran away from home for good, became a nun, and entered the forest for ten years of practice. Wandering around in winter in light cotton robes, eating leaves and grass, Sunim slept under pine trees and meditated in a hole dug in the sand near a river. Her skin was cracked and bleeding, her bones sticking out, her wild hair tied up in a ball with a stick. Her koan became "Daddy!" or *Appa!* in Korean. She constantly inquired, "Who is Appa? Where is Appa?" The answer arose, "You should die, then you will see you."

After several failed attempts to kill herself, she made a final resolve. Looking for a place where no one would have to bother with her body, she came to the edge of a cliff on the Han River. But the moment she came to the water, her feet stopped, and she forgot about dying. Sunim stood there for half a day, staring into the water, and finally came to. She walked away. A little time later, she knelt down for a drink from the stream. She saw her exhausted face clearly and wondered why, if her mind felt okay, did her body look so bad? From deep within an answer came, "All is buddha." The nun saw, for the first time, the true nature of her inner "Appa." From this moment of deep awakening, Sunim went on to be tested by the greatest Zen master of the day. After passing the exam, the master declared her one of the greatest he'd ever met, and she succeeded, for the next forty years, in establishing herself with hundreds of thousands of followers.

I closed the book. My heart was beginning to break open, but my mind raced with judgment. I thought about how, if this woman had been in America, she'd have been involuntarily committed to a state hospital. We simply don't let people walk around crying, "Daddy," dirty, hungry, and half-naked, trying to throw themselves into rivers. Therefore, she must be truly crazy like my brother, and this biography was just some Zen glorification of insanity, a hagiography in the extreme. Based on that conclusion, I closed my heart and set off for her temple on the outskirts of Seoul.

The meeting in her private quarters was much anticipated by me and the two translators. We walked into a room fit for royalty, with silks, crystal, even a fountain garden; everything was polished and impeccably clean. Senior nuns were fluttering around to make way for the Master. I was anxious, my preconceptions of meeting a Zen master, in addition to someone I thought was probably insane, erupting all at once. Finally, a tiny, old woman came into the room and the nuns came to attention. She had oversized glasses, actually rose-tinted, that matched rosy lips. My preconceptions began melting away. She finally settled onto the couch. Everyone was stiff and formal. She looked right at me, and I suddenly felt about as significant as belly-button lint and very self-conscious. I noticed that my being began kind of voom-vooming, my whole psyche vibrating at a rate I'd never felt before. I was caught off guard. As she talked, in Korean, I felt like I understood what she was saying without translation. Her mind seemed to be having a tremendous effect on mine, without my being able to control it at all. After a few polite questions, she gave me the impression that she thought I was being dishonestly intellectual. I finally got down to it. I said, "Would you mind if I ask you something personal?" She nodded. I asked her, "I read your biography. Like you, my own and my brother's childhood saw a lot of trauma in relation to my father. How do we heal this as Buddhists?"

She told me that our mind and our father's mind were the same mind. I felt horrified, even sick, that such a beast would be any part of me. She said that as I transform my mind to forgiveness, compassion, and purity, it would also begin to transform his mind. This wasn't immediately appealing to me. After all, I had worked so many years unentangling the enmeshment and codependency among my brother, our dad, and me. I had worked hard to find a dispassionate distance at which I could hold a person who'd betrayed the trust of a little girl and boy.

Yet by the end of the meeting, I left knowing that I had met with a great being of high realization. I walked away feeling that there could be a great awakening in the face of trauma, perhaps even inspired by trauma. There was hope for someone like my brother. My heart began cracking open. The wall between my brother and me was crumbling.

These days, I look for the qualities and potentialities of the Zen master in my brother. He has an easiness about our parents' misdeeds that I envy. I still fly into rages when they do the stupid things resembling their past. When we go to Mom's for a holiday, everyone is edgy and distant around me but enjoys sitting on the porch shooting the breeze with my brother as he smokes. He listens carefully to the people in his housing development and takes their suffering seriously, respecting the buddhanature in anyone who comes into his path.

Most of all, I now believe that had it not been for my brother's breakdown, none of the others in my family, including myself, would have been able to begin their paths in healing. Before he became sick, our family was a web of secrets, manipulations, and shame that formed a tight psychic knot no one could untie. I now deeply respect my brother for his unstinting confrontation with suffering and for honestly manifesting the truth of our childhoods, which allowed all of us to loosen that knot. I now understand my brother's difficult years as not simply insanity but as his own meaningful struggle to find freedom.

The Dharma of Social Transformation ⊚⟫

Charles Johnson

Is Buddhism a quietist religion, one devoted to personal realization to the exclusion of social progress? This is a question non-Buddhists frequently ask, and it's true that traditional Buddhism was often nonpolitical or even a defender of the status quo. That has changed as Buddhism has entered the modern world and added a social dimension to its analysis of human suffering. The MacArthur Award–winning novelist and critic Charles Johnson argues that the goal of social transformation actually has an honored place in Buddhist history and is inherent in Buddhist philosophy.

Whenever I'm asked if the dharma makes possible social transformations that are relevant for the specific and seemingly endless problems of the world today (and I'm asked this often), I find myself considering that question in light of a provocative critique presented forty-five years ago by Paul Tillich, the great Christian theologian, who called Buddhism "one of the greatest, strangest, and at the same time most competitive of the religions proper." In 1963, Tillich published *Christianity and the Encounter of World Religions,* a series of lectures he gave one year after his return from a nine-week lecture tour in Japan in 1960. In the book's third chapter, "A Christian-Buddhist Conversation," Tillich takes up the social and ethical consequences, as he sees them, of his religion in contrast to the buddhadharma. Regarding his faith, he states that a Christian's dedication to the passages in the New Testament that describe agape—an unconditional love for others—translates into an energetic form of the social gospel that emphasizes "the will to transform individual as well as social structures."

"The Kingdom of God has a revolutionary character," wrote Tillich. "Christianity . . . shows a revolutionary force directed toward a radical transformation of society. . . . Most of the revolutionary movements in the West—liberalism, democracy, and socialism—are dependent on it, whether they know it or not. There is no analogy to this in Buddhism. Not transformation of reality but salvation from reality is the basic attitude. . . . No belief in the new in history, no impulse for transforming society, can be derived from the principle of Nirvana."

Tillich quickly concedes that a conquering, self-confident will may be problematic because it "leads to the attitude of technical control of nature which dominates the Western world." But for Tillich, while Buddhism's version of agape—*metta,* or loving-kindness toward all sentient beings—can lead to identification with the Other, and thus to empathy, nevertheless "something is lacking: the will to transform the other one either directly or indirectly by transforming the sociological and psychological structures by which he is conditioned."

It is here that the dialogue between Buddhists and Christians (and possibly some social activists) reaches a "preliminary end" for Tillich. At the end of the chapter, Tillich imagines this exchange between a Buddhist priest and a Christian philosopher:

The Buddhist priest asks the Christian philosopher: "Do you believe that every person has a substance of his own which gives him true individuality?" The Christian answers, "Certainly!" The Buddhist priest asks, "Do you believe that community between individuals is possible?" The Christian answers affirmatively. Then the Buddhist says, "Your two answers are incompatible; if every person has a substance, no community is possible." To which the Christian replies, "Only if each person has a substance of his own is community possible, for community presupposes separation. You, Buddhist friend, have identity, but not community."

The distinguished Zen teacher and scholar Masao Abe praised Tillich for being "the first great Christian theologian in history who tried to carry out a serious confrontation between Christianity and Buddhism in their depths." His influence on spirituality in America has been wide and deep; among those he inspired was Martin Luther King, Jr., who based his goal of achieving the "beloved community" on the concept of agape and devoted his dissertation at Boston University to Tillich ("A Comparison of the Conceptions of God in the Thinking of Paul Tillich and Henry Nelson Wieman").

To my eyes, Tillich's assessment of the social and political shortcomings of Buddhism leaves a good deal to be desired, especially since it does not account for the "engaged Buddhism" that emerged in the 1960s. Nevertheless, his sincere misgivings are shared by many non-Buddhists, as well as by some new members of the American convert community as they struggle to integrate their practice into a contemporary need for political activism, which for over two millennia was judiciously separated from the buddhadharma by traditional Buddhist monastics. As students of the dharma, we should be able to clarify Tillich's questions—the relationship between Buddhist practice and our political commitments, and how *anatta* (no-self) fits with a sense of community. This begins with mindfulness of how key historical figures and principles of Buddhism anticipate and resolve the question, "Is a will toward social transformation lacking in traditional Buddhism?"

For one answer, we need only look to the remarkable life and works of Ashoka, ruler of the Maurya kingdom from about 272 to 236 B.C.E. After waging but one military campaign, which conquered the Kalingas around 264 B.C.E. (150,000 were deported, 100,000 were killed, and many more died), Ashoka was so appalled by the carnage and cruelty of war that he embraced the dharma and for twenty-eight years devoted himself to the creation of hospitals, charities, public gardens, education for women, the protection of animals, and caring for everyone in his kingdom. He exercised compassion toward lawbreakers and prisoners, cultivated harmonious relations with neighboring states, and encouraged the study of other religions.

The wise lay Buddhist Ashoka was hardly alone among leaders who translated the virtue of *ahimsa* (nonharm) into civic life. In his book *Inner Revolution,* Buddhist scholar Robert Thurman reminds us that the revered second-century monk Nagarjuna was the mentor of the South Indian king Udayi; he told him, "O King! Just as you love to consider what to do to help yourself, so should you love to consider what to do to help others!"

According to Thurman, Nagarjuna, whose counsel is recorded in the five hundred verses of *The Precious Garland,* "taught his friend the king how to care for every being in the kingdom: by building schools everywhere and endowing honest, kind, and brilliant teachers; by providing for all his subjects' needs, opening free restaurants and inns for travelers; by tempering justice with mercy, sending barbers, doctors, and teachers to the prisons to serve the inmates; by thinking of each prisoner as his own wayward child, to be corrected in order to return to free society and use his or her precious human life to attain enlightenment." Thurman observes, "This activism is implicit in the earliest teachings of the Buddha, and in his actions, though his focus at that time was on individual transformation, the prerequisite of social transformation."

Buddhist history, with which Tillich may not have been well acquainted, offers us time and again concrete examples of how the dharma has inspired enlightened social policies. But, like many Western intellectuals, Tillich was unable—or perhaps unwilling—to accept the doctrine of anatta and worried a bit more than he should have about defining nirvana. Yet we cannot dismiss too quickly the pivotal questions he raised: Without a belief in true individuality, a discrete ego that is enduring, immutable, and independent from other essences, can there be a community of individuals in the dharma? Is there truly no will to transform the lives of others in Buddhism, but only the intention to secure one's own salvation from reality?

Clearly, asking these questions from the standpoint of nirvana is as nonsensical as asking, "What is the distance from one o'clock to London Bridge?" Ultimate truth (*paramartha-satya*) is a nonconceptual and nondiscursive insight into ourselves and the world. *Nirvana* literally means "blowing out" (Sanskrit: *nir*, "out"; *vana*, "blown") craving and a chimerical sense of the self, like a candle's flame, allowing us to experience things in their true impermanence, codependency, and emptiness (*shunyata*). "In Buddhism," Thich Nhat Hahn reminds us, "we never talk about nirvana, because nirvana means the extinction of all notions, concepts, and speech."

However, Buddhism also acknowledges a region of conventional, relative truth (*samvriti-satya*) that is our daily, lived experience, and for this reason, Shakyamuni Buddha in the sutras can refer to his disciples individually and by name. Here, in the realm of relative truth and contingency, of conditioned arising, each person presents to us a phenomenal, historical "substance," which due to custom and habit we refer to as "individuality."

The same things have not happened to or shaped us all since birth. Our lives differ so radically and with such richness that, personally, I prefer to see the Other as a great and glorious mystery about which I can never make any ironclad assumptions or judgments. The very act of predication is always risky, based as it is on partial information that is subject to change when new evidence arises.

Thus, what is required of us in the social world is nothing less than vigilant mindfulness. Even though we can say that each person has a "separate" history, the dharma teaches—as does quantum mechanics—that we are really a process, not a product: We are each an "individuality," ever arising and passing away, every one of us a "network of mutuality," as Martin Luther King, Jr., famously said. In the ontology of the buddhadharma, everything is a shifting assemblage of five *skandhas,* the "aggregates" that make up individual experience, with no "essence" or "substance" discernible in the concatenation of causes and conditions that create our being instant by instant. For this reason, if I am practicing mindfulness, phenomena ever radiate a surprising and refreshing newness. The "cold" and "wetness" of the water I drank at noon can never be the same "cold" and "wetness" of the water I drink at night. My wife of thirty-six years is hardly—as she will quickly tell you—the same young woman I wooed when we were both twenty years old. (Nor am I the same naive young swain I was back then, thank heaven!) Far from being "salvation from reality," as Tillich stated, Buddhist meditation is instead a paying of extraordinarily close attention to every nuance of our experience.

Something I find worthy of contemplation is how in the dialectic between samsara and nirvana, the dreamworld of samsara is logically prior to and quite necessary for the awakening to nirvana. Discussing tantric Buddhism, scholar Gunapala Dharmasiri says, "We make a Samsara out of Nirvana through our conceptual projections. Tantrics maintain that the world is there for two purposes. One is to help us to attain enlightenment. As the world is, in fact, Nirvana, the means of the world can be utilized to realize Nirvana, when used in the correct way."

Perhaps a more concrete way of expressing this in terms of social action is to say we come to the buddhadharma precisely because the suffering we have experienced in the world of relativity forces us to relentlessly question "conventional" truth and the status quo, as Ashoka discovered after his slaughter of the Kalingas brought him no happiness, or as the now-Buddhist monk Claude AnShin Thomas realized after killing civilians during the Vietnam War. Or we can consider the case of a black American born in the late 1940s, as I was, a person who knows firsthand the reality of racial segregation in the South and North fifty years ago, and the subtler forms of discrimination in the post–Civil Rights period, which I call "Jim Crow–lite." He (or she) discovers that many Eurocentric whites project fictitious racial "substance" (or meaning) onto people of color, never seeing the mutable individual before them—just as unenlightened men do with women. They dualistically carve the world up in terms of the illusory constructs of "whiteness" and "blackness" and, on the basis of this mental projection, create social structures—as Tillich declared—that fuel attachment, clinging, prejudice, and what the dharma describes as the "three poisons" of ignorance, hatred, and greed. A black poet expressed powerfully his pain at this reality when he wrote, "Must I shoot the white man dead / To kill the nigger in his head?"

Fortunately, a black American who has been exposed to the buddhadharma sees that these racial illusions, so much a part of conventional reality—just as the caste system was in the time of the Buddha—are products of the relative, conditioned mind. He realizes that while he is not blind to what his own valuable yet adventitious racial, gender, or class differences reveal to him, neither is he bound by them; and those very phenomenal conditions may, in fact, spark his dedication to social transformations intended to help all sentient beings achieve liberation. The Buddha employed *upaya kaushalya* (skillful means) when he taught the truth of anatta and said he would teach a doctrine of self if his followers became attached to the idea of no-self. Always, his teachings bring to the foreground the importance of a radical freedom.

As the first line of the *Dhammapada* says, "All that we are is the result of what we have thought." Thus, the transformation of sociological and psychological structures must take place initially in our own minds—and those of others—if we truly hope to address the root cause of social suffering. The Four Noble Truths, the five precepts observed by laity and monks alike, the Eightfold Path, and the ten *paramitas* (perfections) make up a time-honored blueprint for revolutionary change, first in the individual, then in the community of which he or she is a part.

We must, I believe, agree with Tillich when he proclaims that Buddhism is one of the "most competitive religions proper." Without reliance on a higher power, it is competitive exactly to the degree that it is noncompetitive and nondualistic, an orientation toward life that avoids the divisions and divisiveness that are the primary causes of our social problems. This rare quality, together with an answer for how relative individuality can be reconciled with our nirvanic "original face," is beautifully present in a biographical detail from the life of Hui-neng, the sixth patriarch of Zen. When he presented himself to the abbot of Tung-shan monastery in the Huang-mei district of Ch'i-chou in hopes of study, Hui-neng portrayed himself as a poor "commoner from Hsin-chou of Kwangtung."

The abbot rebuked him: "You are a native of Kwangtung, a barbarian? How can you expect to be a buddha?" "Although there are northern men and southern men, north and south make no difference to their buddhanature," replied Hui-neng. "A barbarian is different from Your Holiness physically, but there is no difference in our buddhanature."

Healing the Earth ☙

Stephanie Kaza

When the Buddha achieved enlightenment, the first thing he did was reach down and touch the earth. If he did that today, the earth would cry out in pain. To heal the wounded earth, we must understand our complete interdependence with nature, all living creatures, and the planet itself. Because interdependence is a key Buddhist principle, says Stephanie Kaza, Buddhism offers some important guidelines for environmental activism.

These days it can be overwhelming to think about the state of the environment. Ravaging consumption, exploding population growth, and high-impact technologies now circle the globe; the problems seem intractable. Methods of resource extraction have become rapacious in their efficiency, and ecosystem health is plummeting on every continent. In the midst of such a challenge to planetary stability, what can one person really do? This is the question my students ask every semester, and it is crucial to have some answers or we cannot move forward toward any hope of sustainability.

Often people ask me, "Where should I begin?" I usually ask in reply, "What do you care about the most?" Because most environmental work is incremental and cumulative, strong motivation is essential to hang in there for the long haul. And since the problems are endless, no one can possibly address all of them effectively. So it is important to choose a specific area in which to do some work, to be grounded in the physical, political, and economic realities of a specific situation. I won't tell you where you should put your energy, but I would like to offer several Buddhist approaches that can be applied to any environmental work.

Being with the Suffering

If you look at the state of the world today, the suffering is enormous. Global agriculture, urban sprawl, and industrial development have caused wide-scale loss of habitat, species extinction, land and water degradation, and unstable climate. In the last century, the rate of loss has accelerated significantly, to the point of threatening ecosystem health and the continuity of life.

One of the earliest Buddhist teachings, the Four Noble Truths, begins with the suffering of impermanence. Birth, sickness, old age, and death—every stage of life for every form of existence is conditioned by the inevitability of change and loss. Facing this suffering and the delusions it generates is the place where all Buddhist practice begins. In his precepts of the Order of Interbeing, Thich Nhat Hanh urges, "Do not avoid contact with suffering or close your eyes before suffering." He directs students to be present with suffering to understand the nature of existence. This requires patience and equanimity in the face of upsetting realities, whether it is a clear-cut forest reduced to stumps, a once-fertile wetland deadened by chemical waste, or a coral reef blasted by fishing dynamite. It is not easy to gaze clear-eyed at these troubling manifestations of human activity.

Most of the time we would rather not consider the consequences of such activities. Yet from a Buddhist perspective, this is the best place to start, for it is grounded in reality, undistorted by visionary ideals. Mindful awareness supports what Zen teachers call "direct knowing," or direct experience of the actual state of things. Such authentic perception is freeing and motivating at the same time. Practices that quiet and focus the mind provide a stable mental base from which to observe the full range of human impact.

To be with environmental suffering means being aware of the suffering produced by our own cultural conditioning toward other beings. Those of us in the West have been raised with views that emphasize objectivity: seeing plants and animals, forests and rivers as autonomous objects and potential resources. This human-centered bias, so central to Western politics and economics, is one of the greatest deterrents to being fully present with other living beings. If we see the environment as primarily for human use—whether for food, shelter, recreation, or spiritual development—it is hard to see the intrinsic nature of another being and how it suffers under the thumb of human dominance.

Part of being with the suffering is learning what is actually going on in any given environmental conflict. The Four Noble Truths can be applied as a framework for diagnosis through four questions, each corresponding to one of the truths. First, what is the problem or suffering? Second, what are the causes of the suffering? Third, what would put an end to the suffering? And fourth, what is the path to realize this goal? This analysis is deceptively simple, yet it is radical in including all forms of suffering—people, animals, trees, species, habitats, ecosystems. This method of questioning provides straightforward guidelines for how to become more informed and therefore more able to bear witness to the suffering involved. It also provides some analytical balance to the inevitable emotions that arise when you glimpse the nature of another being's suffering.

Cultivating Systems Mind

Analyzing environmental problems almost always requires some understanding of ecological principles, or what I call "systems thinking." Buddhist philosophy provides an excellent foundation for systems thinking in the law of dependent co-arising, or interdependent origination. According to this perspective, all events and beings are interdependent, interrelated, and mutually cocreating. The universe is dynamic in all dimensions and scales of activity, with every action affecting and generating others in turn.

A Chinese Buddhist metaphor for this view is the "Jewel Net of Indra." Imagine a fishnetlike set of links extending infinitely across horizontal and vertical dimensions of space. Then add more nets crisscrossing on the diagonals. And then imagine an infinite number of these nets crisscrossing every plane of space. At each node in every net, there is a multifaceted jewel that reflects every other jewel in the net. There is nothing outside the Net and nothing that does not reverberate its presence throughout this Net of infinite capacity. The jewels and the infinite links across space are all changing constantly and always reflecting each other in that process.

From an ecological perspective, this metaphor makes obvious sense: ecological systems are exactly such complex sets of relations, shaping and being shaped over time by all the members in the system. You do not have to study formal ecological science to understand this; it is a matter of observing cause and effect in whatever system you engage closely—your family, the workplace, your backyard. Systems thinking develops through looking at patterns in time and space, such as seasonal cycles or animal paths. For an ecologist, these are essential tools. For a mindful citizen, these tools enable you to ask very useful questions in addressing environmental concerns. Rather than focusing too narrowly on only one or two actors in the drama, you can ask about the origin and history of the conflict, about the patterns in policy that have determined decisions, the economic and social needs of the parties involved, and the specific ecological relations at stake. A systems thinker looks across several scales of time and space, always piecing together the puzzles of relationship, of the many causes and the many effects.

Astute observers of systems can decipher the patterns of feedback that reflect the dominant shaping forces. Too much heat, the cat seeks shade. Too much cold, the cat finds a warm car hood to sleep on. Systems are created by self-regulating patterns, such as those that keep you at a constant body temperature, and by self-organizing patterns that allow the system to adapt and respond when new opportunities arise.

Self-regulation (which maintains the stability of the system) and self-organization (which allows the system to evolve or "learn") are both happening all the time at all levels of activity in every system. You can practice observing this in your own body/mind to see how such feedback works. How do you respond to rainy days? To the short days of the year? To being hungry? To getting enough and not enough sleep? You can practice observing yourself in nature to see which places nourish you, and why and in what season. This is all very useful for developing a systems mind to address complex environmental situations.

So far this is fairly straightforward biogeophysical reality. From a Buddhist perspective, however, the law of interdependence, or systems thinking, as I'm calling it, also includes the role of human thought and conditioning. Intention and mental attitudes count; they are a significant force in the universe. So Buddhists see human thought as a very critical part of any environmental dialogue. What people think about the environment will have a major determining effect on what they choose to do. The serious Buddhist systems thinker taking up a perplexing environmental controversy would want to know as much about the human actors and their attitudes as about the affected trees and wildlife.

This leads to a key aspect of systems thinking, *agency:* who is actually doing what? It can be intoxicating to taste the grand interdepending awe of the whole universe, that "oneness" experience where everything makes sense. But this is only a first step of insight. It is crucial to keep going—to study closely what is actually going on and who is causing what to happen. With environmental issues, this means determining who is responsible for the decisions or actions that impact the earth and human community. It means tracing the chain of cause and effect back to those who have generated the environmental damage and who are in a position to reverse their course of action.

The vast web of relations in the dynamic unfolding is not made up of equal partners. Some agents definitely carry more weight than others, and identifying key actors and policy decisions can be very helpful in choosing appropriate strategies to reorient systems to healthy goals.

Liberty Hyde Bailey, an American naturalist at the turn of the twentieth century, said, "The happiest life has the greatest number of points of contact with the world, and it has the deepest feeling and sympathy with everything that is." I believe he is describing the experience of a systems thinker, who brings awareness to all their relationships with specific human and nonhuman beings. A Buddhist might call it a penetrating experience of interdependence. The point is that such awareness is available to everyone and is foundational to doing effective environmental work. If you learn the topography of local rivers and mountains, if you hike their latitudes in all seasons, if you converse with those who use and protect the local rivers and mountains, this becomes the basis for seeing yourself as one who is shaped by—as well as shaping—the relations of Indra's Web.

Taking Up the Path of Nonharming

All religions and cultures have established ethical guidelines and moral frameworks to guide human actions. Historically, and more so recently, a number of these have been interpreted to support environmental protection.

In Buddhist ethics, there is one central principle to all ethical teachings: the practice of nonharming, or *ahimsa*. This is the first precept of the monastic vows, and it informs all other ethical commitments. Understanding how deeply life is conditioned by suffering at many levels, the Buddhist student aims not to add to the suffering and to reduce suffering where possible; in other words, to cause minimal harm. In its deepest sense, *ahimsa* means the absence of even the urge to kill or harm. Such a compassionate response arises naturally out of a broadly felt connection to other beings.

Nonharming is not meant as an unreachable ideal, but rather as a pragmatic basis for making choices. It can serve as a guiding principle for environmental decisions. The U.S. National Environmental Protection Act (NEPA) was written with this intention: environmental impact statements were mandated as a way to measure how much suffering would be caused by a federal project and to suggest mitigation measures to reduce the impact. That can mean changing harvest methods, for example, from clear-cutting to selective cutting. It can mean providing protection for endangered species that are close to extinction. It can mean forming a watershed council so that all voices are included in decisions about watershed basin planning.

The practice of nonharming has been codified in the Mahayana model of the bodhisattva, the enlightened being who returns lifetime after lifetime to help all suffering beings. The bodhisattva's vow is all-encompassing, requiring endless compassion. Green Buddhists have coined the term *ecosattva* to conjure an archetypal bodhisattva pledged to ending environmental suffering. Ecosattvas take their work into any field of environmental concern. Agriculture, water pollution, climate stabilization, wilderness protection—the opportunities are endless—and their work carries the strength of the bodhisattva vow to help all who are suffering. Having such a vow as a reference point relieves some of the anxiety about getting quick results. Many environmental problems are quite intractable and will take lifetimes to turn around. A steady intention can provide a grounding point for what may be a very long battle for environmental stability.

Two places where I hear a lot of discussion these days about reducing harm are in relation to food and energy. The suffering of modern meat production for both animals and workers has been well documented (see *Fast Food Nation* by Eric Schlosser, for example). Likewise, industrial agriculture has been exposed for its chemical assaults on soil and human health. Many people are choosing ethical principles for eating that reduce harm to animals, plants, soils, and the human body. For some, this means eating food produced organically, and if possible, grown by local farmers, which reduces the energy use of long-distance transportation. For others, this means choosing fair trade products that reduce the suffering of field laborers and producers caught in a global economic system. Some people are committed to reducing the anonymity of food shopping by participating in community-supported agriculture food shares.

College students are especially concerned about alternative energy choices. They know that oil production will peak in their lifetime and that other sources of energy must be developed. Biodiesel fuel is quite popular, since it offers a way to recycle used vegetable oil. Wind and solar energy are both seen as causing relatively little harm to the environment, while other potential energy sources, such as hydrogen fuel cells, are questioned because of their high costs of production. Many students would love to have a hybrid electric vehicle, because with better gas mileage they would be less dependent on the petroleum economy. While "nonharming" may not be a key word in the conversation, the direction seems clear to these students: why cause any more harm to the environment? Hasn't there been enough already, enough Chernobyls and Love Canals and Exxon Valdez oil spills? Getting "off-grid" is seen as a moral ideal, a way to reduce your ecological footprint and be a better neighbor to the rest of the world.

Getting to Peace

William Ury, an internationally recognized conflict negotiator, has laid out a number of principles for "getting to peace," meaning solutions that stabilize political conflicts at many levels. His work applies well to environmental issues, which often involve conflict between different parties and different points of view. Some have said that we are now fighting World War Three—the ongoing war not against terrorism, but against the environment. Pesticides, nuclear waste, toxic chemicals, clear-cutting—all these and more are direct assaults on life forms of many kinds. Getting to peace would mean finding a less harmful way of living with the environment, a way that supports peaceful, loving relations with other beings.

In his book, *Getting to Peace,* Ury lays out a role for what he calls "the third side," a party outside the immediate conflict but with a vested interest in a peaceful outcome. This seems to me to be a useful role for people concerned about the environment. The third-side party can clarify differences, provide protection to threatened parties, and educate where knowledge is needed. Someone with Buddhist sensibilities in these roles can draw on the three approaches outlined above: being with the suffering, cultivating systems mind, and practicing nonharming. Holding to such an intention in itself can help to stabilize an ongoing conflict. Ury sees the third-side role as an active one—it engages the conflict but doesn't take sides. For most of us groomed in polarizing thinking, which is so caustic and destructive in modern politics, such a third side can be hard to imagine. But over and over again in a wide variety of conflict situations, Ury has observed the third-side role as crucial in finding a way forward.

Ury describes ten roles for the third side that address reasons why conflict escalates. These he categorizes as preventing, resolving, or containing conflict. All of them might apply to environmental situations, but I'd like to focus on three roles that seem particularly well suited for a Buddhist approach.

Among the roles that prevent conflict from escalating or getting started in the first place, the bridge-builder role seems appropriate for Buddhist sensibilities. The bridge-builder works to strengthen weak relationships between human parties or between human and nonhuman parties. An example is efforts to protect the Everglades built on conversations among cotton growers, wildlife biologists, and tourism operators. Very often environmental problems arise from overuse of a resource or an area; with shared discussions among the users, it is possible to achieve some restraint and coordination of activities. This is essential in recreation conflicts between, for example, Jet Skiers and canoers, or hunters and hikers. A third-party role would support creative problem solving through bringing the parties together to discuss the situation.

To resolve existing conflicts or environmental problems, Ury suggests roles that settle disputed rights and power imbalances. Of the four prevention-oriented roles, I imagine the role of healer, one who cares for injured relationships, would be well supported by Buddhist practice. With relational thinking at the heart of systems mind and compassionate action, a Buddhist practitioner is both skilled and sensitized to the health of relationships. Where relations have been injured, the Buddhist third party would work to heal brokenness and damage. This would take diplomacy, courage, and patience, depending on the degree of injury. A third-side party with clear intention to heal and to serve with compassion would be a valuable asset in moving a situation out of the stuck place of conflict. One could bring this healer role to cases of bad neighbor relations, where injury has been caused through felling a beloved tree or spraying a lawn with pesticides. One could be proactive in healing relations with the soil through local community gardens or by supporting organic agriculture.

In cases where environmental conflict has become entrenched and resolution is not obvious, the third-side role requires more courage. I think of the massive gold mining operations in Indonesia, for example, where the mining company pays the military to support its ravaging of the land in search of gold. Such a deeply ingrained history of assault, which has engaged local political, economic, and military systems to sustain it, will not be easy to resolve. Here a good role for the Buddhist would be as witness—to offer active attention, to make public what is happening, and to articulate the impacts on plants and animals and impaired ecosystems.

The third-side witness documents and records what is going on. This can be the role of a journalist or a tour guide or a scientist. Within government agencies, third-side witnesses are often whistleblowers who reveal illegal or improper activity. This role, as the others, is not without risk and difficulty. When what is being exposed is very threatening to an agency or business, they may decide to eliminate the messenger. Whistle-blowers have lost their jobs; journalists have been killed. A Buddhist approach is not necessarily more effective than other approaches, but it may be less prone to adding antagonism to the situation. The Buddhist can take a systems view and act compassionately toward all parties involved, bearing witness without accusation, reporting facts without condemnation.

To carry out such challenging environmental work, it is essential to regard yourself as an active and effective agent in Indra's Net. This is part of the peacekeeping effort. Thich Nhat Hanh refers to this as planting seeds of joy and peace internally, actively choosing to do environmental work with clear intention and a joyful heart.

Such joy may come from sensory contact with the natural world or quiet meditative practices that renew the heart. By cultivating an internal reference point of joy, independent of changing circumstances, a spiritually committed environmentalist is prepared to work for the long haul. In the ancient tradition of *gathas,* or meditation poems, Zen teacher Robert Aitken offers such a long-haul vow:

Hearing the crickets at night
I vow with all beings
to find my place in the harmony
crickets enjoy with the stars.

Reciting such a mantra or vow of intention can be a force of renewal in the universe, opening up your creativity in peace negotiations. When you actively cultivate an attitude of loving-kindness, it encourages others to plant seeds of joy, and this joy can spread to catalyze the desperately needed transition to ecological sustainability.

His Holiness the Dalai Lama advocates a policy of kindness no matter how troubling the situation. This is practicing Buddhism with a small *b,* taking up the everyday challenge of getting along peacefully with the environment. A policy of kindness toward trees, rivers, sky, and mountains means paying caring attention to all the relations that make up Indra's Net. Engaging environmental problems is not easy work; it is not for the fainthearted. But working with these Buddhist principles—being with the suffering, cultivating systems thinking, and getting to peace—the task seems more possible.

So I haven't told you whether to get involved with climate protection or waste reduction. I haven't said whether population or consumption are causing more damage to the earth. There are many fine resources in print and online that take up just these questions. What I hope is that anyone working at any level, as a citizen or professional, as a parent or student, can take up these Buddhist approaches and put them to good use. The Buddha felt the true test of his teachings was whether they were helpful in everyday life. Those I've offered here are core to my environmental work; may they be of good use to you, dear reader, in whatever small piece of the puzzle you take on.

Mindful Marriage

Christopher Germer

Romance is one of the things we long for most—it's the source of so much song and poetry, after all—but when we find it, the relationship that follows can be one of our biggest challenges. There are no magic formulas for a happy marriage, but couples therapist Christopher Germer says some Buddhist practices can help.

Over the years I've come to a conclusion: Human beings are basically incompatible. Think about it. We live in different bodies, we've had different childhoods, and at any given moment our thoughts and feelings are likely to differ from anybody else's, even those of our nearest and dearest. Given the disparities in our genetic makeup, conditioning, and life circumstances, it's a miracle we get along at all.

Yet we yearn to feel connected to others. At the deepest level, connectedness is our natural state—what Thich Nhat Hanh calls "interbeing." We are inextricably related, yet somehow our day-to-day experience tells us otherwise. We suffer bumps and bruises in relationships. This poses an existential dilemma: "How can I have an authentic voice and still feel close to my friends and loved ones? How can I satisfy my personal needs within the constraints of my family and my culture?"

In my experience as a couples therapist, I've found that most of the suffering in relationships comes from disconnections. A disconnection is a break in the feeling of mutuality; as the psychologist Janet Surrey describes it, "we" becomes "I" and "you." Some disconnections are obvious, such as the sense of betrayal we feel upon discovering a partner's infidelity. Others may be harder to identify. A subtle disconnection may occur, for example, if a conversation is interrupted by one person answering a cell phone, or a new haircut goes unnoticed, or one partner falls asleep in bed first, leaving the other alone in the darkness. It's almost certain that there's been a disconnection when two people find themselves talking endlessly about "the relationship" and how it's going.

The Buddha prescribed equanimity in the face of suffering. In relationships, this means accepting the inevitability of painful disconnections and using them as an opportunity to work through difficult emotions. We instinctively avoid unpleasantness, often without our awareness. When we touch something unlovely in ourselves—fear, anger, jealousy, shame, disgust—we tend to withdraw emotionally and direct our attention elsewhere. But denying how we feel, or projecting our fears and faults onto others, only drives a wedge between us and the people we yearn to be close to.

Mindfulness practice—a profound method for engaging life's unpleasant moments—is a powerful tool for removing obstacles and rediscovering happiness in relationships. Mindfulness involves both awareness and acceptance of present experience. Some psychologists, among them Tara Brach and Marsha Linehan, talk about radical acceptance—*radical* meaning "root"—to emphasize our deep, innate capacity to embrace both negative and positive emotions. Acceptance in this context does not mean tolerating or condoning abusive behavior. Rather, acceptance often means fully acknowledging just how much pain we may be feeling at a given moment, which inevitably leads to greater empowerment and creative change.

One of the trickiest challenges for a psychotherapist, and for a mindfulness-oriented therapist in particular, is to impress on clients the need to turn toward their emotional discomfort and address it directly instead of looking for ways to avoid it. If we move into pain mindfully and compassionately, the pain will shift naturally. Consider what happened to one couple I worked with in couples therapy.

Suzanne and Michael were living in "cold hell." Cold-hell couples are partners who are deeply resentful and suspicious of each other and communicate in chilly, carefully modulated tones. Some couples can go on like this for years, frozen on the brink of divorce.

After five months of unsuccessful therapy, meeting every other week, Suzanne decided it was time to file for divorce. It seemed obvious to her that Michael would never change—that he would not work less than sixty-five hours a week or take care of himself (he was fifty pounds overweight and smoked). Even more distressing to Suzanne was the fact that Michael was making no effort to enjoy their marriage; they seldom went out and had not taken a vacation in two and a half years. Suzanne felt lonely and rejected. Michael felt unappreciated for working so hard to take care of his family.

Suzanne's move toward divorce was the turning point—it gave them "the gift of desperation." For the first time, Michael seemed willing to explore just how painful his life had become. During one session, when they were discussing a heavy snowstorm in the Denver area, Michael mentioned that his sixty-four-year-old father had just missed his first day of work in twenty years. I asked Michael what that meant to him. His eyes welling up with tears, Michael said he wished his father had enjoyed his life more. I wondered aloud if Michael had ever wished the same thing for himself. "I'm scared," he replied. "I'm scared of what would happen if I stopped working all the time. I'm even scared to stop worrying about the business— scared that I might be overlooking something important that would make my whole business crumble before my eyes."

With that, a light went on for Suzanne. "Is that why you ignore me and the kids, and even ignore your own body?" she asked him. Michael just nodded, his tears flowing freely now. "Oh, my God," Suzanne said, "I thought it was me—that I wasn't good enough, that I'm just too much trouble for you. We're both anxious—just in different ways. You're scared about your business and I'm scared about our marriage." The painful feeling of disconnection that separated Michael and Suzanne for years had begun to dissolve.

From the beginning of our sessions, Michael had been aware of his workaholism. He even realized that he was ignoring his family just as he had been ignored by his own father. But Michael felt helpless to reverse the intergenerational transmission of suffering. That began to change when he felt the pain of the impending divorce. Michael accepted how unhappy his life had become, and he experienced a spark of compassion, first for his father and then for himself.

Suzanne often complained that Michael paid insufficient attention to their two kids. But behind her complaints was a wish—not unfamiliar to mothers of young children—that Michael would pay attention to her first when he came home from work and later play with the kids. Suzanne was ashamed of this desire: she thought it was selfish and indicated that she was a bad mother. But when she could see it as a natural expression of her wish to connect with her husband, she was able to make her request openly and confidently. Michael readily responded.

A little self-acceptance and self-compassion allowed both Suzanne and Michael to transform their negative emotions. In relationships, behind strong feelings like shame and anger is often a big "I MISS YOU!" It simply feels unnatural and painful not to share a common ground of being with our loved ones.

We all have personal sensitivities—"hot buttons"—that are evoked in close relationships. Mindfulness practice helps us to identify them and disengage from our habitual reactions, so that we can reconnect with our partners. We can mindfully address recurring problems with a simple four-step technique: (1) feel the emotional pain of disconnection; (2) accept that the pain is a natural and healthy sign of disconnection and the need to make a change; (3) compassionately explore the personal issues or beliefs being evoked within yourself; (4) trust that a skillful response will arise at the right moment.

Mindfulness can transform all our personal relationships—but only if we are willing to feel the inevitable pain that relationships entail. When we turn away from our distress, we inevitably abandon our loved ones as well as ourselves. But when we mindfully and compassionately incline toward whatever is arising within us, we can be truly present and alive for ourselves and others.

Nirvana ☼))

Gil Fronsdal, Anam Thubten Rinpoche, and Roko Sherry Chayat

Nirvana, or nibbana *in the original Pali, is renowned as the ultimate goal of Buddhism. Or is it? Some schools of Buddhism see it as the end point of the path; others see it as a diversion on the way to complete enlightenment. Some strive to achieve it; others defer it to carry on the work of helping others achieve enlightenment. Three well-known Buddhist teachers of different schools—Theravada, Zen, and Vajrayana—wrap up this book by contemplating this elusive topic. It is the end. Or is it the beginning?*

GIL FRONSDAL

Nibbana is the ultimate good news of Theravada Buddhism: it means "complete liberation." Naturally, people want to know about the nature of nibbana, but from the Theravada standpoint, knowing *how* a person is transformed in attaining nibbana is more important than understanding *what* it is.

When a person is thirsty, what's important about water is not its chemical properties, but that it quenches thirst. Similarly, for someone who is suffering, what's important about nibbana is not so much its nature, but that its attainment extinguishes suffering.

Nirvana (Sanskrit) and *nibbana* (Pali, the language of the earliest Buddhist texts) literally mean "to go out"—like a fire—and "to cool." Applied to the mind, it refers to extinguishing the fevers of greed, hate, and delusion, the three roots of suffering. The Buddha's choice of this term was intimately tied to the imagery of his famous Fire Sermon. Here he said: "Everything is on fire; the eyes are on fire; sights are on fire; visual perception is on fire . . . ; the ears are on fire . . . ; the nose is on fire . . . ; the tongue is on fire . . . ; the body is on fire . . . ; the mind is on fire. . . . They are on fire with greed, hate, and delusion" (from the *Mahavagga* of the Theravada Vinaya).

In the language of the Buddha, the word for fuel and for clinging is the same: *upadana*. The Buddha understood that suffering arises from and is fueled by clinging. When the fuel is removed, suffering is extinguished. By understanding how deep-rooted and subtle clinging is in our own unliberated minds, we come to appreciate the mind of nibbana as refreshingly cool and peaceful.

Nibbana is the end of samsara. Contrary to a popular misunderstanding, neither nibbana nor samsara is a place. In attaining nibbana we don't escape from one location to another. For the Buddha, samsara is the process by which clinging gives rise to suffering, which, in turn, gives rise to further clinging. He understood that this self-perpetuating process continues over lifetimes as the "fuel" for rebirth, just as the fire from one burning house is carried to a neighboring house by the wind. Nibbana is what is realized when the clinging of greed, hate, and delusion is brought to an end.

Some later Buddhist traditions equate nirvana and samsara. However, they likely attribute very different meanings to these words than those understood by the earliest Buddhist tradition. In Theravada teachings, samsara cannot be nibbana any more than a clenched fist can be an open hand, any more than holding a burning ember in your fist can be the same as letting it go. For the Buddha, nibbana had quite positive associations—after all, it is a simile for ultimate freedom and awakening. At times he used other similes to describe this state: "the blissful, the secure, the pure, the island, the shelter, the harbor, the refuge, the ultimate."

Other, more perplexing, synonyms include "the unconstructed, the ageless, the deathless, the featureless." These refer to the idea that nibbana does not exist as something that can be made, shaped, or willed. It is not a "ground of being" from which anything subject to death can arise. Although there is a consciousness, "featureless, infinite, and luminous all around," that is associated with nibbana, it is not dependent on the conditioned world. Nor does it produce the conditioned world. Rather, it is a dimension of consciousness totally independent of circumstances in the world or in one's personal life. Because nibbana is independent, people who fully realize it are said to be "unestablished"—in other words, free from any clinging that would confine their consciousness to any point in space or time.

Experiencing nibbana is like taking a dip in a refreshing pond. A quick dip and we are slightly refreshed. With a long soak, we are thoroughly refreshed. Even the first, brief dip into nibbana is a powerful lesson in the possibility of a great happiness, freedom, and peace not dependent on the conditions of the world. As long as someone believes happiness can only be found through the right conditions, it makes sense to cling to those conditions—even when knowing full well that all conditioned phenomena are subject to change. But when there is a direct, visceral experience of an alternative, the enchantment that fuels this clinging lessens dramatically.

The function of attaining nibbana is to reduce and finally end all clinging. In Theravada Buddhism, the desire to walk the path to nibbana has an honored place. Once that desire is fulfilled, it naturally subsides and the mind clings to nothing, not even to nibbana itself.

Walking the path toward the complete ending of clinging and suffering is the noblest thing a person can do. It opens the fist of the mind and allows a person to walk in the world with gift-bestowing hands.

Anam Thubten Rinpoche

The human mind has the tendency to manufacture concepts and beliefs in relationship to things that are inherently transcendental.

This often leads us to suffer the old curse of "mistaking the finger pointing to the moon for the moon itself." The cause of this mistaken perception is the ego, since the ego's only occupation is to sustain its flimsy existence or world of illusion. It always tries its best to create hindrances to the realization of truth.

Every thought about nirvana can be credited to the ego's attempt to jeopardize one's entry into nirvana itself. Yet this situation should not cause us to lose hope of discovering nirvana. Many men and women have already realized it. One may know about nectar very well from reading and listening to others' experiences of tasting it. This is still simply intellectual understanding. One honestly doesn't know how nectar tastes until it is touched by one's own tongue. In the same way, you have to directly experience nirvana in order to know its true flavor. This realization requires the dropping of everything that one is shamelessly trying to hold on to. It means a spiritual death—dying to the illusion of self. This is different from physical death.

We come across various terminologies and symbols created by spiritual traditions to describe this inner liberation. We even find slightly different ways of understanding nirvana within Buddhism. The point of view within the Vajrayana is that it is an awakened state endowed with wisdom and love. It is ecstatic. It is regarded as *maha-sukha,* which literally means "great bliss." This word alone can immediately create a misconception of the true state of liberation. It has nothing to do with ordinary bliss that we experience through our senses, like taking drugs or having sex. It is not necessarily some titillating or altered state of mind that inspires you to frolic in the meadows. Otherwise, hedonism and self-indulgence would be a short cut to enlightenment, which is not the case. The Vajrayana position is to counter the dry notion that nirvana is a dead end: the terminus of every experience from sorrow to bliss. The Vajrayana doctrine regards this as a pseudonirvana, which is nothing more than a pain-free vegetative state. It defines awakening as a state that is not only free from sorrow, but also the embodiment of transcendent love, wisdom, and ecstasy.

All schools of thought in Buddhism seem to agree that great cessation is true nirvana. Buddha himself taught that nirvana is the realm of inner peace in which all gross and subtle turbulence of mind has subsided. This comes into being by awakening to the sacred nature of all things. Vajrayana postulates that nirvana is an awakening in which one sees all things as divine, the universe itself as Buddha paradise, living beings as deities. Its unique outlook is that ultimate truth is not just *shunyata,* or emptiness, but all-pervading sacredness, which is called *dakpa rabjam* in Tibetan. One of the main features in the Vajrayana practices is to visualize beings as deities in accordance with traditional iconography as a means to gaining realization. Such practice may not be found in other traditions.

Vajrayana starts from the premise that nirvana cannot only manifest in one lifetime, but also at any time—mostly when one is not expecting it. This holds true for both women and men. It's said that even sinners can be enlightened in one lifetime without incurring the ultimate punishment of being born in hell. The Tibetan saint Milarepa supposedly took the lives of many in his early years through the use of black magic, and then later embraced the spiritual path and became one of the most revered masters in Tibetan Buddhism. There are many people who doubt the existence of nirvana in the first place. This doubt is the product of not finding many examples of those who are enlightened or the experience of encountering those who are regarded as enlightened by their followers but turn out to be just a big divine joke.

Of course, nirvana is not a myth. It's a possibility for everyone, but an individual must believe in its existence in order to have any motivation to be on the path to the everlasting freedom. The essence of our consciousness is already love and wisdom. Karma, concepts, and emotional patterns are only temporarily preventing our consciousness from unfolding its enlightened nature. Nirvana is nothing more than being awakened to the enlightened nature of our consciousness. That awakened nature is who we truly are from the very beginning. In accordance with this reasoning, we are destined to be enlightened. If not in this lifetime, then definitely at some point in the distant future.

Roko Sherry Chayat

What is enlightenment? What was it that the young prince of the Shakya clan realized that caused him to be called Buddha, the awakened one?

To answer in the usual discursive, conceptual way cannot convey the truth of this experience, an experience that is not limited to some past event, does not belong to some great historical figure, but is ours to discover. Enlightenment is not a thing, not a condition, not an event, not a goal, not an accomplishment. That which is without limits cannot be defined. Yet the question is a burning one for Buddhists. Even though we may be too hip to ask it, deep down, we want to know what it is that we are practicing. But in truth, we are practicing enlightenment! It is always and already here! There is not a hair's breadth of separation between what we perceive as our separate, burdensome selves and buddhanature. But until this truth has been experienced, a little voice is always asking, "Why?" "What for?" "How come?" We want an answer, we want access to someone else's understanding, we want some reassurance that what we are doing makes sense. And a good teacher's response is guaranteed to pull the rug out from under us, to frustrate our acquisitive seeking after the attainment of something outside.

Someone asked the great T'ang dynasty teacher Unmon Bunen, "What is Buddha?" Unmon answered, "Shit-wiping stick." A more modern answer was given by my dharma grandfather, Soen Nakagawa Roshi: "A piece of toilet paper." This may seem blasphemous: How can one compare Buddha to something that is used to wipe away shit? Indeed, if we think buddhanature is that which is sacred, as opposed to everything else that is profane, then of course it sounds blasphemous. But from the vista of realization, what's blasphemous is making this separation between sacred and profane. This is the same dualistic mind-set that creates the fiction of a separate self and condemns us to suffering.

In the *Mahaparinirvana Sutra,* Shakyamuni Buddha teaches, "All living beings are buddhanature," or, as Zen master Dogen phrased it, "All that there is without anything missing, there-is [is] the buddhanature." Shit-wiping stick, toilet paper, birds singing, cars passing by, ants crawling on the ground, itchiness around your ear, sleepiness, everything, all that there is is nothing but buddhanature. What is lacking?

The Zen master Rinzai said, "Followers of the Way, it is urgently necessary for you to attain true insight." And then he continued, "Just don't strive!" Then what about that urgent necessity for attainment? How do we experience true insight without striving? How do we come to see that this very moment, this very place, just as it is, has nothing lacking, nothing superfluous—that we are "all done" just as we are?

In the fascicle "The Buddha-nature" in his *Shobogenzo,* Dogen wrote, "The principle of the Buddha-nature is that one's Buddha-nature remains incomplete as long as one is not awakened, and that it is completed only from the moment one is awakened; the Buddha-nature and awakening can only be simultaneous. You must deeply penetrate this principle in your practice of concentration. Twenty or thirty years of grinding effort are necessary."

That doesn't appeal to us. We don't like the idea of long years of grinding effort. Despite what the Buddha says in the *Diamond Sutra*—"There is no formula for supreme enlightenment"—we long for some guidelines, some diagram, yes, a formula for quick success. We want what our teachers have, and we want them to give it to us without delay. And therein lies the problem in at least two of its guises: we think there is something to have; and we think it's good to get something for nothing—when, in fact, this practice of ours requires giving everything for nothing!

One of my favorite sayings of Rinzai's teacher, Obaku, is, "Those who seek the Way must enter it with the suddenness of a knife thrust. Full understanding of this must come before they can enter." Every koan requires this from us: entering with the suddenness of a knife thrust, giving everything for nothing, having no preconceived ideas of attainment or accomplishment, just sitting down and emptying the room so that the koan can reveal itself in ourselves, through ourselves, as ourselves. This is effortless effort: difficult, for it flies in the face of all our conditioning; easy, for it requires nothing but an utter giving up and entering into this unlimited, unbounded moment. The more we sit in this dumbfounded way, the more our heart-minds are purified. What we think is the obstacle is the very encouragement we need to open, to give unconditionally, to enter with the swiftness of a knife thrust into what has never been hidden. This is koan practice. We empty the room, and the Way is everywhere apparent.

When there's nowhere to turn, nowhere to run, we discover an inner motivation, a strong determination: "I'm going to sit down and shut up. I'm sick and tired of this endless round of confusion and fear. I resolve to enter into the clear, awakened mind of my innate buddhanature, so that true compassion can flower, can bloom in my very being."

Motivation is so important. If we don't have motivation, of course we're going to sit there feeling bored, irritated, and in pain. With motivation, we can dedicate our lives: "I am here, fully present, and I vow to wake up fully so that all beings may be released from suffering." It's that simple. Vow and bow, wholeheartedly, and sit down. Then, having entered with "the suddenness of a knife thrust," we can drink of the refreshing spring called "the readiness of time."

Contributors

AJAHN AMARO is co-abbot of Abhayagiri Buddhist Monastery in Mendocino County, California. He graduated from London University with degrees in psychology and physiology in 1977, and in 1978 he took up residence in a forest meditation monastery in the Ajahn Chah lineage in northeast Thailand. He returned to England to join Ajahn Sumedho at Chithurst, a newly founded forest monastery in Sussex, and in 1996 he founded Abhayagiri Monastery, where he has been based ever since. His forthcoming book, *The Island: An Anthology of the Buddha's Teachings on Nibbana,* was written with Ajahn Pasanno, co-abbot of Abhayagiri.

NANCY BARDACKE, RN, MA, is a nurse-midwife, mindfulness teacher, and founding director of the Mindfulness-Based Childbirth and Parenting (MBCP) program. She teaches MBCP at the Osher Center for Integrative Medicine at the University of California–San Francisco Medical Center, where she is an assistant clinical professor in the department of family health care nursing. Bardacke teaches mindfulness-based programs for parents-to-be, patients, and health care professionals, and she is currently writing a book on mindfulness practice as preparation for childbirth and parenting.

ROKO SHERRY CHAYAT is abbot of the Zen Center of Syracuse (New York). She began Zen practice in 1967 with Eido Shimano Roshi at New York Zendo Shobo-ji, where she attended the teachings of Hakuun Yasutani Roshi and also practiced with the late Maurine Stuart at the Cambridge Buddhist Association. A creative writing graduate of Vassar College, she studied painting at the New York Studio School and was a reviewer for *ARTnews* in the late 1960s. Chayat has written, compiled, and edited several books, including *Endless Vow: The Zen Path of Soen Nakagawa* and *Subtle Sound: The Zen Teachings of Maurine Stuart.* She travels widely to teach and lead retreats, and she is a member of the Cabinet of Faith Leaders of Syracuse Interfaith Works.

PEMA CHÖDRÖN is an American Buddhist nun whose root teacher was the renowned meditation master Chögyam Trungpa Rinpoche. Since his death in 1987, she has studied with his son, Sakyong Mipham, and with her current principal teacher, Dzigar Kongtrul Rinpoche. Pema Chödrön is resident teacher at Gampo Abbey in Nova Scotia, the first Tibetan monastery in North America established for Westerners. Her many popular books include *The Places That Scare You, When Things Fall Apart,* and *Start Where You Are.*

LEONARD COHEN is a poet, novelist, and troubadour of a generation. His gravelly voice, powerful lyrics, and beautiful melodies have made him one of the best-known singer-songwriters in the world, one whose themes and art continue to evolve as he enters his seventy-third year. For seven years in the 1990s, Cohen lived at Mount Baldy Zen Center near Los Angeles, where he studied with and attended Joshu Sasaki Roshi.

HIS HOLINESS THE DALAI LAMA is the spiritual and temporal leader of the Tibetan people and winner of the Nobel Peace Prize. Unique in the world today, he is a statesman, national leader, spiritual teacher, and deeply learned theologian. In talks and teachings throughout the world, he advocates a universal "religion of human kindness" that transcends sectarian differences.

DANIEL DANCER lives in an earth-sheltered home in a model eco-community he founded near Hood River, Oregon. After getting his MA in psychology at the University of Kansas, he left the academic world to pursue a career as an outdoor photographer. Dancer now leads a popular artist-in-residency program called Art of the Sky, which culminates in the formation of a giant living painting that can be seen properly only from the sky. This image represents the power of collaboration, the beauty of impermanence, and the interconnection of all life. Dancer is the author of *Shards and Circles: Artistic Adventures in Spirit and Ecology.*

NORMAN FISCHER is an author, poet, and Zen priest. He is founder of and teacher at the Everyday Zen Foundation, whose mission is to open and broaden Zen teaching and practice for contemporary society. Fischer practiced and taught at the San Francisco Zen Center for twenty-five years and served as abbot there from 1995 to 2000. His latest collection of poetry is *I Was Blown Back* (Singing Horse Press), and 2008 will see the publication of *Sailing Home: The Spiritual Journey as an Odyssey of Return* (Free Press), his reflections on Homer's *Odyssey* as a map of the human inner journey.

GIL FRONSDAL is the primary teacher for the Insight Meditation Center in Redwood City, California. He was a Theravada monk in Burma in 1985, and in 1989 he began training with Jack Kornfield to be a Vipassana teacher. In 1995 he received dharma transmission from Mel Weitsman, abbot of the Berkeley Zen Center. Fronsdal has an undergraduate degree in agriculture from the University of California–Davis and a PhD in religious studies from Stanford University. He also teaches at Spirit Rock Meditation Center, where he is a member of the teachers collective.

PERRY GARFINKEL has been a journalist for thirty-five years, working for such newspapers as the *Boston Globe* and *Newark Star-Ledger.* He is a longtime contributor to the *New York Times* and *National Geographic.* Precariously straddling the fence between skeptic and believer, he has covered the convergence of East and West since returning from his first trip to India in 1973. He was among the group that founded *New Age Journal* in the mid-1970s. His closet career is as a professional drummer, having been a high school all-state drummer and played in blues bands, wedding bands, and jazz ensembles.

CHRISTOPHER GERMER is a clinical psychologist in private practice and a founding member of the Institute for Meditation and Psychotherapy. He is also a clinical instructor in psychology at Harvard Medical School and leads continuing education courses for therapists nationwide. He practices in the Theravada tradition and teaches at the Barre Center for Buddhist Studies.

CAROLYN ROSE GIMIAN is a freelance editor and writer who has edited many of Chögyam Trungpa Rinpoche's books, including *The Collected Works of Chögyam Trungpa* and the recent compilation *The Sanity We Are Born With: A Buddhist Approach to Psychology*. She is the director emeritus of the Shambhala Archives, which she helped to establish in 1989, and the director of the Chögyam Trungpa Legacy Project. Gimian is currently editing a number of forthcoming books by Chögyam Trungpa and working on a book of essays. She is also a meditation teacher.

NATALIE GOLDBERG is the author of eleven books, including the popular *Writing Down the Bones* and, most recently, *The Great Failure*. Her forthcoming book is *Old Friend From Far Away: How to Write a Memoir*. Her paintings are displayed at the Ernesto Mayans Gallery in Santa Fe, and with filmmaker Mary Feidt, she has recently completed the documentary *Tangled Up in Bob*, about Bob Dylan's childhood on the Iron Range in northern Minnesota. She has been a Zen practitioner for more than thirty years and teaches workshops and retreats on writing as a Zen practice.

DANIEL GOLEMAN, PHD, is a psychologist, best-selling author (*Emotional Intelligence*), and journalist who has been nominated twice for the Pulitzer Prize. He is a founding member of the Mind

Life Institute, which is dedicated to building bridges between science and Buddhism, and he has played a key role in a series of dialogues between Western scientists and the Dalai Lama.

KHENPO TSULTRIM GYAMTSO RINPOCHE was born in eastern Tibet in 1934. After completing his early study of Mahayana texts, he roamed the charnel grounds and caves of central Tibet for five years practicing meditation. After the Chinese invasion of Tibet in 1959, he led a group of nuns to safety in India, where many of them continue to study with him. Since the late 1970s, he has traveled and taught extensively in the West and has become renowned for his clear and lively presentation of the most profound teachings of Vajrayana Buddhism.

THICH NHAT HANH is a Zen teacher, poet, and founder of the Engaged Buddhist movement. A well-known antiwar activist in his native Vietnam, he was nominated for the Nobel Peace Prize by Martin Luther King, Jr. In 2005 he returned to Vietnam for the first time since his exile in 1966. The author of more than forty books, Thich Nhat Hanh resides at Buddhist practice centers in France and Vermont.

BELL HOOKS is one of America's most versatile and prolific social critics. Best known for her groundbreaking book on feminism and race—*Ain't I a Woman?*—she is a leading thinker on the search for love and community in a society marked by many forms of power imbalances. She is currently distinguished professor in residence at Berea College in Berea, Kentucky.

CHARLES JOHNSON is a novelist, a scholar, and an essayist who combines his study of Buddhism with a deep knowledge of the African-American struggle for liberation. Johnson holds the S. Wilson and Grace M. Pollock Professorship for Excellence in English at the University of Washington in Seattle. He has been the recipient of many awards, including a Guggenheim Fellowship and a MacArthur Foundation grant. His novels include *Dreamer* and *Middle Passage,* for which he won a National Book Award.

STEPHANIE KAZA is an associate professor of environmental studies at the University of Vermont, where she teaches religion and ecology, ecofeminism, and unlearning consumerism. A longtime student of Zen, she is coeditor of *Dharma Rain: Sources of Buddhist Environmentalism* and editor of *Hooked: Buddhist Writings on Greed, Desire, and the Urge to Consume.*

DZONGSAR KHYENTSE RINPOCHE is a student of Khenpo Appey Rinpoche and is responsible for the education of approximately sixteen hundred monks among six monasteries and institutes in Asia. He is the founder of several dharma centers in the West and three nonprofit organizations: Siddhartha's Intent, Khyentse Foundation, and Lotus Outreach. He is also the director of the acclaimed films *The Cup* and *Travelers & Magicians.*

MICHAEL KRASNER, MD, is a specialist in internal medicine, practicing primary care in Rochester, New York. He is a student of Roshi Bodhin Kjollhede of the Rochester Zen Center and of Jinen Jason Shulman, founder of A Society of Souls, with whom he is studying integrated kabbalistic healing. Krasner has been teaching mindfulness-based stress reduction to patients, medical students, and physicians for more than six years and is currently directing a project called Mindful Communication: Bringing Intention, Attention, and Reflection to Clinical Practice. This yearlong program will train seventy-five primary care physicians in mindfulness practice, narrative medicine, and appreciative inquiry.

JENNIFER LAUCK has known nearly every human difficulty from direct experience. Following the deaths of her mother, father, and brother, she was homeless, abandoned, raped, beaten, and relocated in and out of twenty-seven different homes and several different families—all by the time she was eighteen years old. For ten years of her adult life, she devoted herself to a personal spiritual journey to transcend the trauma of her life and turn her challenges into a course of healing. As part of this journey, she penned three memoirs: *Blackbird*, a *New York Times* best seller; *Still Waters;* and *Show Me the Way.* Lauck has created the Blackbird Feather Fund, a scholarship fund devoted to the empowerment and healing of women through creativity.

JUDITH LIEF began studying Buddhism with Chögyam Trungpa Rinpoche in 1975. Her path as a student led her to take on many roles and positions, working closely with Trungpa Rinpoche as a teacher, meditation instructor, editor, and head of the Naropa Institute (now Naropa University). In 1976, she begin to work with and learn from the dying, people working with the dying, and people facing loss and change. This led her to write the book *Making Friends with Death: A Buddhist Guide to Encountering Mortality.* Lief is a senior teacher (*acharya*) in Shambhala International.

DONNA LOVONG was born in Thailand near the Laotian border. She has a BA in sociology and conducts public health research. She enjoys reading, traveling, and practicing eating meditation.

LAYLA MASON (a pseudonym) grew up in a meditation community in the 1970s and early 1980s. She currently works at a dharma center, where she lives with her husband and daughter.

JARVIS JAY MASTERS is an African American imprisoned on death row at San Quentin state prison in California. He is a student of the late Chagdud Tulku Rinpoche. His book, *Finding Freedom: Writings from Death Row* (Padma Publishing), can be ordered from the Buddhist Peace Fellowship. He is currently at work on his second book, titled *That Bird Has My Wings: Autobiography of an Innocent Man.*

KAREN MILLER is a priest in the Soto Zen lineage of Taizan Maezumi Roshi and a student of Nyogen Yeo Roshi. In her daily life, as a mother to her young daughter, Georgia, and as a writer, she aims to resolve the enigmatic truth of Maezumi Roshi's teaching, "Your life is your practice."

DIANA MUKPO was born in England in 1953 and attended the prestigious Beneden School until she left at the age of sixteen to marry the Tibetan lama Chögyam Trungpa Rinpoche. She moved to the United States in 1970, where she participated in Trungpa Rinpoche's historic career as a pioneer of Buddhism in the West until his death in 1987. During their marriage, Mukpo pursued an intensive study of dressage, and she is now the owner and director of Windhorse Dressage, a riding academy in Providence, Rhode Island. She also teaches frequently at the Shambhala dharma centers established by her late husband.

MATTHIEU RICARD is a Buddhist monk who left a promising career in cellular genetics to study Buddhism in the Himalayas. A close student of the late Dilgo Khyentse Rinpoche, one of the great Buddhist teachers of the twentieth century, Ricard is an author, translator, photographer, and leading participant in scientific research on the effects of meditation on the brain. Two of his books, *The Monk and the Philosopher* and *The Quantum and the Lotus*, have been best sellers in France.

SEUNG SAHN, the seventy-eighth patriarch in his line of Korean Buddhism, was the first Korean Zen master to live and teach in the West. He was founding teacher of the Kwan Um School of Zen, an international organization of more than one hundred centers and groups. In 2004 he received the title "Great Master" from the Chögye Order of Korean Buddhism in appreciation for his lifetime of teaching. Seung Sahn died in 2005 at the age of seventy-seven.

GARY SNYDER is a longtime practitioner of Zen Buddhism, a key member of the Beat generation of poets and writers, and a powerful voice in defense of the environment. Reflecting his literary, ecological, and public policy interests, in 1997 he was awarded both the Bollingen

Prize for Poetry and the John Hay Award for Nature Writing. He is a member of the Ring of Bone Zendo, and in 1998 he was the first American literary figure to receive the prestigious Buddhism Transmission Award from the Buddhist Awareness Foundation of Japan. Since 1985 he has taught at the University of California–Davis.

JOHN TARRANT is the author of *Bring Me the Rhinoceros—and Other Zen Koans to Bring You Joy, The Light Inside the Dark: Zen, Soul and the Spiritual Life,* and many poems. He is the director and a senior faculty member of Pacific Zen Institute and one of the foremost koan teachers in the United States. He has a PhD in psychology and helped develop the Art of Medicine curriculum for the Fellowship in Integrative Medicine at the University of Arizona. Now he teaches physicians and executives at Duke Integrative Medicine and works on alliance integration for a green energy company.

KHENCHEN THRANGU RINPOCHE is a teacher and scholar in the Kagyu school of Tibetan Buddhism and the abbot of several monasteries in Asia and North America. He has traveled extensively in Europe and the United States and has a retreat center in Crestone, Colorado.

ANAM THUBTEN RINPOCHE was born in Tibet and recognized as an incarnate lama (*tulku*) when he was a young boy. He has been teaching in the West since the 1990s and serves as the main dharma teacher for the Dharmata Foundation, based in Point Richmond, California. He is a Buddhist scholar and writer whose first book in English is titled *No Self, No Problem.*

ALICE WALKER is a poet, a novelist, and an essayist whose work addresses themes of violence, isolation, troubled relationships, multigenerational perspectives, sexism, and racism. In 1983 she won the Pulitzer Prize for her novel *The Color Purple.* At sixty-four, she continues to write and is active in environmental and feminist causes and issues of economic justice.

Credits

Ajahn Amaro, "Reflections on My Mother's Love." From the Summer 2006 issue of *Buddhadharma: The Practitioner's Quarterly*.

Nancy Bardacke, "Birthing." Reprinted by permission from the Spring 2006 issue of *Inquiring Mind: A Semiannual Journal of the Vipassana Community*, www.inquiringmind.com.

Pema Chödrön, "Turning Your Whole Way of Thinking Upside Down." From *Practicing Peace in Times of War* by Pema Chödrön, © 2006. Reprinted by arrangement with Shambhala Publications Inc., Boston, MA. www.shambhala.com.

Leonard Cohen, "My Life in Robes." From *Book of Longing*, copyright © 2006 by Leonard Cohen. Reprinted by permission of HarperCollins Publishers. Originally published in the United States by Ecco, an imprint of HarperCollins Publishers.

His Holiness the Dalai Lama, "How to See Yourself as You Really Are." Reprinted with the permission of Atria Books, a Division of Simon & Schuster, Inc., from *How to See Yourself as You Really Are* by His Holiness the Dalai Lama, translated and edited by Jeffrey Hopkins, PhD, Copyright © 2006 by His Holiness the Dalai Lama.

Daniel Dancer, "Impermanence Rocks!" From the Spring 2006 issue of *Turning Wheel*.

tics: A Buddhist Guide to Making the World a Better Place, © Melvin
McLeod, 2006. With permission of Wisdom Publications, 199 Elm
Street, Somerville, MA 02144 U.S.A., www.wisdompubs.org.

Dzongsar Khyentse Rinpoche, "What Makes You Not a Buddhist."
From *What Makes You Not a Buddhist* by Dzongsar Jamyang
Khyentse, © 2006. Reprinted by arrangement with Shambhala Pub-
lications Inc., Boston, MA. www.shambhala.com.

Michael Krasner, "Through the Lens of Attention." From the Spring
2006 issue of *Zen Bow.*

Jennifer Lauck, "Reentry." From the January 2006 issue of *Mandala.*

Judith Lief, "Letting Go." From the Fall 2006 issue of *Tricycle: The
Buddhist Review.*

Donna Lovong, "Are You Joining a Cult?" Reprinted from *The Buddha's Apprentices: More Voices of Young Buddhists,* © Sumi D. Loundon, 2006. With permission of Wisdom Publications, 199 Elm Street,
Somerville, MA 02144 U.S.A., www.wisdompubs.org.

Layla Mason, "What's Crazy, Really?" Reprinted from *The Buddha's
Apprentices: More Voices of Young Buddhists,* © Sumi D. Loundon,
2006. With permission of Wisdom Publications, 199 Elm Street,
Somerville, MA 02144 U.S.A., www.wisdompubs.org.

Jarvis Jay Masters, "Pitbull." From the Spring 2006 issue of *Turning
Wheel.*

Karen Maezen Miller, "Momma Zen." From *Momma Zen* by Karen
Maezen Miller, © 2006. Reprinted by arrangement with Shambhala
Publications Inc., Boston, MA. www.shambhala.com.

Diana Mukpo and Carolyn Rose Gimian, "Married to the Guru." From
Dragon Thunder: My Life with Chögyam Trungpa by Diana Mukpo